how to pray

NICK FAWCETT

how to
pray

kevin mayhew

First published in 2006 by
KEVIN MAYHEW LTD
Buxhall, Stowmarket, Suffolk, IP14 3BW
E-mail: info@kevinmayhewltd.com
www.kevinmayhew.com

9 8 7 6 5 4 3 2 1 0
ISBN 1 84417 690 8
Catalogue No. 1500948

Cover design by Sara-Jane Came
Edited and typeset by Katherine Laidler

Printed and bound in Great Britain

Contents

Part Four: RESOURCES FOR GROUP AND PERSONAL DEVOTION

Acknowledgements

Unless otherwise stated, prayers are by Nick Fawcett and are taken from the following publications:

Are You Listening?
Heart to Heart
Heaven Touching Earth
Selected Prayers for Public Worship
Touching Down
Touching the Seasons
Touched by His Hand
The Unfolding Story

The Publishers wish to thank all those who have given their permission to reproduce copyright material in this publication:

Part Two: Using our senses
Page 88: If we knew how to listen to God . . . (Michel Quoist), extract from *Prayers of Life* © 1965 Gill & Macmillan.

Part Three: Praise
Page 113: O world, I cannot hold thee close enough . . . (Edna St Vincent Millay), *Modern American Poetry*. Ed. Louis Untermeyer © 1919 Harcourt, Brace & Howe.
Page 123: Almighty and most merciful Father . . . (*Book of Common Prayer*). Administered by the Crown's patentee, Cambridge University Press.

Part Three: Thanksgiving
Page 146: Almighty God, Father of all mercies . . . (*Morning and Evening Prayer*) © The Archbishop's Council; reproduced by permission.

Part Three: Intercession
Page 192: Where restless crowds are thronging . . . (Thomas Curtis Clark) © Hymn Society in America/Hope Publishing Co. Administered by CopyCare. Used by permission.

Part Four: Expressing our thanks
Page 407: My heart gives thanks . . . (William Stanley Braithwaite), *The Book of American Negro Poetry*. Ed. J. Weldon Johnson © 1922 Harcourt, Brace & Co.

Every effort has been made to trace the owners of copyright material and we hope that no copyright has been infringed. If the contrary be the case, a correction will be made in any reprint of this book.

Lord, teach us how to pray

Luke 11:1b

Introduction

'Well, well,' she said, clearly impressed, 'so you write books, do you? What sort, exactly?' I knew well enough what was coming next. The moment I mentioned prayer her face changed from fascination to disappointment, even disdain. 'Oh, I see,' came the response, and it wasn't long before the conversation petered out as my questioner took the earliest possible opportunity to move away. Had I written on another subject, it might have been different; even, funnily enough, had I said I wrote on spirituality, but *prayer* rang all the wrong bells.

What do you make of that? Is it yet another example of our increasingly secular society; proof, if any were needed, of a growing disinterest in God? Actually I don't think so – quite the contrary. People are as hungry today as they've ever been for a sense of the divine, the spiritual, the Other – call it what you will – but they're turned off by the way the Church presents this, and often with good reason: organised religion too easily stifles what it sets out to safeguard. With prayer that's as true as anything. The language can seem archaic, the repetitiveness boring, the jargon incomprehensible, the approach stuffy or over-familiar, and so I could go on. Many, furthermore, have inherited stereotypical images of what prayer should be, believing it, in consequence, to have little relevance to daily life.

Even those committed to prayer frequently struggle with it; many Christians, in my experience – and yes, myself too at times – finding it a burden rather than blessing, a duty instead of joy. They feel it should come naturally, but it doesn't; that they should pray far more often, yet struggle to pray at all; and that there's a certain way to pray, even though they can't quite fathom what it is.

This book is written with two objectives in mind. One is to provide a resource for prayer, both in terms of approach and in providing material for devotional use ranging from poetry, hymns, music and meditations, together with words from Scripture, historic prayers, and material of my own. Part Four illustrates how these various aspects can be put together, this being divided into five sections focusing, respectively, on praise (worship), confession, thanksgiving, petition and intercession. Twenty prayer sessions are offered for each theme, these being available, should you wish to purchase them, on CDs produced by Kevin Mayhew.

You will find here some of the material cited in the first three parts of the book, together with a great deal more, these providing a resource for either group or individual devotions.

The second aim is to broaden horizons to show that prayer is far wider than anything we do in church or in a few moments set aside with head bowed and eyes closed; rather, it embraces every aspect of life. At times, for reasons of copyright and space, I've only been able to recommend resources rather than cite them in full. Equally, when it comes to silence or responding to God in everyday life, I can only point at this on paper, or indeed on the companion CDs, but I've attempted at least to give a flavour of what I mean. I'd like to have written more, for there's so much about prayer that could be said, but hopefully at least something in these pages may offer ideas you can carry over into your own devotional life.

There's one final point I'd like to make. Despite the invitation to write this book, I'm no expert in prayer – far from it. More to the point, I hope I'll never consider myself such, for, to me, expertise and prayer simply don't belong together. There's no right or wrong way to pray – it all depends on the individual and the way they experience God. I stand with Teresa of Avila who described praying to God as 'nothing more than a friendly conversation with One who we know loves us'; with Father Willie Doyle, SJ, who urges, 'Make your prayer simple, as simple as you can. Reason little, love much, and you will pray well'; with Dom Chapman who advised, 'Pray as you can and do not try to pray as you can't'; with St Dimitri of Rostov, who saw prayer simply as 'turning the mind and thoughts towards God'; and perhaps most of all with St Anthony, who observed, 'They pray best who do not know that they are praying.' If anything in this book makes those ideas ring true for you, then it will have done its job.

NICK FAWCETT

Part One

APPROACHING PRAYER

What is prayer?

What do we mean by prayer? The word is so much a part of religious language that we rarely if ever ask that question, yet if prayer is to be as meaningful a part of our Christian life as it should be, it's one that we need to consider, for only then can we escape from the shackles imposed by our preconceptions.

For many, prayer is something we do in church, or perhaps at the beginning and end of each day – seen, in other words, as a 'religious' activity, requiring suitably pious and reverent language, perhaps also with our heads bowed, eyes closed and hands together. I can well understand that, for all too often it's how I perceive prayer myself; this was the way many of us were taught to pray from early years. And it's not that there's anything inherently wrong with any of the above perceptions; quite the contrary. Sunday worship offers invaluable times of prayer for many, helping them to draw close to God in a way they otherwise find hard. Praying first thing in the morning or last thing at night can be a simple but effective way of staying in touch with God in the press of a busy lifestyle. Shutting our eyes can help blot out distractions, kneeling can express our sense of awe and humility, and bowing our heads can likewise express reverence and wonder. Each, in other words, can have a very real place in our devotional life, yet all of them together are but a part of prayer, not the whole.

The downside of the perceptions we've mentioned is that many people feel unable to measure up to expectations, considering their grasp of language or depth of spirituality to be inadequate for the task. Some are unsure what to pray for, others find the words just don't come, others again feel that words aren't enough . . . and if all that's hard enough to cope with, then a bigger problem still is understanding just what it is we're meant to be doing. Why *do* we pray? What do we hope to achieve? How do we think prayer works? What should we expect to happen? And so we could go on.

Part of the difficulty, I have to confess, rests with people like me, for Christian leaders and teachers across the years have frequently spoken all too blithely of prayer being a *dialogue*, a conversation with God in which we both talk to him *and hear his voice*. Is that what it actually involves? Well yes, I believe it is, but not in any simplistic sense. No one

I know actually hears God speaking to them, spelling out his answers word for word. And if someone did start hearing voices in their head we'd soon start questioning their sanity. Yes, lots of people believe God has answered their prayers, and I'm sure they're right, but this typically comes through a *sense* of what he wants rather than receiving clear instructions, and there are occasions, all too many, when it turns out we were wrong in what we thought God was saying. There are times also when we pray but don't feel we've got through; or when the answer we're looking for doesn't come; or when it's only weeks, months, even years later that we realise, with the benefit of hindsight, that our prayers have indeed been answered. Popular hymns may speak of prayer being like a telephone, a hotline to God, but for the average person – me included – it's most definitely not.

So where does that leave us? Have we been misled, carried away by religious fervour? No, I'm convinced not. The problem is that, with prayer, as with anything else to do with God, we're trying to put into words what's finally beyond language; trying, that is, to express the inexpressible. We have no choice, for when it comes to articulating our thoughts, language is the chief tool at our disposal. But it's not the only one, not by a long way, as we shall see during the course of this book. Although prayer uses words, it goes far beyond them, being not so much about *talking* to God or even *listening* to him, as simply and consciously *being in his presence.*

To understand what that means, think of those you're most close to in the world. You can spend time with them quite comfortably in silence, can't you, such moments being just as meaningful as when you use words? Even though nothing is actually said, you are still sharing together, still relating one to another. Of course, were you never to speak it would be a strange relationship indeed, but the point is that words arise naturally rather than being in any way forced. Most of the time you simply know your loved one's mind, just as he or she knows yours. Enjoying that person's company is what matters. We may talk or be quiet, share the important or the trivial, communicate through a look, a word or a gesture – each reflects the closeness of our relationship. So it is with prayer. It doesn't always need words, often being more a case of recognising God's presence wherever we are. Similarly, when language *is* used it doesn't need to be of a special kind, but should come naturally, using whatever words feel real and right at a given moment. As for God's reply, that can come in a host of ways, from the words of Scripture or a sermon, the advice of a friend or stranger, the voice of conscience or sudden insight, or simply through the world around us or events of daily life.

In short, then, prayer is much wider than the models mentioned earlier, those being but a fraction of something infinitely bigger. To discover the riches it has to offer we need to explore more widely, using all the resources God has given: resources such as music and pictures, every-day items, events and experiences, as well, of course, as words and silence. In this book, I'll be attempting to do just that, offering further thoughts on prayer, together with a host of examples, to show how it can engage all our senses and touch every part of life. First, though, let's explore some of the questions and issues that people most commonly raise about prayer.

When, where and how should we pray?

Is there a right or wrong time to pray? The obvious answer to that is of course not, prayer being appropriate at any time, all the time. But if that's the ideal, most of us find it hard to get anywhere near it, all too easily praying none of the time. There can be a host of reasons for that, as we will explore later, but it begs the question of whether we need to cultivate a regular pattern or discipline in our prayer life in order to prevent it falling by the wayside. Some people, for example, make a point of praying first thing in the morning and last thing at night, or at a specific time each day, while others prefer to pray as and when it feels appropriate or simply whenever they can snatch a moment. Similarly, some find it helpful to use a book of prayers or devotions, others may use the same prayer day in, day out, while others again prefer to extemporise. As with most things in life, there are arguments on both sides.

Many find a structured prayer life enormously helpful, not least, of course, religious orders, which across the centuries have based their day and night around set cycles of prayer. Likewise, several hugely respected devotional writers of the last century, among them George Appleton, Leslie Weatherhead and John Baillie, used the morning and evening format, or something similar. Without some kind of routine, prayer can be crowded out by other concerns, so that we end up going from one day to the next without giving God a second thought.

The downside with structured prayer, though, is that it can become mechanical, offered more out of habit or duty than from the heart, and though we continue to go through the motions, deep down we feel dissatisfied, well aware that our words no longer come from the heart. Perhaps worse still, we can feel guilty if for some reason our usual pattern is disrupted, convinced that we've somehow let God down by failing to pray at a certain time or to pray in the right way.

At the risk of fudging the issue, I firmly believe we need to steer a middle course, borrowing as far as possible from all traditions and recognising the value of different ways to approach prayer. A set time may indeed be valuable, and if you can build that into your daily schedule by all means do so, but don't feel it's set in stone. A particular book or collection of prayers may offer much-needed inspiration, but don't be afraid of using other resources too, and don't worry if you miss out on a few days before coming back to it. It may be that on some days words simply flow whereas at other times your mind's a blank. Again, it's not a problem – as the old saying goes, there's more than one way to skin a cat. You may very well find it helpful to use one approach for a month or so and then switch to another, ringing the changes to keep your prayer life fresh and vibrant. With prayer, as with so much else, variety is the spice of life, change literally good for the soul. So be prepared to experiment and to go with what works for you.

Finally, does it matter *where* we pray? The answer is yes and no. On the one hand, I'm convinced that prayer should never be restricted to a specific place – as we will see during the course of this book, that would be to contradict much of what I believe – but where we pray does, without doubt, affect the sort of prayers we offer. To pray during the course of our favourite TV programme, for example, or while busy working, or while playing a game of cards, or in the middle of a heated conversation, would be difficult to say the least, simply because our attention is almost wholly focused elsewhere. It's not easy either to pray at any length when we're rushing about doing household chores, or in company, or doing the weekly shopping; although, as I attempt to show in the sections of this book concerned with reflective prayer and using our senses, very meaningful prayers can in fact often be offered precisely within the hustle and bustle of the daily routine, even if these are only a word or thought hastily offered to God, or simply a vague perception of his presence. Such prayers are enough to transform the ordinary into the special, the secular into the sacred, but in order to sustain them we need, I believe, other times when we're able to focus more deliberately on God, setting aside quality time both to offer our prayers and seek his voice. Just as Jesus built quiet times into his routine away from the crowds and demands of his ministry, so we need to find moments and places free of distraction. Such times aren't always easy to find, but it's worth taking the trouble to secure them. I personally find it helpful sometimes to sit quietly in the garden as dusk is falling, or to reflect on God while out walking. Equally, you may find it helpful to pop into a church building for a few minutes, to kneel by your bed, or even to have a quiet place in the home where, perhaps, you light a candle, place a Bible or hang a cross as an aid to reflection.

What I'm saying, in other words, is that we need a balance between drawing away from the world and being part of it. It's important sometimes to find a quiet place for reflective personal devotion, but important also to understand that prayer is not and cannot finally be tied to any one place.

The following prayer makes the point:

I'll never forget it, Lord,
 that moment as I stood on that hilltop
 and took in the sight before me –
 the sun golden on the horizon,
 the sea stretching out into the distance, blue as topaz,
 the cliffs white as snow,
 and the seagulls soaring overhead in lofty splendour.
It was magnificent,
 a taste of paradise,
 the world as I'd never seen it before,
 full of beauty and wonder.
I heard cows lowing and sheep calling their young,
 birds singing in the distance
 and bees droning among the heather,
 the laughter of the waves
 and the playful whispering of grass stirred by the breeze,
 each joining to create a jubilant chorus,
 an outpouring of celebration,
 a hymn of praise.
And my heart joined in the dance,
 leaping with delight,
 skipping with pleasure,
 crying out in adoration.
For here was freedom and inexpressible loveliness,
 life as it ought to be,
 creation in all its glory.
It was wonderful, Lord,
 a glimpse of your majesty,
 a revelation of your handiwork,
 a sign of your love –
 and in that moment,
 as never before,
 I gave you my worship.

My child,
    this may come as a surprise,
    but that moment was as precious to me as it was to you,
    for the wonder in your eyes and the joy in your face
    was a prayer greater than all words,
    an expression of gratitude I shall always treasure.
So thank you for your worship,
    and thank you for taking time to stop and stare,
    to glimpse my presence in the beauty of creation,
    to reflect on my handiwork and know me by your side.
Don't lose that sense of awe,
    for it is a gateway to heaven,
    a foretaste of my eternal kingdom.
Yet remember also there is more to discover –
    that if you found me once in a moment of quietness,
    you must find me always in every place and every moment.
Make time to withdraw, of course,
    but then return,
    back to the daily round of life.
Make time to pause,
    but then resume,
    picking up where you left off.
Make time to reflect,
    but then to act,
    seeing my presence in the place where I have placed you,
    for when you have learned that, my child,
    we shall dance together for all eternity.

What should we pray for?

What sort of things should we ask for in prayer? Is it acceptable to present God with a list of requests, asking him for this, that and the other, or should our prayers be more a question of 'not my will but yours be done'? The words of Jesus on the subject give what seem to be conflicting messages. On the one hand, he told the crowd listening to the Sermon on the Mount that God knows all our needs before we ask him, so instead of focusing on trivial concerns we do better to seek the kingdom of heaven and his righteousness. On the other hand, passages like Luke 11:9 or Matthew 21:22 tell us that whatever we ask for in prayer we will receive, provided our faith is strong enough. Consider the implications if that's true. Effectively, Jesus would be offering us a blank cheque, a guarantee that we can have whatever we want whenever we want it. Can that really be what he had in mind? If so, it's a disturbing prospect. Not only would it be open to abuse in terms of praying for riches, success, power and such like, but there would be a distinct possibility of some people praying for one thing and others for precisely the opposite, each with equal faith. What would God do then? There seems no way in which both prayers could be answered. More disturbing still, if we can receive whatever we ask, then effectively we have usurped the place of God.

The key to the problem is a little proviso Jesus added to his promise: namely that we will receive what we ask if, and only if, we ask *in his name*. In the context of Judaism that qualification is all-important, for a 'name' was not just a label but symbolic, connoting a person's character and personality. To ask in someone's name meant to ask with that person's approval and authority, so what Jesus is saying here is that if we ask according to his purpose, looking for his will to be done in our lives, *then* we shall receive. The same idea is spelt out yet more clearly in 1 John 5:14, 15: 'We approach God in this confidence: that if we ask for something in accordance to his will, he hears us. And if we know that he hears us, whatever it is that we may ask, we know equally that we have that which we asked him for.'

If this interpretation is correct, however, then why not simply pray, 'Your will be done' and have done with it? Isn't it best simply to place everything in God's hands and concern ourselves with it no further, just as Jesus did in the garden of Gethsemane when, faced with the prospect of death, he uttered those famous words: 'not my will but yours be done' (Mark 14:36). Here is the ultimate prayer of faith, yet for most of us prayer is not that simple. For one thing, unlike Jesus, most of us are unsure what God wants from us, his will for our lives anything but clear. Prayer offers an opportunity to ask for his guidance and understand the way ahead. Equally, God won't force his wishes upon us, for we are not puppets, at the behest of his every whim. He wants us to make our own choices, and so he invites us freely to respond and say yes to his purpose.

The temptation when praying is to expect God to pander sometimes to our every whim, almost as though he's duty bound to deliver, such as in this prayer called 'The dispensing machine':

Tea,
  coffee,
  soup,
  chocolate –
  just a small selection of the drinks on offer.
Insert coins . . .
  select option . . .
  wait.

Lord, I treat *you* like a dispensing machine sometimes,
  as if all I have to do is press the right buttons
  and you will pander to my wishes.
A drop of devotion and touch of faith,
  with a hint of penitence thrown in,
  and you're bound to come up with the goods,
  whatever I may ask.
Forgive me for seeking to exploit rather than worship you,
  and teach me to focus on what I can give
  instead of dwelling on what I might receive.
Amen.

Such an approach, however, doesn't make any sense if God is who we say he is. Of course, we'll inevitably bring to God all kinds of things in prayer that, in the long run, are trivial and incidental, and equally, many of our prayers will focus on what are ultimately selfish concerns – our own future, welfare, loved ones and so on. We'd be less than human if that wasn't so. Yet the requests we make should, above all, be for deeper things: a closer relationship with God, deeper spiritual insight, greater love and compassion for others, strength to resist temptation and other such gifts and qualities. Praying for ourselves needs a healthy balance between the two: an understanding that everyday life matters to God but also a desire to share more in *his* life, his kingdom not of this world. The following meditation sums up this point:

'Help me,' I prayed.
'Take away this problem.'
'Provide those funds.'
'Grant that job.'
In these, and a host of other ways, Lord,
    I've come to you in prayer,
    asking for first this,
    then that –
    as though you are a blank cheque,
    a guarantee card
    assuring that I will secure whatever blessing I seek.
But it's not like that, is it?
You may say yes, of course –
    indeed, you often do –
    but you may equally say no,
    faith not a promise of earthly comfort
    but of heavenly blessing.
You want me to ask, certainly,
    to seek and to knock at the door,
    but you've made clear also
    what the object of my asking should be,
    the goal of my search,
    the purpose of my knocking –
    each concerned with your kingdom
    and your righteousness;
    with leading me closer to you
    and teaching me more of your way,
    so that I might know and serve you better.

I'll still ask as I used to, Lord,
    still seek your blessing in the daily affairs of life,
    for I need your guidance and help so much,
    but teach me also and especially to ask for what really matters,
    to search for eternal riches,
    to knock at the gates of life in all its fullness,
    knowing that you will be there,
    waiting to fling them open and welcome me in.

What language should we use in prayer?

How easy do you find the language of Shakespeare? Personally I don't find it easy at all, much of it sounding odd if not incomprehensible, yet, paradoxically, I love Shakespeare's plays and poems, for there is so much poetry and skill in his use of language once you're able to tune into it. I wouldn't want to speak Shakespearean English all the time, of course, but I'd be profoundly sorry if this rich part of our heritage were lost to posterity. All of which leads us to the question above: what sort of language should we use in prayer? Sometimes Christians get very hung up about linguistic matters, preferring either old or new idioms – a conflict seen across the years in debates concerning the merits of the King James version of the Bible as opposed to modern translations, or of the Book of Common Prayer as opposed to revised or contemporary liturgies. Personally I see no reason why we shouldn't have the best of both worlds, finding a place for each in our worship. Habitually to use 'thee' and 'thou', let alone 'whithersoever', would seem strange, given that we don't use such terms in daily conversation today, but they are nonetheless integral to some of the great prayers, poems and hymns of antiquity, and to update them would be to lose much of their poetry. In many places, then, within this book I've retained traditional language, this complementing the more familiar but prosaic language of today.

When it comes, though, to the language we use in our own prayers, the issues are wider. Even modern or extemporary prayers in the context of public worship tend to have an indefinable 'churchy' feel to them, and subconsciously we can try to imitate that, almost as though there's a specific way we should frame our prayers: prescribed terms to address God, a correct way to finish, a proper way to express what it is we want to say. If you think that, then think again, for I'm sure it's mistaken. Prayer is about opening up before God in whatever way comes naturally, and there are no more rules here than in any other relationship. If there's one piece of advice I'd offer, it's this: don't *pray* to God, *talk* to him!

Honesty in prayer

I may be wrong, but I suspect there are some things we would never dream of including in our prayers, it just not seeming the done thing. Which of us, for example, would tell God that we are angry or frustrated with him, disappointed at what he has done or failed to do? Which of us would pour out our feelings of resentment, bitterness and even dislike concerning others? In other words, which of us feels able to come before God as we are, and lay our thoughts and emotions on the line? You may, of course, be the exception that proves the rule, but most of us are more circumspect, our prayers couched in a language that we consider God will deem acceptable. After all, we tell ourselves, it's God we're talking to, the creator and Lord of all, so it stands to reason we must watch our P's and Q's, show a little respect. All this contains a degree of truth, yet when we look at the Psalms, biblical prayers *par excellence*, we find no coy and restrained piety, but a blunt spelling out of whatever the writer happened to be feeling at the time of writing, whether it was joy or sorrow, praise or anger, faith or doubt. The God the Psalms address is involved in daily life; sovereign, yes, but eminently approachable, ready both to listen and to answer. He doesn't simply *invite* them to be themselves; he *wants* them to be, for it is only through coming as they are that his grace can help them become the people he would have them be.

Prayer, then, means opening your soul to God. If you're angry, tell him! If you're puzzled and confused, tell him! If you're tired and frustrated, dispirited and disillusioned, tell him! If you've lost heart, lost your way, even lost your faith, tell him! Whatever your feelings and failings, no matter how shocking they may seem, he is big enough to take them, surely preferring a prayer from the heart to words that sound good but mean little. Too easily, prayer can become a matter of going through the motions, telling God what we think he wants to hear rather than expressing our true feelings. Such prayer does nothing for us and nothing for him. We need to say what we mean and mean what we say, or, more accurately, to pray what we mean and mean what we pray. Do that, and then we will know what it means to take everything to God in prayer!

The following meditation illustrates the point I'm trying to make. It emphasises the importance of being true to oneself before God, not

speaking in a prescribed language or necessarily about spiritual things,
but coming as we are and bringing our down-to-earth needs and concerns
to him in prayer.

It's me, O Lord –
    not the person I pretend to be,
    nor who I want to be,
    but me, as I am,
    with all my strengths,
    all my weaknesses,
    all my faith,
    all my doubt –
    me, as I've rarely dared come before,
    reaching out to you in prayer.
I've no right to be here, I know that,
    for I'm nothing special,
    nothing to write home about,
    and I've little idea what I'm going to say,
    still less how to say it.
But you tell us if we truly seek, we shall find,
    if we're really sorry, you'll forgive,
    if we keep on asking, you will answer.
So I'm here, Lord,
    in all my ugliness and sin –
    weak,
    selfish,
    greedy,
    thoughtless –
    but I'm here,
    and I'm asking you despite it all,
    hear my prayer.

My child,
    don't stop,
    keep talking,
    for I'm here too,
    delighted to listen,
    drinking in your every word.

It's a joy to hear you, believe me,
    music to my ears –
    no need to apologise or excuse yourself.
I've looked forward to this moment for so long,
    your coming openly and honestly to meet me.
For it's you I want to talk to,
    not the mask you wear for the world –
    you as you really are –
    the face you show, the face you hide,
    the person you love, the person you hate.
They're both you,
    two halves of the same whole,
    inseparable as light and dark, substance and shadow,
    and unless you bring all, openly and honestly before me,
    you bring nothing.
You're not perfect, I know that,
    but I don't ask you to be –
    it's not me who twists the knife, but you.
I love you as you are,
    with all your faults and fragile faith,
    and I'll go on loving you day after day,
    drawing you closer to me not as a condition
    but as an expression of that love.
So come now, gladly and confidently;
    bring yourself with head bent low but soul held high,
    and find in me your kindest critic
    and truest friend.

Too busy to pray?

'I'd like to pray, believe me, but there just isn't time. I've 101 jobs to get done and I've barely even started, so yes, I'll find time for prayer eventually, but not now.' We've all been there, haven't we, believing ourselves to be so snowed under with demands and responsibilities that prayer is a luxury we cannot afford. So we put it off, and put if off again, feeling increasingly guilty as we do so.

What's the best way to cope at such times? Well, partly, of course, that depends on how busy we actually are. It may be that those things we have to get done aren't as important as we like to think and that many of them could be put off for a while. It may even be that our 'busyness' consists largely in trivia – watching the latest soap on TV, going to the football, reading the paper, or enjoying a drink with friends. Or it may simply be that we need to organise our time better, too much of it being wasted through a failure to plan or work properly. If any of those is the case, then we probably need most of all to be a little more honest with ourselves.

But let's suppose we really are busy, to the point that we're run off our feet – what then? The first thing I'd like to say is this: God understands. Contrary to what we sometimes imagine, he's not waiting to condemn us if we fail to offer prayer, ticking our names off on a register to make sure we're meeting our quota. So if life *is* such a rush that you're too exhausted even to pray, tell him about it in as few words as possible, and ask his help to get through. Having said that, perhaps we do well to remember the story of Martha and Mary, and its important lesson concerning priorities. If we're not careful, we can *always* be too busy for God, for, let's face it, there's always something else that needs doing if we look hard enough. More to the point, if we forget the spiritual dimension to life, then every part suffers, the law of diminishing returns starting to kick in, so that, despite all the effort we put in, we get less and less done. Make time for God and it's surprising how often we find time for everything else as well, whereas when we forget him things quickly pile up on top of us until we feel overwhelmed by them all. The following meditation makes the point:

God, I'm busy,
    rushed off my feet,
    running around like a headless chicken
    with scarcely a moment to breathe.
I hardly know what I'm doing one day to the next,
    always something else waiting,
    someone else demanding my time –
    another job,
    another need,
    another cry for help.
Lord, I'm exhausted,
    just about fit to drop,
    for I've given everything,
    the last drop of blood.
Yet I can't afford to stop,
    not yet anyway,
    for if I do, who will pick up the pieces –
    who will ensure the job gets done?
I've done my best, no one can argue with that,
    but there's so much still to do and so little time to do it.
Lord, give me strength,
    give me a break,
    give me something!

My child,
    you *are* busy,
    your energy astonishing,
I honestly don't know how you do it!
But be careful, please,
    for even *you* need to stop some time.
You can't take on everything, and you mustn't try,
    however strong the urge may be.
I know it's hard to leave a job undone,
    a task unfinished,
    but occasionally you need to, or you'll pay the price –
    believe me, I've seen it all too often.
So step back a little,
    and think about what you're doing and why you're doing it.

Is it really so urgent?
Won't it wait till tomorrow?
Does it have to be you?
You see, sometimes we can be so busy
 we lose sight of what really matters.
There's a time for busyness, don't get me wrong,
 for doing instead of simply talking,
 but there's a time also for being still
 and reflecting on what really counts.
So stop a minute and pause for breath,
 for perhaps then,
 and only then,
 you may find the rest that you crave.

There's one more thing to say, and it's perhaps the most important of all. To pray effectively you haven't necessarily got to stop what you're doing, because, properly understood, prayer is a part of life. We'll touch more on this later but the point is this: a few words, even a thought, can suffice in prayer and be as meaningful as any. Yes, we need longer times too if we're to nurture and sustain our faith, but as well as finding God in times away from the world, prayer is equally about finding him within it.

Too fed-up to pray?

Few of us, thankfully, have to wrestle in life with clinical depression, but equally few escape times when we feel decidedly down. I don't just mean waking up with the Monday morning blues, though that can be hard enough; I'm thinking, rather, of those occasions when life puts us through the mill through illness, tragedy, bereavement or some other traumatic experience that knocks us for six. At such times what we usually take in our stride becomes an effort, and that can include prayer as much as anything, it suddenly becoming a burden instead of a blessing, pain instead of pleasure, and the lower we feel, the less we can be bothered with it. Yet, as the old saying has it, a problem shared is a problem halved, and prayer offers an ideal opportunity to put that into practice, sharing the load with another. So if you're feeling down, life having lost its sparkle, tell God how you feel; pour out your sorrows to him, instead of offering well-intentioned but hollow platitudes. Don't think you need to apologise for how you're feeling, for you don't. Don't think it's wrong to feel as you do, for it's not. Don't expect to come away from your prayer with everything magically resolved, for you almost certainly won't. And don't think you have to balance any negative thoughts with positive ones, tossing in a little praise and thanksgiving to make up for your moans and groans, for that is to have a skewed idea not just of prayer but of God himself. His first desire is to respond to your need, his greatest wish for you to know him as a friend, and part of that is being able to open up and express your feelings honestly. So if you're feeling down, tell him about it, and if the only prayer you can offer is a list of woes, never mind, offer it anyway, for though it may not always seem like it, he *will* hear and listen, even if you come away afterwards feeling that you've been beating your head against a brick wall. There's no criteria you have to meet for your prayer to be acceptable; what matters is that you're true to yourself, for only then can you be true to God. The following meditation illustrates the point:

> Lord, I can't carry on much longer!
> Do you hear me?
> I'm fraying at the edges,
>   coming apart at the seams,

and it's only a matter of time
   before I fall to pieces completely.
What's happened, Lord?
I thought I was in control,
   master of my own destiny,
   one of the few survivors in this rough old world of ours.
All right, I had my problems, I admit it –
   the nagging worries,
   hidden fears,
   pent-up emotions,
   but we all have those, don't we – *all* of us.
I'd learned to live with them over the years,
   even welcome them in a funny way,
   for I felt that knowing my weaknesses
   somehow gave me control.
But not any longer,
   for suddenly the world's been turned upside down,
   everything I'd put my trust in –
   seemingly so solid and certain –
   all at once so insecure.
And now I'm on the edge of a precipice,
   a deep dark cavern opening up beneath me.
I'm slipping, Lord!
I'm falling!
Are you listening?
Help!

My child,
   you *can* carry on, believe me.
You may not think so,
   but you have the resources to keep going,
   or do you really think I'd have brought you this far
   simply to abandon you now?
Of course not!
I'm with you always,
   in the good and the bad,
   the pleasure and the pain,
   the joy and the sorrow.

Whether you see me or whether you don't,
    I'm there beside you,
    watching over you with a love that will never let you go.
But I can't do it all, tempting though it is,
    for that would be no help to either of us in the long run.
You may not *welcome* the hard times,
    but they're as necessary as any,
    for there can be no light without darkness,
    no laughter without tears,
    no beauty without ugliness,
    no life without death.
I'm afraid that's the way it has to be,
    but when you finally reach the end of the tunnel,
    as you surely will,
    it will be to find your faith deeper
    and yourself stronger than you've ever dared to dream.

Too confused to pray?

How easy did you find it to pray when the massive double tsunami struck the Asian Pacific with such catastrophic consequences late in 2004, or when, in the following year, a series of bombs exploded in London, an earthquake devastated Pakistan, a daily catalogue of death and destruction scarred the country of Iraq, and a succession of hurricanes ripped apart the southern states of America? Much in life, albeit generally far removed from us, is hard to reconcile with faith, leaving us grappling with questions and unable to stifle all kinds of doubts. Why does God allow such suffering, we ask ourselves? Why doesn't he step in and help? How can we speak of a loving purpose in the face of such heart-ache? All too easily we can end up questioning the very existence of the one we're praying to and the value of prayer itself, and when that happens, continuing with it can be very hard, if not impossible. Wouldn't it be more honest, we wonder, to wait until our doubts are resolved? Is there any point praying if we can't make sense of what we're doing? Well, yes and no. It goes back to what I was saying about being honest in prayer. There's no point in going through the motions, saying what you think is expected of you. Such prayer would be empty, true neither to us nor to God. If you're wrestling with questions of faith and unable to find answers, open up about it, even if your prayer is simply 'Lord, I'm not sure I believe anything any more', or, perhaps, 'Lord, I believe; help with my unbelief.' Ask God's help in facing the questions and finding answers. Run away from the challenge, and faith will almost certainly be undermined. Face it, and God can lead you to deeper understanding and maturity. The following meditation develops the point:

> Lord, I'm not sure any more –
> not like I used to be.
> There was a time when it was all so clear,
> everything black and white.
> But now?
> I just don't know.
> And I'm lost and frightened.
> It's not that I don't believe any more –

simply that the edges have become blurred,
the picture fuzzy, no matter how I try to focus it.
And I can't say why, that's what really frightens me –
there's no one moment I can put my finger on
and say that's where it all started,
where the rot set in,
where the damage was done.
It's rather that,
slowly,
like it or not,
my view on life has changed,
few things as certain as I once thought,
few truths as uncomplicated as I once imagined.
What I see one way, those around me see another.
What's right in one place is wrong in the next.
What seemed obvious yesterday is a mystery today.
Why, Lord?
What's happening to me?
What's gone wrong?
I'd like it to be different,
to be like it always was before,
and I feel as if I'm failing you because it isn't –
letting the side down almost,
though that's the last thing I want to do.
Yet what option is there?
I could pretend,
put on a show,
go through the motions.
And yes, I might fool others,
maybe even myself,
but never you, Lord,
that's the trouble –
never you.

My child,
stop torturing yourself,
stop apologising!

I'm glad you're not sure,
     for there are few people I like less
     than those convinced of their own rightness.
Oh, I know it's not easy, living with doubt.
I know you'd love to have everything crystal clear,
     mapped out to the last detail.
But do you honestly think that would be faith?
Let me tell you this –
     if you think you know it all, you don't,
     if you imagine you've understood, you haven't,
     if you believe you've got it right,
     you've almost certainly got it wrong.
Or do you really imagine you're like me –
     your thoughts my thoughts,
     your ways my ways?
No, don't be ashamed of doubt,
     for it's not answers I'm finally looking for,
     it's a willingness to ask the questions –
     to keep on looking,
     keep on striving,
     keep on accepting there's another step still to be taken
     just when you thought the end was in sight.
It may be hard to live with, I'm well aware of that,
     but, believe me, it's not doubt that will destroy you,
     despite what some people may say –
     it's a faith that will not question.

Unanswered prayer

Why does prayer sometimes seem to go unanswered? Why are we often left disappointed, even when we're sure we're asking for the right thing? Of all the questions we may have concerning prayer, this surely is the one that perplexes us most. Is it my fault, we wonder? Am I asking in the wrong way or am I not as close to God as I should be? Have I done something wrong, causing him not to listen? Is God there at all? A look at the Bible shows that such feelings are nothing new. 'How long, O Lord?' wrote the psalmist (Psalm 131:3a). 'Will you forget me for ever? How long will you hide your face from me? Consider and answer me, O Lord my God!' And again: 'Hear my prayer, O Lord; let my cry come to you. Do not hide your face from me in the day of my distress. Incline your ear to me; answer me speedily in the day when I call' (Psalm 102:1, 2). 'My God, my God, why have you abandoned me? Why are you so far from helping me, from heeding my groans? I cry out by day, O God, but you do not answer; and by night, but gain no respite' (Psalm 22:1, 2). Time and again the psalm writers make no secret of their despair and frustration in the face of God's apparent refusal or inability to answer.

So how can we make sense of this? One answer is given to us by the Apostle Paul, who knew firsthand the pain and confusion occasioned by unanswered prayer, having three times begged God to rid him of what he termed a 'thorn in the flesh' – some unnamed problem that clearly caused him huge distress. His request was not granted, but for Paul this was an answer in itself, God's way of saying, 'My grace is all you need, for in your weakness my power is perfected' (2 Corinthians 12:9). Here, then, is one possible explanation of the riddle of 'unanswered' prayer – namely, that *no* answer may be *the* answer, or at least the answer we're given is not the one we want or expect. I am reminded of that often-told story of a man who falls off a ship and then stubbornly spurns every attempt to rescue him, each time protesting, 'God will save me.' 'What happened?' he asks God, when, having drowned, he finds himself in heaven. 'Where were you?' 'I don't understand it,' comes the reply. 'I threw down a lifebelt, then sent a lifeboat, then a helicopter. Didn't you see them?' A simplistic analogy, I know, but it contains an important truth nonetheless. How often do we fail to recognise God's reply because we've already decided what it should be?

Another possibility is that we're simply not tuned in to God. I don't want to push the metaphor too far, but just as we need an aerial, cable, digibox or satellite dish to pick up various radio and television signals, so we need to be on God's wavelength to 'pick up' his voice. As Jesus put it on more than one occasion, 'Those with ears to hear, let them hear.' In other words, unless we are receptive to God, we will not hear what he is saying, however hard we try. If we expect an answer, we must first get close enough to listen.

There are many other reasons why our prayers may not seem to be answered. Perhaps we're asking for the wrong things, more concerned with serving self than others. Perhaps God has other and better plans for us, knowing what's best better than we do ourselves. Perhaps his answer is 'yes, but not yet', or perhaps he has done his bit and is waiting for us to do ours. Perhaps his hands are tied in some way by our refusal to listen, change or respond as he needs us to, or perhaps we're simply asking for what, in terms of this world, is impossible, its fulfilment only possible in the life to come. Whatever the case, we have God's assurance that he *does* listen and *will* answer, no prayer that we offer passing unheard. So however frustrated you may feel, however much you may seem to be beating your head against a brick wall, don't give up, for even now God may be working in ways you do not yet see. The following meditation sums up that truth.

You're here, Lord!
How did I never see it before?
How did I go so long,
    aching,
    thirsting,
    searching,
    when all the time you were here,
    standing by my side,
    right before my very eyes?
It's astonishing, yet it's true,
    day after day I've gone through life oblivious to your presence.
I've knelt in prayer and begged you to hear me,
    I've shared in worship, hungry to meet you,
    I've studied your word, thirsting for guidance,

yet when you answered,
  when you touched my soul,
  I never knew it, even when you called my name.
Why, Lord?
Wasn't I listening?
Was my mind distracted,
  my attention elsewhere?
I thought I was ready,
  tuned in and waiting,
  but I wasn't,
  for somehow I missed you when you were there all along.

My child,
  there's no mystery, strange though it all seems to you.
You *were* listening,
  as eagerly and intently as I could have wished for,
  except for one thing –
  it was for *your* answer,
  in *your* time,
  on *your* terms.
That's what muddled you.
When I told you to wait, you wanted to hurry;
  when I answered no, you shouted yes;
  when I asked for patience, you chafed with frustration;
  when I urged you forward, you wandered back.
It wasn't me you were looking for,
  much though you thought it was,
  but yourself –
  me made in your image rather than you made in mine,
  and that's why you never heard.
But I was there for all that,
  just as I always am,
  just as I'll always be,
  speaking my word,
  leading you by the hand,
  offering you my guidance,
  and waiting till you respond.

So next time you do not see me,
   when you call my name
   and I do not seem to answer,
   look within and ask yourself,
   are you really listening,
   and do you want to hear?

How long should we keep praying?

'If at first you don't succeed, try, try, try again.' Generally speaking, that's good advice; it is those with sufficient resolve and resilience to bounce back from disappointment who find their way to success. Many famous authors had their early manuscripts rejected before finally having a book published. Untold motorists needed to take their driving test several times before eventually managing to pass. And countless childless couples experience years of trauma before their dream of a child comes true. In such cases, persistence by no means guarantees success, but it certainly helps increase the chances. On the other hand, there are times when persistence is inappropriate. Some would-be authors will never have a book published no matter how many manuscripts they submit – their writing is simply not good enough. Some would-be drivers are a threat to others and themselves when they get behind the wheel; they could retake their test a thousand times and still fail to get through. And all too many couples are biologically predestined never to have a child, however hard they try. What we deem persistence in one case looks like stubbornness in another; tenacity being just another word for pigheadedness, depending on how you look at it.

So how about when it comes to prayer? Should we carry on praying for something when God doesn't seem to answer, or should we admit defeat, accepting that he's saying no or leading us in another direction? At first sight, the teaching of Jesus seems to imply we should persevere come what may. Take, for example, the story of the Canaanite woman who came to Jesus begging him to heal her daughter. Jesus' first answer was cagey, to say the least: 'I have been sent solely to the lost sheep of the house of Israel.' And when that failed to put her off, he was still more blunt: 'It wouldn't be right to take the children's food and hurl it to the dogs' (Matthew 15:24, 26). Hardly the most encouraging of replies, but incredibly the woman kept on asking and eventually got what she wanted: 'Woman, you have enormous faith,' said Jesus. 'Your plea is granted' (Matthew 15:28). Add to that the parable of a man who turned up at a friend's house late one night asking for bread, just when the friend had locked up and settled down to sleep. Once again, a refusal to take no for an answer finally wins the day, the friend reluctantly rousing himself and getting some food in order to get rid of his unwanted visitor. The implication seems to be that if we're dogged enough, we can wear God down until he caves in to our requests.

Can that be true? Is prayer really about making such a nuisance of ourselves that eventually God will capitulate and bow to our every whim? Well, if it is, pity help us, for what sort of God would that make him, and what kind of world would we end up with? But is this actually what Jesus was saying? I don't think so. His aim was to contrast, not liken, the unjust judge to God. If even a corrupt old reprobate will eventually respond to requests for help, he says, then how much more will God! That's the point here: not that we have to twist God's arm but that he delights to bless us and longs, whenever possible, to shower us with good things. Far from having to bludgeon God into submission, we need only to approach him for him to respond in love. Yet, having said that, there are times when God has to say no to our requests, either because they're not right for us or not right for others. What should we do then? If, as we claim, we believe God knows best, then what do we think we're doing by pushing him to say yes? Too often we're happy to accept God's answer so long as it fits in with our wishes, but if it doesn't, we decide we must pray harder and keep on praying until God gives the answer we're looking for. It's a slippery road to tread.

But that's not quite the end of story, for there are times, I think, when God wants us to persist, and for a variety of reasons. It may be we need time to reflect on what we're asking for and what granting it will mean. It may be we have to show we're serious, that our request is for something we truly want or need rather than a passing whim. Or it may be we're not yet ready for what we're asking, God needing to prepare the ground first. How do we know when to persist and when to let go? Sadly, there is no foolproof rule we can apply. It's possible to persevere too much, consciously or unconsciously trying to force God's hand when, in fact, he's answered already, only we don't like his reply. Equally, we can persist too little, giving up at the drop of a hat. Getting the balance right is far from easy. Admitting we've got it wrong is harder still.

The following meditation, based upon the unjust judge in Luke 18:1-8, explores further what persisting in prayer may involve:

> I didn't like to ask again,
>> for I'd come before God in prayer so many times before,
>> and I was afraid if I kept on he'd get fed up with me,
>> sick and tired of the same old refrain, day after day.

There's no denying it, I'd been like a dog with a bone,
    refusing to let go
    until even *I* had become wearied by the whole business,
    never mind what *he* must have felt.
Yet, for all my pleading, I was no further forward,
    my prayers seeming to fall on deaf ears –
    hardly a surprise, then, that I lost heart.
It was time to give it a rest,
    for if God wanted to answer me
    he'd surely have done so by now,
    it stood to reason –
    even *his* patience has some limits!
Only I couldn't have been more wrong,
    not just about that but about everything,
    as Jesus was to show me so simply yet so powerfully that day.
Which of you, he said, wouldn't grant a request
    if pushed hard enough?
If someone made a sufficient nuisance of themselves,
    how many of you wouldn't give in? –
    with bad grace perhaps,
    against your better judgement,
    but eventually any inconvenience worth it for a bit of peace.
I thought he was saying the same about God –
    that if even *we* finally acquiesce,
    then *he* is bound to do the same –
    and perhaps that *was* part of it,
    in the sense that we must never give up in prayer,
    never feel he hasn't heard or doesn't care.
But then Jesus continued:
    'Ask, and it will be given you;
    search, and you will find;
    knock, and the door will be opened for you' –
    and I realised he wasn't so much comparing
    as contrasting God with us,
    reminding us that, though it may not seem like it,
    he is always listening,
    always ready to respond,
    always looking to grant his blessings to us.

So I'm here again,
   kneeling before God,
   offering once more my old familiar prayer,
   and suddenly the answer is becoming clear –
   goodness knows why I didn't see it before.
I should have understood
   and I will next time,
   for I know now God doesn't grudgingly reply when we call –
   our prayers an unwelcome irritation –
   rather, he delights to hear us,
   and waits eagerly to shower his gifts without reserve
   on all those who ask him.

Part Two

RESOURCES FOR PRAYER

The Old Testament on prayer

You'd have thought, wouldn't you, given the emphasis Christians and the Church place upon prayer, that the Bible would have a good deal to say on the subject, but it actually says surprisingly little. There are references to people praying, certainly, and without doubt it's taken as read that prayer is a daily part of Christian life, but there's a paucity of explicit teaching about it. There is nonetheless much that the Bible can teach us, and, contrary to what you might expect, it's the Old Testament that provides a particularly valuable resource. Nowhere is this more so than in the Psalms, for although these were designed to be sung, they are essentially a collection of prayers, and a wonderful assortment at that. For example, there are joyful outbursts of praise:

> Praise the Lord! Let my soul praise the Lord! I will extol the Lord all my days; I will honour him my whole life long with songs of worship. What a joy it is and how appropriate to sing praises to our God. *Psalm 146:1, 2; 147:1b*

> I will bless the Lord at all times; his praise will constantly be upon my lips. *Psalm 34:1*

> You, Lord, are enthroned high over all the earth, exalted above all gods. Your constant love is higher than the heavens and your truth reaches up to the skies. To you belongs glory, O God, for you are enthroned high in heaven. Let your glory illuminate the earth. *Psalm 97:9; 108:4, 5*

> The heavens acknowledge your mighty deeds, O Lord; and the congregation of the holy ones proclaims your constancy. No one among the gods is like you, O Lord, nor are any deeds like yours. All people that you have made will come and bow in homage before you, O Lord, and give glory to your name, for you are great and do breathtaking things. You alone are God. *Psalm 89:5; 86:8-10*

> My heart is constant, O God, resolute within me. I will sing and make music. I will publicly give you thanks, Lord, and sing praise

among the nations, for your unfailing love reaches up to the heavens, and your constancy extends beyond the clouds. Let your name be honoured, O God, above the heavens, and your glory known across the earth!   *Psalm 57:7, 9-11*

I will hope continually, and will praise you more and more each day.   *Psalm 71:14*

I will praise you, for your constant love is better than life itself. I will worship you all my days, lifting up my hands and calling on your name.   *Psalm 63:3, 4*

Equally, there are outpourings of confession coupled with pleas for mercy:

I lift up my voice to the Lord; crying out to him for mercy. Listen to my pleas for mercy, Lord, and in your faithfulness and righteousness, respond to my appeal.   *Psalm 142:1; 143:1*

While I remained silent, my body grew weary with my constant groaning, for day and night your hand weighed heavily upon me; my strength dried up like sap in the heat of summer. Then I acknowledged my sin and did not conceal my guilt from you; I said, 'I will confess my disobedience to the Lord,' and you absolved me from my guilt and sin.   *Psalm 32:3-5*

From the depths of despair I call out to you, Lord! Hear my voice, I beg you, and listen to my cry as I plead for mercy! If you, Lord, were to keep an account of our sins, which of us could lift up our head before you? In you, though, is forgiveness, and consequently you are worshipped.   *Psalm 130:1-4*

I admit my faults and am truly sorry for my sin.   *Psalm 38:18*

Then there are pleas for protection, comfort, guidance, justice and strength:

Lord, you have been our home across the centuries. Before the mountains were formed and before you fashioned this world we live in, from eternity to eternity you are God. You return us to dust, saying, 'Back to what you once were, you mortals!' A thousand years are like a passing day in your sight, as short-lived as the night-watch. Our fleeting span is seventy years, perhaps eighty if we are strong; throughout they are filled with struggle and sorrow, here today and gone tomorrow. Teach us to make the most of our days and so to discover the secret of inner wisdom.

Psalm 90:1-4, 10, 12

I cry out to the Lord, I lift up my voice begging him for mercy. I pour out my grievance before him; I tell him openly of my trouble.

Psalm 142:1, 2

God, rescue me, for the waters have risen to my neck. I sink in a deep swamp, where I can find no footing; I have slipped into deep waters, and the flood engulfs me. I am tired of this weeping, throat dry and eyes blurred with tears, while I wait for my God. Lord, I bring you my prayer. In your own time, O God, and out of the greatness of your unfailing love, answer me. Faithfully hear me, once more, and rescue me from sinking in the swamp; deliver me from my adversaries and from the deep waters. Do not let the flood overwhelm me, or the deep swallow me, or the pit close up over my head.

Psalm 69:1-4, 13-15

Satisfy us each morning with your unswerving love, so that we may rejoice and celebrate all our days.

Psalm 90:14

Do not be far from me, for trouble is at hand and I have no one to help me. Please, Lord, don't keep your distance. Hurry and help me, come to my aid.

Psalm 22:11, 19

You, O God, are *my* God. I look for you, my spirit yearns and my whole being hankers after you, just as someone in a parched and arid desert longs for water.

Psalm 63:1

I take shelter in you, O Lord; grant that I may not be humiliated. Deal justly and come to my aid: bring deliverance; listen and save me. You are my rock and fortress; be those to me now!

Psalm 71:1, 2

Then, there are prayers for others:

> Grant blessing, Lord, to those who are good, those who are honest
> in heart.   *Psalm 125:4*

> Rescue your people, grant blessing on your heritage; be a shepherd
> to them and bear them in your arms for ever.   *Psalm 28:9*

> Grant justice to the weak and orphaned; uphold the entitlements
> of the deprived and destitute. Save the vulnerable and disadvantaged;
> redeem them from the clutches of the corrupt.   *Psalm 82:3, 4*

There are simple declarations of faith and trust:

> Even though I walk through the darkest of valleys, I fear no evil;
> for you are with me, your rod and staff a constant source of comfort.
> You prepare a table before me in the presence of my foes; you
> anoint my head with oil; my cup brims over.   *Psalm 23:4, 5*

> I will sing of your devoted love for ever, O Lord; my mouth will
> declare your faithfulness to the end of time.   *Psalm 89:1*

> Lord, my heart does not get above itself nor do I lift my eyes higher
> than I can hope to see. I do not dwell on matters beyond my compre-
> hension, too wonderful for me to fathom. No, I see myself instead as
> a weaned child, as one whose mother has set its soul at rest. That's
> what my soul's like: a child gently soothed by a mother's love.
>   *Psalm 131:1, 2*

> O Lord, you have searched me and known me. You know when I
> sit down and when I rise up; you discern my thoughts from far
> away. Such knowledge is too wonderful for me; it is so high that I
> cannot attain it. Where can I evade your spirit? Where can I flee
> from your presence? If I soar up to heaven, you are there; if I
> make my bed in Sheol, you are there. If I sail on the wings of the
> morning and settle at the uttermost limits of the sea, even there
> your hand will lead me, your right hand holding me firm. If I say,
> 'Surely darkness will steal over me, night will envelop me,' dark-
> ness is not dark to you; the night is as bright as day; for you dark
> and light are the same.   *Psalm 139:1, 2, 6-12*

I will lie down and sleep in peace; for you alone, O Lord, make me lie down in safety.   *Psalm 4:8*

The Lord has listened to my plea; he will accept my prayer.
                                                        Psalm 6:9

There are words of acknowledgement and thanksgiving:

I had become like a broken pot . . . but you heard my pleas when I cried out for help.   *Psalm 31:12b, 22b*

When I thought, 'My foot is starting to slip,' your love, O Lord, supported me. I am constantly with you; you hold my right hand. I will acclaim you, O Lord, for I was at rock bottom and you lifted me up.   *Psalm 94:18; 73:23; 30:1a*

I will praise the name of the Lord in song; I will magnify him with thanksgiving.   *Psalm 69:30*

I am contented deep within, like someone who has enjoyed a sumptuous meal. When I lie awake at night, reflecting during the hours of darkness over all you have done, my mouth worships you, songs of joy on my lips, for you have helped me, encircling me in the shadow of your wings.   *Psalm 63:5-7*

I will sing unceasingly of your unfailing love, O Lord; I will declare your faithfulness to all generations. Your constant love is unchanged from the beginning of time, and your faithfulness is as permanent as the heavens.   *Psalm 89:1, 2*

I give thanks to the Lord with all my heart. I offer thanks in your name for your unfailing love and constancy; your name and your love are exalted above everything.   *Psalm 138:1a, 2*

There are exclamations of frustration, doubt and dismay, and at times what can only be described as tantrums, as the psalm writer vents his spleen on God:

I call to you, O Lord my rock: do not refuse to listen, for if you keep silent I shall be like those who go down into the depths.

Hear my entreaty as I beg you for help, and as I lift up my hands towards your dwelling place. *Psalm 28:1, 2*

Why, O Lord, are you so distant? Why do you hide yourself from me in my hour of need? My God, my God, why have you abandoned me? Why are you so far from helping me, from heeding my groans? I cry to you by day, O God, but you do not answer; and by night, but gain no respite. *Psalm 10:1; 22:1, 2*

How much longer, Lord? Are you going to hide yourself away for ever? Where, Lord, is your steadfast love of old? Do not stay silent, O God; do not remain quiet and do nothing. I lift up my voice and cry to the Lord, entreating him for help. I pour out my complaint, spelling out my troubles before him.

Psalm 89:46a, 49a; 83:1; 142:1, 2

Hear my prayer, Lord, let it reach you. Please don't turn your face from me at my time of need. Give ear to my cry, and when I call to you answer me swiftly. *Psalm 102:1, 2*

And there are some prayers that are downright vindictive, shocking in the intensity of their emotions:

Break the arms of the sinful and wrongdoers; root out their wickedness until there is none left anywhere. *Psalm 10:15*

Let those who cast aspersions on me be humiliated and destroyed; let those who try to hurt me be utterly put to shame, ridiculed and dishonoured. Multiply their guilt upon them and refuse them any prospect of acquittal. Expunge their names from the book of the living, and do not grant them any place among the roll of the righteous. Let them disappear like water that trickles away; let them be trodden underfoot like grass and wither away. Let them be like a slug putrefying in its own slime, like a stillborn child that never sees the light of day.

Psalm 71:13; 69:27, 28; 58:7, 8

Not every psalm, then, as you can see, is a perfect example of prayer – indeed, some are quite the opposite – but together they speak of a living relationship with God, of one whom the writers felt able to address not in formal religious language but from the heart, freely expressing what they thought and felt. If you're ever struggling to pray, as happens to most of us at some time or other, then you could do a lot worse than turn to the book of Psalms, for, whatever it is you want to say, the chances are you'll find words there to say it for you.

The New Testament on prayer

Read through the New Testament, and Paul's letters in particular, and it's clear that prayer was central to the life of the Church, even though we're given few examples of the actual prayers used. 'All the disciples, without exception,' says Acts 1:14, 'along with the women, Mary the mother of Jesus, and his brothers, single-mindedly dedicated themselves to prayer.' 'Exult in hope,' wrote Paul to the church in Rome (Romans 12:12), 'be long-suffering in times of trial, and be steadfast in prayer.' And it's a similar message elsewhere. Ephesians 6:18: 'In all your requests and entreaties, pray at all times in the Spirit . . . pleading for all the saints.' Philippians 4:6: 'Do not brood about anything, but thankfully bring all your needs to God through your prayers and petitions.' Colossians 4:2: 'Persevere in prayer, remaining constantly alert in it with thanksgiving.' And finally 1 Thessalonians 5:17: 'pray without ceasing'. Quite clearly, then, prayer was seen as inseparable from Christian discipleship, the idea of there being one without the other simply not an option. But equally clearly, unless Paul intended us all to live a monastic hermit-like existence, prayer was seen as far more than a 'religious' activity that somehow had to be fitted into one's daily routine; it should arise naturally in day-to-day situations as each moment is consecrated to God.

Don't go away, though, with the impression that Paul found prayer easy, for revealing words in his letter to the Romans indicate he found it anything but. 'We do not know how to pray,' he writes, 'or what to pray for, but the Spirit pleads on our behalf with entreaties that are beyond words, and the one who searches our hearts knows the Spirit's mind, because he intercedes constantly on behalf of the saints seeking the fulfilment of God's purpose' (Romans 8:26, 27). Encouraging words indeed, and vital to remember at those times when prayer doesn't come easily or doesn't come at all. The Holy Spirit, says Paul, is able to articulate our thoughts to God, even when *we* find it impossible to do so. More than that, Christ himself is constantly interceding on our behalf, expressing our unspoken needs and requests. Prayer may start with us but it doesn't end there. However much it may sometimes feel like it, we are never alone in our attempts. That's not to encourage casualness or complacency, for prayer is for our benefit rather than God's, but if you can't quite find the right words, or genuinely can't give to it the time that you'd like, don't despair, for your prayer will get to him nonetheless.

If that's what Paul makes of prayer, what about Jesus? Surprisingly, he has less to say on the subject than we might imagine, but what he *does* say has much to teach us. There's advice concerning asking in prayer, a parable about persistence, prayers of Jesus in Gethsemane and on the cross, and, of course, the celebrated words that have come to be known simply as the Lord's Prayer, and we'll look at each of these more carefully during the course of this book. But it's not just what Jesus *said* that's important but also what he *did*, repeatedly spending quality time alone with God. For him, too, prayer was not tagged on to daily life but it underpinned each moment of every day: the vital ingredient that sustained his faith and ministry and without which he could never have continued.

What, finally, of specific examples of prayer within the New Testament? Few and far between they may be, but they include some of the most memorable words of Scripture, many of which will be familiar to us as blessings at the close of worship:

> Now to the one who, in line with the gospel I preach and Lord Jesus Christ I proclaim, is able to build you up through the unfolding of the mystery – obscured for so long but now, at God's command and in order to secure obedient faith, divulged and made known through prophetic words to all people – to that God, the only source of true wisdom, be glory now and always, through Jesus Christ! Amen. *Romans 16:25-27*

> Blessed be the God and Father of our Lord Jesus Christ, who has bestowed on us in Christ every spiritual blessing in the heavenly realms. *Ephesians 1:3*

> Now to him who by his power at work within us is able to achieve inestimably more than anything we can ask or even dream of, to him be glory in the Church and in Christ Jesus in this and every generation, now and always. Amen. *Ephesians 3:20, 21*

> Now may the God of peace, who through the blood of the eternal covenant brought our Lord Jesus – the great shepherd of the sheep – back from the dead, provide you with all good things, so

that you may be able to do his will and offer service pleasing in his sight, through Jesus Christ, to whom be eternal honour. Amen.

Hebrews 13:20, 21

To him who is able to keep us from slipping and to present us faultless and brimming over with joy into the glorious presence of God, to him be glory and majesty, dominion and power, now and for evermore. Amen.

Jude vv. 24, 25

Classic prayers

What is that makes a prayer unforgettable? That's a hard question to answer, for there's no simple formula to follow, and indeed it would be a sad thing if there were, but if there are two things we might highlight, they are probably a poetic use of words coupled with deep spiritual insight. These, when wedded together, are able to speak to the heart and soul. So it is that certain prayers have spoken to generations across the years, touching a chord deep within. Take, for example, the memorable prayer of St Ignatius of Loyola (1491–1556):

> Teach me, good Lord,
> to serve you as you deserve:
> to give, and not to count the cost;
> to fight, and not to heed the wounds;
> to toil, and not to seek for rest;
> to labour, and to ask for no reward,
> except that of knowing that I do your will;
> through Jesus Christ my Lord.
> Amen.

Another famous prayer – the so-called 'Anima Christi' – dates from around the fourteenth century:

> Soul of Christ, sanctify me.
> Body of Christ, save me.
> Blood of Christ, inebriate me.
> Water from the side of Christ, wash me.
> Passion of Christ, strengthen me.
> O good Jesus, hear me.
> Within thy sacred wounds hide me.
> From the wicked enemy defend me.
> In the hour of my death call me
> and bid me come to thee
> that with thy saints I may praise thee
> for ever and ever.
> Amen.

Or again, there's the simple but unforgettable prayer of St Augustine of Hippo (354–430):

Everlasting God,
    in whom we live and move and have our being:
    you have made us for yourself,
    and our hearts are restless until they rest in you.

Likewise, the prayer of St Patrick (387–461), commonly known as St Patrick's Breastplate:

Christ be with me, Christ within me,
Christ behind me, Christ before me,
Christ beside me, Christ to win me,
Christ to comfort me and restore me;
Christ beneath me, Christ above me,
Christ in quiet, Christ in danger,
Christ in hearts of all that love me,
Christ in mouth of friend or stranger.

And how about the following prayer attributed to Clement XI (1649–1721), generally known as the 'Universal Prayer':

Lord, I believe in you: increase my faith.
I trust in you: strengthen my trust.
I love you: let me love you more and more.
I am sorry for my sins: deepen my sorrow.
I worship you as my first beginning.
I long for you as my last end.
I praise you as my constant helper,
    and call on you as my loving protector.
Guide me by your wisdom,
    correct me with your justice,
    comfort me with your mercy,
    protect me with your power.
I offer you, Lord, my thoughts: to be fixed on you;
    my words: to have you for their theme;
    my actions: to reflect my love for you;
    my sufferings: to be endured for your greater glory.

I want to do what you ask of me:
    in the way that you ask,
    for as long as you ask,
    because you ask it.
Lord, enlighten my understanding,
    strengthen my will,
    purify my heart,
    and make me holy.
Help me to repent of my past sins
    and to resist temptation in the future.
Help me to rise above my human weakness
    and to grow stronger as a Christian.
Let me love you, my Lord and my God,
    and see myself as I really am:
    a pilgrim in this world,
    a Christian called to respect and love all whose lives I touch,
    those in authority over me or those under my authority,
    my friends and my enemies.
Help me to conquer anger by gentleness,
    greed by generosity,
    apathy by fervour.
Help me to forget myself and reach out towards others.
Make me prudent in planning,
    courageous in taking risks.
Make me patient in suffering,
    unassuming in prosperity.
Keep me, Lord, attentive in prayer,
    temperate in food and drink,
    diligent in my work,
    firm in my good intentions.
Let my conscience be clear,
    my conduct without fault,
    my speech blameless,
    my life well-ordered.
Put me on guard against my human weaknesses.
Let me cherish your love for me,
    keep your law,
    and come at last to your salvation.

Teach me to realise that this world is passing,
 that my true future is the happiness of heaven,
 that life on earth is short,
 and the life to come eternal.
Help me to prepare for death with a proper fear of judgement,
 but a greater trust in your goodness.
Lead me safely through death
 to the endless joy of heaven.
Grant this through Christ our Lord.
Amen.

And so we could go on. We have at our disposal a great repository of riches built up across the centuries; a treasure-trove of spiritual wisdom and insight that we do well to make use of. Such prayers can't always speak for us, and if we use them too often their impact will be diminished, but on occasions they can be an invaluable aid to devotion, helping us to meet with God in a special way. We can find them in all kinds of places. Browse, for example, in your local library or bookshop, or perhaps in a second-hand bookstall, or simply look online, searching under 'Classic prayers' or similar keywords. Build up a personal collection of prayers that speak most powerfully to you, and make a point of dipping into them, regularly using this resource.

Music in prayer

It's good sometimes in prayer to escape from words, for although they can help express our feelings, they can also trap them, tying us down to earth rather than allowing us to soar in spirit up to heaven. To a point, that limitation can be overcome simply through setting words to music; at other times music alone is sufficient to capture our imagination, transporting us into another dimension. How far music can be useful in prayer depends partly on the music itself and partly on how we use it. Much obviously depends on the taste of the listener, what moves one entirely failing to stir another. The key thing is that it helps us to focus our thoughts on God, and whatever music we make use of, it's important to keep that objective in mind. Much ancient music was written specifically for devotional purposes, from the monastic plainchant of monks to untold hymns and anthems, the innumerable cantatas of Handel and Bach and the celebrated requiems and masses of the great composers, to name but some. In these we find expressions of praise, confession, thanksgiving and much else. That tradition is continued today by a host of talented musicians and writers, devotional musical resources available as never before. You'll find many recommended in the resource section (Part Four) of this book.

There's a danger, when listening to music in this way, of forgetting why we do so, prayer taking a back seat as we simply savour the piece or allow our thoughts to wander where they will; but don't let this put you off making use of this wonderful resource which is able like few others to speak both *to* and *from* the heart, carrying us in spirit into the very presence of God. The following reflective prayer, 'The symphony', makes the point:

> It stirred my heart,
>> bringing a lump to my throat,
>> the emotions it aroused so powerful,
>> almost overwhelming,
>> that my spirit soared with the melody,
>> transported to new heights,
>> an ecstasy of delight.

May the same be true, Lord, of knowing you,
　　your presence causing me to catch my breath in wonder,
　　to exult and marvel.
Instead of being an arid issue of the mind –
　　an intellectual assent to truth –
　　may faith be an affair of the heart,
　　capturing my imagination,
　　lifting me up and transporting me into your presence,
　　so that, overwhelmed with joy and filled with awe,
　　my spirit may rise to you each day,
　　in rapturous praise and grateful worship.
　Amen.

Poetic prayers

People find some forms of prayer more helpful than others, and that's almost certainly so when it comes to using poems, poetry leaving many people completely cold. Yet you only have to look at the success of writers like Helen Steiner Rice to see that many people find this a hugely valuable resource, offering inspiration, comfort, challenge and reassurance. Of course, not all poems are suitable for personal prayer, in the sense of directly articulating our thoughts. Some, certainly, may speak to us powerfully, opening up new perspectives on life and fresh insights into the world around us, and thus play a real part in our devotional life, but if you take time to look, there are also many poems written on specifically religious themes, and often in the first person, enabling us to identify with the writer's thoughts and in some way make them our own. Take, for example, the following:

My prayers must meet a brazen heaven

My prayers must meet a brazen heaven
and fail and scatter all away.
Unclean and seeming unforgiven
my prayers I scarcely call to pray.
I cannot buoy my heart above;
above I cannot entrance win.
I reckon precedents of love,
but feel the long success of sin.

My heaven is brass and iron my earth:
yea, iron is mingled with my clay,
so harden'd is it in this dearth
which praying fails to do away.
Nor tears, nor tears this clay uncouth
could mould, if any tears there were.
A warfare of my lips in truth,
battling with God, is now my prayer.

Gerard Manley Hopkins (1844–89)

Love bade me welcome

Love bade me welcome; yet my soul drew back,
guilty of dust and sin.
But quick-eyed Love, observing me grow slack
from my first entrance in,
drew nearer to me, sweetly questioning
if I lack'd any thing.
A guest, I answer'd, worthy to be here:
Love said, You shall be he.
I the unkind, ungrateful? Ah, my dear,
I cannot look on thee.
Love took my hand, and smiling did reply,
Who made the eyes but I?
Truth, Lord, but I have marr'd them: let my shame
go where it doth deserve.
And know you not, says Love, who bore the blame?
My dear, then I will serve.
You must sit down, says Love, and taste my meat:
so I did sit and eat.

George Herbert (1593–1633)

The tables turned

Up! up! my Friend, and quit your books;
Or surely you'll grow double:
Up! up! my Friend, and clear your looks;
Why all this toil and trouble?

The sun, above the mountain's head,
A freshening lustre mellow
Through all the long green fields has spread,
His first sweet evening yellow.

Books! 'tis a dull and endless strife:
Come, hear the woodland linnet,
How sweet his music! on my life,
There's more of wisdom in it.

And hark! how blithe the throstle sings!
He, too, is no mean preacher:
Come forth into the light of things,
Let Nature be your teacher.

She has a world of ready wealth,
Our minds and hearts to bless –
Spontaneous wisdom breathed by health,
Truth breathed by cheerfulness.

One impulse from a vernal wood
May teach you more of man,
Of moral evil and of good,
Than all the sages can.

Sweet is the lore which Nature brings;
Our meddling intellect
Mis-shapes the beauteous forms of things –
We murder to dissect.

Enough of Science and of Art;
Close up those barren leaves;
Come forth, and bring with you a heart
That watches and receives.

William Wordsworth (1770–1850)

Nirvana

Could my heart but see Creation as God sees it – from within;
See his grace behind its beauty, see his will behind its force;
See the flame of life shoot upward when the April days begin;
See the wave of life rush outward from its pure eternal source;

Could I see the summer sunrise glow
    with God's transcendent hope;
See his peace upon the waters in the moonlit summer night;
See him nearer still when, blinded,
    in the depths of gloom I grope –
See the darkness flash and quiver with the gladness of his light;

Could I see the red-hot passion of his love resistless burn
Through the dumb despair of winter,
  through the frozen lifeless clod –
Could I see what lies around me as God sees it, I should learn
That its outward life is nothing, that its inward life is God.

Vain the dream! To spirit only is the spirit-life revealed:
God alone can see God's glory: God alone can feel God's love.
By myself the soul of Nature from myself is still concealed;
And the earth is still around me, and the skies are still above.

Vain the dream! I cannot mingle with the all-sustaining soul:
I am prisoned in my senses; I am pinioned by my pride;
I am severed by my selfhood from the world-life of the Whole;
And my world is near and narrow,
  and God's world is waste and wide.

Vain the dream! Yet in the morning,
  when the eastern skies are red,
When the dew is on the meadows,
  when the lark soars up and sings –
Leaps a sudden flame within me from its ashes pale and dead,
And I see God's beauty burning through the veil of outward things.

Brighter grows the veil and clearer, till, beyond all fear and doubt,
I am ravished by God's splendour into oneness with his rest;
And I draw the world within me, and I send my soul without;
And God's pulse is in my bosom, and I lie upon God's breast.

Dies the beatific vision in the moment of its birth;
Dies, but in its death transfigures all the sequence of my days;
Dies, but dying crowns with triumph all the travail of the earth,
Till its harsh discordant murmurs swell into a psalm of praise.

Then a yearning comes upon me to be drawn at last by death,
Drawn into the mystic circle in which all things live and move,
Drawn into the mystic circle of the love which is God's breath –
Love creative, love receptive, love of loving, love of love.

God! the One, the All of Being! let me lose my life in Thine;
Let me be what Thou hast made me, be a quiver of Thy flame.
Purge my self from self's pollution; burn it into life divine;
Burn it till it dies triumphant in the firespring whence it came.

Edmond Gore Alexander Holmes (1850–1906)

The labourer's noon-day hymn (excerpt)

Up to the throne of God is borne
The voice of praise at early morn,
And he accepts the punctual hymn
Sung as the light of day grows dim:

Nor will he turn his ear aside
From holy offerings at noontide:
Then here reposing let us raise
A song of gratitude and praise.

Lord! since his rising in the East,
If we have faltered or transgressed,
Guide, from thy love's abundant source,
What yet remains of this day's course:

Help with thy grace, through life's short day,
Our upward and our downward way;
And glorify for us the west,
When we shall sink to final rest.

William Wordsworth (1770–1850)

I've recently taken this idea of poetry further, writing a collection of
rhyming prayers myself. The following gives a flavour of these:

A love that conquers death

Give me greater faith, Lord, in your love that conquers death,
a love that keeps on burning beyond our dying breath,
a purpose that continues unchanged for evermore,
and when this life is over still holds the best in store.

Speak of the special future you want us to enjoy,
the blessings of your kingdom that nothing can destroy;
a realm of awesome beauty where joy will never cease,
no hatred there or warfare, but everlasting peace;
a place of hope and healing where tears are washed away,
and those oppressed by darkness will bask in endless day.
Although my heart is heavy, although I need to grieve,
Lord, nurture trust within me and help me to believe.
Remind me truth is greater than I can comprehend:
however much it seems so, the grave is not the end.

The promise of new life

Lord, autumn leaves are falling,
the trees will soon be bare;
a multitude of endings
surround me everywhere.
So much that bloomed so brightly
now seems a world away,
its glory but a memory,
supplanted by decay.

Yet, hidden in the darkness,
beneath the silent earth,
already shoots are forming –
a promise of new birth.
And softly you are saying
to those with ears to hear,
though death for now brings sorrow,
keep hope and do not fear.
Yes, life may seem extinguished,
but days to come will bring
beginnings after endings,
in place of winter, spring.

Faith, come what may

Though this day brings good or bad,
makes me happy, leaves me sad,
leads to smiles, ends in tears,
answers hopes or bears out fears;
whether I prove weak or strong,
do things right or get them wrong;
gracious Lord, through good or ill
in your love enfold me still.

A world in need

In a world of hurt and need,
scarred by selfishness and greed,
touched by sorrow, racked with pain,
such that hope can seem in vain;
in this mix of toil and strife
where so much devalues life,
gracious Lord, I pray be there,
showing all how much you care.

Renewed commitment

Lord of life, direct my ways,
help me love you all my days.
Though my faith is flawed and frail,
though I all too often fail,
take my heart, my hands, my feet –
reach out now to all I meet.
Teach me how to serve and when.
Guide my footsteps, Lord. Amen.

Of course, what appeals to one person may not appeal to another, but there is no shortage of poetry around for you to choose from, whether it be rhyming or blank verse. You may find it helpful to browse through an anthology of poetry or perhaps you have a soft spot already for certain poems. Alternatively, there are numerous books of Christian poetry on the market. A search on Amazon brings up over 200 titles, including the following:

Mortal Beauty, God's Grace: Major Poems and Spiritual Writings of Gerard Manley Hopkins (Vintage Books USA, Vintage Spiritual Classics, 2003)

Words to Comfort, Words to Heal: Poems and Meditations for Those Who Grieve, ed. Juliet Mabey (Oneworld Publications, 1998)

The Poems of the Cross, Saint John et al., George Herbert, ed. Peter Washington (Everyman's Library, 2004)

Run, Shepherds, Run: Poems for Advent and Christmas, L. William Countryman (Continuum International Publishing, 2005)

Poems, George Herbert *et al.* (W. W. Norton and Co, 1980)

The Poems of Rowan Williams (Wm. B. Eerdmans Publishing, 2004)

Out of the Ordinary: Prayers, Poems, and Reflections for Every Season, Joyce Rupp (Ave Maria Press, 2000)

Hearing the Stranger: Reflections, Poems and Hymns, Michael Hare Duke (Cairns Publications, 1994)

I Am with You Always: A Treasury of Inspirational Quotations, Poems and Prayers, Douglas Bloch (Pallas Communications, 1998)

Poems To Help You through the Week: Inspiration for Every Day, ed. Andrea Skevington (Lion Hudson, 2004)

Images of Grace: 33 Christian Poems, Regis Martin (Franciscan University Press, 1995)

As well as these and innumerable other publications, there are various magazines and websites offering Christian poetry, much of it free but varying in quality. Probably the best sites I've come across are:

http://www.bartleby.com, where a search for 'God' under 'Verse' brings up a staggering 2554 entries;

http://www.poetseers.org/ offers access to a wide range of spiritual poetry from all kinds of religious traditions.

Other sites Google came up with, when I searched for 'Christian poetry', include the following:

http://www.angelfire.com/tx2/christianpoetry/

http://www.catholicplanet.com/poems/

http://www.christianpoetry.org/

http://www.christianpoets.com/

http://www.netpoets.com/poems/christian/

http://www.poetry-online.org/christian-poetry-index.htm

http://www.whatsaiththescripture.com/WStS.Poetry.html

Scout around for resources, and, once again, if this form of prayer works for you, then build up a collection as a pool to draw on when words run dry.

Hymns of prayer

Some resources for prayer are obvious, others less so, but perhaps one of the places we're least likely to look is a hymnbook, and that's a pity, for, like the psalms, though written for public worship many hymns are essentially poetic prayers. Some are written in unforgettably expressive language, including many all-time favourites. Who can fail to be moved, for example, by the celebrated words of James William Elliott (1833–1915):

O Jesus, I have promised,
to serve thee to the end;
be thou for ever near me,
my Master and my friend:
I shall not fear the battle
if thou art by my side,
nor wander from the pathway
if thou wilt be my guide.

O let me feel thee near me;
the world is ever near;
I see the sights that dazzle,
the tempting sounds I hear;
my foes are ever near me,
around me and within;
but, Jesus, draw thou nearer,
and shield my soul from sin.

O let me hear thee speaking
in accents clear and still,
above the storms of passion,
the murmurs of self-will;
O speak to reassure me,
to hasten or control;
O speak and make me listen,
thou guardian of my soul.

O Jesus, thou hast promised,
to all who follow thee,
that where thou art in glory
there shall thy servant be;
and Jesus, I have promised
to serve thee to the end:
O give me grace to follow,
my Master and my friend.

O let me see thy foot-marks,
and in them place mine own;
my hope to follow duly
is in thy strength alone:
O guide me, call me, draw me,
uphold me to the end;
and then in heaven receive me,
my Saviour and my friend.

Just as well loved is the following, by the prolific hymn-writer Charles
Wesley (1707–88):

Love divine, all loves excelling,
joy of heaven, to earth come down,
fix in us thy humble dwelling,
all thy faithful mercies crown.

Jesus, thou art all compassion,
pure unbounded love thou art;
visit us with thy salvation,
enter every trembling heart.

Breathe, O breathe thy loving Spirit
into every troubled breast;
let us all in thee inherit,
let us find thy promised rest.

Take away the love of sinning,
Alpha and Omega be;

end of faith, as its beginning,
set our hearts at liberty.

Come, almighty to deliver,
let us all thy grace receive;
suddenly return, and never,
never more thy temples leave.

Thee we would be always blessing,
serve thee as thy hosts above;
pray and praise thee without ceasing,
glory in thy perfect love.

Finish then thy new creation,
pure and spotless let us be;
let us see thy great salvation
perfectly restored in thee.

Changed from glory into glory,
till in heaven we take our place,
till we cast our crowns before thee,
lost in wonder, love, and praise.

Less well known, but equally powerful, is this hymn written by John Hunter (1848–1917):

Dear Master, in whose life I see
all that I long, but fail to be,
let thy clear light for ever shine,
to shame and guide this life of mine.

Though what I dream and what I do
in my poor days are always two,
help me, oppressed by things undone,
O thou, whose deeds and dreams were one.

And if the words of those seem just a shade archaic, there are many modern hymns to choose from. Here's one of my own:

For the days when you feel near,
for the times when all is clear;
when your presence seems so real
that it colours all we feel –
for the blessings of such days,
Lord, accept our grateful praise.

For the times when you feel far,
when we wonder where you are;
when we call and call again,
but our prayers appear in vain –
when it seems you just don't care,
Lord, assure us you're still there.

For the truth that day by day
you are present, come what may:
when we see you, when we don't;
when we trust you, when we won't –
for the peace such love imparts,
Lord, we come with grateful hearts.

You may think you know many hymns back to front, having sung them more times than you care to remember, but don't be so sure, for *singing* a hymn is a very different proposition to *reading* it. Often it's the tune rather than words that grabs us, what the hymn actually has to say more or less passing us by. If you doubt that, then pick up a hymn book now and try reading a few of your favourites; I'm fairly sure you'll come across some details you've never considered before. Of course, the tune can speak to you as well as the words, that being the essence of a well-written hymn, and if, having made the message your own you feel moved to sing along, then so much the better, but to get the most out of them I'd urge you to read first, sing second.

Not every hymn, by a long way, is suitable for personal devotion, but many are, and, as with classic prayers of the past, it's well worth putting together a collection of your favourites as a resource to turn to for encouragement and inspiration. You'll find many other hymn texts later in this book as well as in the resources section (Part Four) of this book, each showing just how useful a prayer tool they can be.

Silent prayer

Making use of hymns, visual images, music and so forth in prayer may not be familiar to most of us, but we can find a place for such things happily enough, readily understanding how valuable they might be. But if there's one thing many of us find extraordinarily hard coming to terms with, it's spending time in silence. Partly, perhaps, because we're just not used to it, our world being one of noise, whether it's the roar of traffic, hum of conversation, whirr of a computer or sound of radio and television. For many, though, the problem runs deeper. On the one hand, we can feel guilty about spending even a few moments in silence, there being so much else we could do with the time instead. And, let's face it, it's hard enough to find a suitable space for prayer as it is, so when we do, shouldn't we make the most of it, cramming in as many words as possible rather than frittering it away in airy-fairy reflection? On the other hand, if we *do* find time, we're not quite sure what we should be doing with it. Typically our attention starts to wander, so that we end up thinking of lunch, that TV programme last night, some pressing problem, or the work we really ought to be getting on with. If only God were to fill the silence we offer him, speaking to us clearly and unmistakably, then it would be more than worth it, but sadly that's rarely if ever the case; as a result we tend to see silence as a luxury we cannot afford.

Believe me, I empathise with such difficulties, for they're as real for me as anyone. But I've no doubt, equally, that quiet times – and I mean truly quiet times – are essential, God using them in ways beyond our imagining. Certainly the psalm writers thought so:

> My spirit waits in silence for God from whom alone comes my salvation. For him and him only do I wait quietly, for in him lies my hope. *Psalm 62:1, 5*

> Be still, and know that I am God. *Psalm 46:10a*

The prophet Isaiah thought the same:

> Thus says the Lord, the holy One of Israel: Come back, be at peace, and you will be safe; your strength lies in quietness and being still. *Isaiah 30:15*

Across the centuries, an emphasis upon silent prayer and reflection has characterised the Christian mystical tradition, exemplified in those like St John of the Cross (1542–91). The following is one of his many prayers and touches upon that need for inner quietness.

> O sweetest love of God, too little known,
>   whoever has found you will be at rest.
> Let everything change, O my God,
>   that I may rest in you.
> How sweet to me is your presence,
>   you who are sovereign good!
> I will draw near to you in silence,
>   and will uncover your feet,
>   that it may please you to unite me with yourself,
>   making my soul your bride.
> I will rejoice in nothing until I am in your arms;
> O Lord, I beseech you, leave me not for a moment.
> Amen.

And the upsurge of interest in recent years in Quiet Days and other reflective events shows that countless others have come to recognise how valuable times of stillness and quiet can be.

So what if our minds *do* wander; perhaps that will be God's way of leading. So what if other things are put on hold; can they really not wait for a moment? So what if we come away without feeling God has spoken; might it not be that those few moments of inner tranquillity have inwardly nurtured us in body, mind and spirit? The value of silence is impossible to quantify but that shouldn't cause us to downplay it. In our hectic, impatient and stress-filled world we need it more than ever.

Reflective prayer

There are times, aren't there, when we come to prayer wanting to receive rather than give, hungry for inspiration, encouragement, comfort or guidance? Perhaps we're at the end of our tether, perhaps physically or emotionally drained or perhaps unsure of our faith – whatever the reason, we yearn in prayer, more than ever before, to hear God speaking to us rather than simply to articulate our needs. At such times, having a resource of reflective prayers – or what we might term meditations – to turn to can be enormously helpful. In the introduction to some of my recent books I wrote of my personal debt to the great Catholic writer Michel Quoist (1921–2000), whose spiritual classic *Prayers of Life* sold millions of copies across the world, touching people who previously had barely given a thought to prayer. The prayers were written in refreshingly different language – honest, direct, and very often couched in the form of a dialogue with God. Clearly God had spoken profoundly to the author, and through the book he was able to speak in turn to others.

I've found many other books inspirational across the years, *Lord of the Seasons* by Peter Firth, *Prayers for Impossible Days* by Paul Geres and *Break of Glory* by Michael Hare Duke to name but some. Today there are probably more such books than ever before, and the success of writers such as Eddie Askew is eloquent testimony to the way reflective prayer continues to speak to Christians today. I've adopted a similar approach myself in several of my publications and I include prayers from these in the resources section (Part Four) of this book, but the following examples give a feel of the approach.

First, a reflection on the theme of love:

Lord, I saw a photograph today,
    a picture of a mother desperately shielding her baby
    from a hail of bullets,
    sacrificing herself to protect her little one.
And there I saw love,
    total love –
    not the pale imitation we pass off in its place,
    but the real thing,
    concerned only to give,

pouring itself out oblivious to the cost.
I admired that, Lord,
   and I longed to share it.
No, not the pain and sacrifice,
   but the ability to love
   with even a fraction of that selfless devotion –
   for I know deep down that I don't.
I speak of love often enough –
   sign off with it in a letter,
   send it casually over the phone –
   but it's just a word,
   well intentioned but hollow.
And even with those dearest to me,
   my friends and family,
   though I care deeply about them,
   more than they will ever know,
   my love is still imperfect,
   as much about *me* as them –
   my happiness,
   my desires,
   my wishes,
   my well-being.
I'm not good at loving, Lord, and that troubles me,
   for it strikes at the very heart of my faith.
Love your enemy,
   love your neighbour,
   love one another –
   isn't that what you tell us to do?
And it all sounds wonderful,
   a recipe for heaven.
But it's one thing to bandy such fine words as theory –
   I do it all the time –
   it's another to mean them,
   let alone to make them real.

My child,
   it's quite true what you say –
   love *is* difficult,

more costly and demanding than most people ever imagine;
and it's true also that your love is less than it ought to be,
as much about yourself as others.
But that's not so terrible,
for I tell you this, unless you learn to love self
you will never love anyone else.
Besides, there is more to you than you give credit for.
That picture you speak of, the mother shielding her child –
you're not so different, despite what you think.
You too could rise to that same devotion and commitment,
that same willingness to sacrifice all.
It would take a lot, I grant you,
and I hope you'll never be put to the test,
but there are those you care about enough
to die for them if necessary.
Believe me, I know,
for I care that much about you, about everyone,
only it cost me more still –
the cruellest of agonies,
the most unimaginable pain.
I came to this world in Jesus,
sharing your human suffering,
bearing your grief and sorrow,
and out of love I watched him give everything,
nailed to the Cross so that you might live.
It was dreadful,
harder than you will ever know not to step in and call a halt –
my child far too precious to die like that.
But I held back, honouring his wishes,
as he laid down his life for all.
So, yes, it's difficult, love, I understand that,
but it's not impossible, not now anyway,
for it's been given freely in the blood my Son shed for you –
and when love like that flows through your veins
it must surely soon beat in your heart.

Next, a reflection concerning the words of Jesus in Matthew 6:34: 'Do not brood about tomorrow . . . take one day at a time, for each has enough problems of its own.'

'Take things as they come,' you say;
    'one day, one moment, at a time.'
And I know it makes sense, Lord –
    that it's foolish to fret –
    for what's done is done
    and what must be will be.
Yet I can't help dwelling sometimes on the past
    and brooding on the future:
    the things I should have done,
    and those I *have* done;
    the things I hope will come,
    and those that *might* come.
I saw the man rushed to hospital
    and I thought that one day it could be me.
I saw the patient in the nursing home
    and I feared one day it *will* be me.
I saw the baby in the photo,
    and I reflected that not so long ago, it *was* me.
Times gone by,
    times to come,
    and both scare me in their way –
    for one is over, lost for ever,
    and the other lies in wait –
    no knowing what it might bring for good or ill.
But I know one thing, Lord;
    remind me of that:
    the truth that your love endures for ever,
    the same yesterday, today and tomorrow.
Teach me, then, that whatever life may bring
    you will be with me in it,
    there by my side to strengthen, sustain,
    succour and support.

In that knowledge may I put all in your hands,
    and live each moment as your gift
    in grateful praise and joyful service.
Amen.

Third, a reflection on the theme of unanswered prayer:

What's happening, Lord?
When are you going to hear me?
You can't say I haven't been patient,
    for it's not just been months now but years –
    long frustrating years of waiting,
    longing,
    hoping –
    and still no sign of an answer.
I've kept faith –
    or at least I've tried to –
    but it's not easy,
    not easy at all,
    for didn't you say, 'Ask, and you will receive,
    Seek, and you will find'?
Well, I've asked,
    I've sought,
    and I'm still seeking,
    but there's no sign of much happening,
    no suggestion you're about to respond.
Lord,
    help me to be patient,
    to recognise that your timing is not the same as mine.
Help me to trust,
    putting faith in your purpose rather than mine.
Teach me that you *do* hear
    and you *will* answer,
    but when and where is down to you,
    and in that assurance may I find the strength to wait
    for as long as you ask.
Amen.

Finally, a prayer titled 'The armchair':

It was comfortable –
   too comfortable –
   enticing me simply to lie back,
   relax,
   and let the world go by.
Nothing wrong with that, of course,
   for work without rest is no good to anyone,
   but I also need exercise and activity,
   these equally vital if I hope to stay in shape.

Forgive, Lord, my laziness in discipleship,
   my inclination to lounge in the comfort zone
   rather than stretch the muscles of faith.
Forgive me for reducing what ought to be a way of life
   to a casual pursuit,
   a couch potato commitment that asks little
   and delivers less.
Teach me to work at my faith
   so that it not only shapes every aspect of life,
   but is also kept in shape in turn.
Amen.

Of course, not every reflective prayer will speak to you, but hopefully some will, helping you to hear God's voice in a way you've never considered before or simply meeting your need at a given moment. Building up your own personal collection of such prayers can once again help provide a valuable resource for personal devotion.

Using our senses – a life of prayer

I spoke earlier of the tradition of praying with hands together and eyes closed. It's a practice inculcated in children during schooldays, and the result is that many grow up believing it's the only way to pray, yet in my view this leaves them immensely impoverished. There are times, yes, when it's helpful to shut out distractions, and adopting a certain posture of prayer can undoubtedly help focus our thoughts as well as expressing worship and humility. But if, as we claim, God is everywhere, intimately involved in daily life, then surely prayer should, at times at least, *involve* our senses rather than shut them out. Personally, I often feel infinitely closer to God listening to the song of a bird, gazing up at a starlit sky, smelling the sea or walking in the countryside than in church or at a prayer meeting. The value of our senses in devotion is highlighted in the following, slightly abridged, prayer of Edward King (1829–1910), Bishop of Lincoln from 1885 to 1910:

> Thank you, O God,
>   for the pleasures you have given me through my senses.
> Thank you for the glory of thunder,
>   the mystery of music,
>   the singing of birds
>   and the laughter of children.
> Thank you for the delights of colour,
>   the awe of sunset,
>   the wild roses in the hedgerows,
>   the smile of friendship.
> Thank you for the sweetness of flowers
>   and the scent of hay.
> Truly, O Lord, the earth is full of your riches!
> Amen.

Equally, a piece of music, the words in a book, a conversation with a friend, the laughter of a baby, a cry of despair, or a symbol, statue or icon can bring home God's word and presence in unexpected ways. As Michel Quoist observes:

If we knew how to listen to God, if we knew how to look around us, our whole life would become prayer. For it unfolds under God's eyes and no part of it must be lived without being freely offered to him . . . Words are only a means. However, the silent prayer which has moved beyond words must always spring from everyday life, for everyday life is the raw material of prayer.

To me, this idea helps make sense of Paul's injunction to pray without ceasing (1 Thessalonians 5:17). We can only do that if prayer is wider than we typically understand it; above all, integrated into our daily activities rather than removed from them. In other words, we need to glimpse God in the things we see, hear, touch, taste and smell, both bringing our world to him through these and hearing his voice speaking through them. That doesn't come naturally, for we find it hard to see beyond ourselves and our immediate concerns, but if we truly seek, then, as Jesus promised, we will find. Be awake to the good things you have to give thanks for, to the temptations you succumb to, to the untold needs around you, to the simple lessons life has to teach, for manifestations of God's greatness, for evidence of his love in others, and so on and so forth. I'm not saying consciously pray about each one, or at least not in the traditional sense, but let your thoughts rest on them for a moment and in doing so they will rest on God.

The idea of involving the senses in prayer is not, of course, new. Many find it helpful to light a candle as an aid to devotion, others to burn incense or gaze at a picture, cross or statue. My nonconformist background makes me wary of these becoming objects of devotion in themselves, but there's no denying they can help focus our thoughts in prayer. Alternatively, or in addition, you may find it helpful to pray as you walk, allowing your thoughts to be guided by the people you meet, and the sights, sounds and scents you come across. I've tried to give expression to this in some of my recent prayers, and the following, spanning all the senses, should give a flavour of what I mean.

The bluebells

What a sight!
What a scent!
What an unforgettable picture they made!

Soon over, it's true,
  but for the month they were in bloom,
  each delicate head nodding in the breeze,
  they turned the woodland into an ocean
  of colour and fragrance,
  a glimpse of Eden,
  a foretaste of paradise I will never forget.

Lord, our human span,
  like the bluebell's,
  is all too brief,
  in the context of the universe just a passing moment,
  a fleeting shadow.
Help me to make the most of the time you give me,
  living each moment to the full
  and, in my own small way,
  reflecting something of your love and glory,
  until that day when I do not merely *glimpse* paradise
  but behold it in all its glory.
Amen.

The handwriting

It was barely legible,
  an indecipherable scrawl,
  yet to the trained eye it was far more,
  every dot, squiggle, line and curve saying as much as the words,
  if not more,
  revealing the quirks, traits, strengths and weaknesses
  of the one who wrote it.

Teach me, Lord, to glimpse you in the daily round of life
  and the wonder of this world.
Where others look and see nothing,
  help me to observe with the eye of faith,
  perceiving the reality beneath the surface.
Open my heart as well as my eyes,
  that I may look and truly see.
Amen.

The recorder player

It was hardly a pleasant sound,
    more of a shrill blast,
    the child having little control of the instrument
    and apparently even less musical sense,
    yet she was enjoying herself,
    letting loose with unbridled glee.

I want to make music for you, Lord,
    to live my life as an exuberant melody of praise,
    offered in gratitude for all you've done
    and everything you'll always mean to me.
It may sometimes be out of tune,
    more of a joyful noise than work of art,
    but receive it, I pray,
    together with what I am and all I long to be,
    for it comes from the heart,
    with love.
Amen.

The feather

It fell from the sky,
    fluttering gently on the breeze
    before landing in the palm of my hand
    with a touch so soft it barely registered.
Yet that same feather had helped carry a bird in flight,
    bearing its weight as wings strained against the wind;
    deceptive strength behind such apparent fragility.

Grant me, Lord, a similar combination:
    strength of faith, character, wisdom and purpose
    coupled with a gentleness of spirit;
    an inner steel
    matched by tenderness and humility in my dealings with others.
Though I am weak,
    may I be strong in you.
Amen.

The rhubarb

I tried to eat it,
> but it was all that I could do –
> the taste bitter,
> bringing tears to the eyes –
> a meal put to waste for want of a little sweetness.

I've seen not just food ruined, Lord, but lives also,
> bitterness destroying what might have been,
> curdling the milk of human kindness,
> souring relationships,
> turning rancid what once brought joy.
Whatever hurts or disappointments I face,
> help me to deal with them and move on,
> lest in making a meal of them,
> they end up making a meal of me.
Amen.

More of these prayers are included in the resources section (Part Four) of this book.

Part Three

ASPECTS OF PRAYER

Praise

Introduction

Of all forms of prayer, you might expect praise to be one of the most natural and spontaneous, an instinctive response to the greatness and wonder of God. Yet, strangely, that's not always the case; many people find expressing their praise far harder than they expect. Why is that? As with prayer in general there are many reasons. Sometimes we can't formulate our thoughts and feelings, try as we might. Sometimes we feel awkward or embarrassed at piling up superlatives. Sometimes we just don't feel like praising God or don't see what there is to praise him for. But perhaps most often of all we simply have too much else to be going on with to devote more than a few cursory moments to prayer in general, and when we do so it's our own needs and concerns that tend to take priority. There's another reason too why we might find praise difficult, though we probably rarely articulate it, and it relates to what we're doing and why. Does God expect, even demand, our praise, being put out or angry if we fail to offer it or if our efforts don't come up to scratch? If that were so, then we'd be quite right to question the sort of God it suggests: one who laps up our plaudits and who feels peeved if he's denied round-the-clock adulation; one who sees fawning upon him as a key aspect of any relationship we hope to enjoy.

If we were talking about *people* here, which of us would want to know someone like that, let alone extol their virtue? We'd find them pompous, overweening, self-centred, conceited, and would almost certainly want as little to do with them as possible. But, as I understand him at least, God isn't anything like that at all, nor does this approximate in any way to the rationale behind prayers of praise. God wants us to acknowledge him, yes – to declare his greatness, offer our worship, affirm his love and celebrate his goodness – but for *our* benefit, not his. He wants it because he longs for us to understand better the extent of his purpose – the breadth of his mercy and depth of his devotion. He yearns for us to be filled with joy and thrilled with wonder, to carry with us, each day, each moment, an awareness of the riches he puts at our disposal and the deeper reality of which we are a part. And often it's only when we stop to consider these things, when we take time to pause and reflect, that we recognise them for what they are. As a well-loved old hymn puts it, 'Count your blessings, one by one'. Unless we do that, recognising what God is and all he has done, and putting all that into words, it so easily and often passes us by.

So, then, where do we start in doing all this? Where, assuming the will is there, do we turn to find help in articulating what we feel inside? There's nowhere better to turn initially than the Psalms, for, as we will see in the next section, this wonderful collections of hymns and songs affords one of the greatest resources for prayer we can ever hope to find.

Praise in the Old Testament

If you're looking for inspiration when it comes to praising God, then the Psalms offer fertile ground, for time and again they positively bubble over in spontaneous, heartfelt worship. Take, for example, the following:

> When I gaze at the heavens, your handiwork, the moon and the stars that you created, what are human beings that you should consider them, mortals that you value them? Yet you have made them scarcely lower than God and crowned them with glory and honour. You have given them authority over your creation and put all things under their feet. *Psalm 8:3-6*

> Because of your constancy, O God, the holy one of Israel, I will extol you on the harp and sing songs of worship accompanied by the lyre. And when I sing those praises my lips will cry out with joy, and so too will my soul, which you have redeemed. With my tongue I will speak of the way day after day you so faithfully come to my aid, thwarting and humiliating those who wished me harm. *Psalm 71:22-24*

> I will sing of your power; each morning I will sing unashamedly of your unswerving love, for in my time of need you showed yourself to be a stronghold and sanctuary. You are my fortress and my strength, a God of unfailing love, so I will sing praises to you. *Psalm 59:16, 17*

Lord God, you have piled high your marvellous deeds and thoughtfulness towards us; none can begin to compare with you! I will make known what you have done to all, speaking of your blessings beyond number. *Psalm 40:5*

I will sing unceasingly of your unfailing love, O Lord; I will declare your faithfulness to all generations. Your constant love is unchanged from the beginning of time, and your faithfulness is as permanent as the heavens. *Psalm 89:1, 2*

I will reflect, O God, on everything you have done, pondering on your mighty acts across the years. You are a God who works wonders, exhibiting your power among the nations, and with your mighty arm you have redeemed your people. *Psalm 77:12, 14, 15a*

I will rejoice and revel in you, O God most high, singing praise to your name. *Psalm 9:2*

My tongue will speak of your righteousness and will praise you all day long. *Psalm 35:28*

God has put a new song into my mouth, a song to him of praise. *Psalm 40:3*

Open my lips, Lord, and my mouth will proclaim your praise. *Psalm 51:15*

I praise you, Lord, for I am astonishingly and awesomely made. You works are truly wonderful; my soul knows it full well. *Psalm 139:14*

And so we could go on, *ad infinitum*. But it's not just in the Psalms we find praise. In 2 Samuel 22:2-51 we find another great prayer of David in which he celebrates deliverance from his enemies and extols God's greatness:

The Lord my God is my rock, stronghold and rescuer – a rock in whom I find sanctuary. For this, O Lord, I will praise you before all people, and sing praises to your name. *2 Samuel 22:2, 3a, 50*

In Isaiah 25 is another outpouring of worship:

> You, O Lord, are my God. I will acclaim you and praise your name, for you have done marvellous things, fulfilling your age-old purpose, dependable and certain.
> *Isaiah 25:1*

Or there are the words of Job, acknowledging that, for all he thought he'd understood, he'd barely begun to grasp the full greatness and wonder of God:

> I realise now you can do anything, and that nothing is able to frustrate your purpose. I have spoken of mysteries I do not understand, things so wonderful they are beyond my comprehension.
> *Job 42:2, 3b*

And, of course, you have only to look at words like the following of the prophet Isaiah to gain inspiration for worship of your own:

> Who has gauged the waters in the palm of his hand and set the boundary between heaven and earth? Who has weighed up the raw materials for this planet, calculating the proportions of hills and mountains? Who advised the Lord's Spirit, offering counsel and instruction? Who did he confer with for guidance, and who showed him the way of justice? Who educated him, and gave him wisdom? Whole countries and cultures are like a drop in a bucket compared to him, little more than dust when weighed in the balance.
> *Isaiah 40:12-15a*

And it's words such as those that reflect the attitude towards God that characterised the people of the Old Testament: their sense of awe, praise and wonder whenever they stood in his presence.

Praise in the New Testament

The New Testament, due to the nature of its writing, has far less in the way of specific praise, but, as the words of Hebrews 13:15 make clear, that's because it was taken as read: 'Let us through Christ continually offer up to God a sacrifice of praise – our lips, in other words, affirming his name.' And though actual prayers are few and far between, they are there if we look. Take, for example, the well-known song of Mary, familiar to many as the 'Magnificat', a song of long ago that still reverberates for many today:

> My soul magnifies the Lord, and my spirit exults within me in God my Saviour, for he has had regard for the humility of his servant. From now on and for all time people will call me blessed, because the Mighty One has done great things for me. Holy is his name! Through successive generations he has shown mercy to those who fear him, displayed strength with his arm. He has scattered the vain thoughts of the proud, humbling the powerful from their thrones and lifting up the lowly. He has filled the hungry with good things but sent the rich away empty. Mindful of his merciful purpose and the eternal pledge he made to our forebear Abraham and his descendants, he has come to the aid of Israel, his servant.
>
> *Luke 1:46-55*

Then there's the following, from the Apostle Paul's letter to the Romans:

> Oh how deep are the riches, wisdom and understanding of God – how far beyond us are his judgements and how unfathomable his ways! 'Who has figured out the Lord's mind, or been his advisor?' 'Who has offered him a gift deserving repayment?' All things are from him, through him and to him. Glory be to him for ever. Amen.
>
> *Romans 11:33-36*

The place above all, though, if we're looking for praise, is the book of Revelation:

> You are worthy, O Lord our God, to receive glory, honour and power, for all things were made by you, their creation and existence down to your will.
>
> *Revelation 4:11*

You are worthy to take the scroll and unseal it, since you were slaughtered, ransoming people for God from every culture, language, race and continent and transforming them into a kingdom and priests to our God, and they will reign on the earth. Worthy is the Lamb that was slain to receive dominion, riches, wisdom, power, veneration, glory and praise! To the one who sits on the throne and to the Lamb be blessing, homage, glory and might, now and always!   *Revelation 5:9, 10, 12, 13b*

Such worship sets the tone not just for the book of Revelation, nor simply the New Testament, but for all who profess the name of Christ.

Classic prayers

When it comes to praise there's no shortage of unforgettable prayers handed down across the centuries. Take, for example, the following, attributed to St Francis of Assisi (1182–1226):

You are holy, Lord, the only God,
    and your deeds are wonderful.
You are strong.
You are great.
You are the Most High.
You are Almighty.
You, Holy Father, are King of heaven and earth.
You are Three and One, Lord God, all Good.
You are Good, all Good, supreme Good,
    Lord God, living and true.
You are love. You are wisdom.
You are humility. You are endurance.
You are rest. You are peace.
You are joy and gladness.
You are justice and moderation.
You are all our riches, and you suffice for us.
You are beauty.
You are gentleness.

You are our protector.
You are our guardian and defender.
You are our courage.
You are our haven and our hope.
You are our faith, our great consolation.
You are our eternal life, great and wonderful Lord,
    God almighty, merciful Saviour.

Another prayer by St Francis (The Canticle of Brother Sun) uses the natural world as a springboard for praise:

All praise be yours, my Lord, through all that you have made,
    and first my lord Brother Sun,
    who brings the day; and light you give to us through him.
How beautiful he is, how radiant in all his splendour!
Of you, Most High, he bears the likeness.
All praise be yours, my Lord, through Sister Moon and Stars;
    in the heavens you have made them, bright
    and precious and fair.
All praise be yours, my Lord, through Sister Water,
    so useful, lowly, precious, and pure.
All praise be yours, my Lord, through Brother Fire,
    through whom you brighten up the night.
How beautiful he is, how gay! Full of power and strength.
All praise be yours, my Lord, through Sister Earth, our mother,
    who feeds us in her sovereignty and produces
    various fruits and coloured flowers and herbs.
All praise be yours, my Lord, through Sister Death,
    from whose embrace no mortal can escape.
Woe to those who die in mortal sin!
Happy those she finds doing your will.
The second death can do no harm to them.
Praise and bless my Lord, and give him thanks,
    and serve him with great humility.

A more recent prayer again celebrates the beauty of creation in an outpouring of praise and thanksgiving. It was written by Walter Rauschenbusch (1861–1918):

O God, I thank you for this universe;
   for its vastness and its riches,
   and for the variety of life which teems within it
   and of which I am a part.
I praise you for the sky and the winds,
   for the clouds
   and for the constellation of the heavens.
I praise you for seas and rivers,
   for mountains and trees,
   and the grass beneath my feet.
I thank you for the senses
   which enable me to see the splendour of the morning,
   to hear the song of the birds,
   and to enjoy the scents of springtime.
Open my heart, I pray,
   to all this joy and beauty,
   and save me from being so burdened by care
   or blinded by greed
   that I fail to notice when even the thornbushes
   are aflame with your glory.
Amen.

Next a prayer dating back to the ninth century and attributed to King Alfred (849–899):

You, Lord, are the supreme Truth, for from you comes all truth,
   and so I pray to you.
You are the highest Wisdom,
   for the wise depend on you for their knowledge,
   and so I bow before you.
You are the supreme Joy, all happiness finally owed to you.
You are the Light of minds, the giver of all understanding.
I love you above all.
I seek and follow you, and am ready to serve you.
I desire to dwell under your power for you are the King of all.
Amen.

Equally memorable are the words of St Augustine of Hippo (354–430):

> O thou Supreme!
> Most secret and most present,
> > most beautiful and strong!
> What shall I say,
> > my God,
> > my Life,
> > my Holy Joy?
> What shall anyone say when they speak of thee?

The prayer of St Boniface (c. 672–754) captures the sense of God's greatness that defies expression:

> O God the Eternal,
> > the refuge and help of all your children,
> > in our weakness you are our strength,
> > in our darkness you are our light,
> > in our sorrow you are comfort and peace.
> We cannot number your blessings.
> We cannot declare your love.
> For all your goodness we bless you.
> May we ever live in your presence,
> > and love the things you love,
> > and serve you with the service of our daily lives,
> > through Jesus Christ our Lord.
> Amen.

On similar lines is a prayer of St John Chrysostom (c.347–407), reminding us of the sovereignty of God, on which all faith finally rests:

> Blessed are you, Lord God of our fathers,
> > to be praised and exalted above all for ever –
> > blessed be your glorious and holy name.
> Yours, Lord, is the greatness and the power,
> > the glory, victory and majesty,
> > for everything in heaven and on earth is yours.

Yours is the kingdom,
> and you, Lord, are exalted as the head over all.

We will sing a new song to you, Lord.

Amen.

Another hugely powerful prayer is the following by St John Vianney (1786–1859):

I love you, O my God,
> and my only desire is to love you
> until the last breath of my life.

I love you, O my infinitely lovable God,
> and I would rather die loving you
> than live without loving you.

I love you, Lord,
> and the only grace I ask is to love you eternally.

My God,
> if my tongue cannot say in every moment that I love you,
> I want my heart to repeat it to you as often as I draw breath.

Amen.

Finally, an extract from a prayer by the celebrated theologian Karl Rahner (1904–84), which captures a sense of the sheer wonder and majesty of who it is we worship.

Almighty, holy God, to you I come, to you I pray.

I acknowledge you, Father, Son and Holy Spirit,
> praise you, glorify you and adore you.

I give you thanks for your great glory.

What can I say to you, my God?

Shall I collect together all the words which praise your holy Name,
> shall I give you all the names of this world,
> you, the Unnameable?

Shall I call you God of my life,
> meaning of my existence,
> hallowing of my acts,
> my journey's end,
> you my most treasured happiness?

Shall I say: Creator, Sustainer, Pardoner,
Near One, Distant One, Incomprehensible One,
God both of flowers and stars,
God of the gentle wind and of terrible battles,
Wisdom, Power, Loyalty, and Truthfulness,
Eternity and Infinity,
you the All-merciful,
you the Just One,
you Love itself?
What can I say to you, my God?
Should I consecrate myself to you?
Should I say that I belong to you with all that I have and am?
O my God, how can I give myself to you,
unless your grace accepts me?
How can I devote myself to your service, unless you call me?
I give you thanks for having called me.
Amen.

You'll find some of these, together with other classic prayers of praise, in Expressing Our Worship, the first section of Part Four of this book. Keep a record of prayers you come across, and build them into your prayer life. You'll find them useful more often than you might imagine.

Worshipful music

In terms of music expressing praise and worship we're truly spoilt for choice. Take for example the work of the great composers, and there's a host of music that celebrates God's wonder and goodness. Below are just a few suggestions:

Adoremus in aeternum (Allegri)
Adoramus te, Christe (Dubois)
Adoro te devote (Plainsong)
Allelujah from *Magnificat* (Scheidt)
Amen from *Messiah* (Handel)
Blagoslovi Dushe Moya [Praise the Lord] from *Vespers* (Rachmaninov)
Exultate, jubilate (Mozart)

Gloria from *Coronation Mass* (Mozart)

Gloria from *Credo Mass* (Mozart)

Gloria from *Gloria* (Vivaldi)

Gloria from *Mass in B Minor* (Bach)

Gloria from *Mass in C* (Beethoven)

Gloria from *Mass No. 1 in F* (Schubert)

Gloria from *Missa solemnis* (Mozart)

Gloria in excelsis deo from *Mass in C Minor* (Mozart)

Gloria Patri from *Dixit Dominus* (Handel)

Hallelujah from *Messiah* (Handel)

Hvalite Imya Gospodne [Praise ye the name of the Lord] from *Vespers* (Rachmaninov)

Jubilate Deo (Mozart)

Laudamus te from *Mass in C Minor* (Mozart)

Laudate dominum from *Solemn Vespers* (Mozart)

Laudate pueri from *Solemn Vespers* (Mozart)

Laudibus in sanctis Dominum from *Cantiones Sacrae* (Byrd)

Magnificat from *Magnificat* (Bach)

Magnificat from *Solemn Vespers* (Mozart)

Magnificat anima mea (Buxtehude)

Magnificat anima mea from *Magnificat* (Scheidt)

O Magnum Mysterium (Palestrina)

Praise God All Christians from *Magnificat* (Praetorius)

Pridite Poklonimsya [O come let us worship] from *Vespers* (Rachmaninov)

Rex tremendae from *Requiem* (Mozart)

Rex tremendae from *Requiem* (Verdi)

Sanctus from *Coronation Mass* (Mozart)

Sanctus from *Credo Mass* (Mozart)

Sanctus from *Mass in C Minor* (Mozart)

Sanctus from *Missa solemnis* (Mozart)

Sanctus from *Requiem* (Fauré)

Sanctus from *Requiem* (Mozart)

Sanctus from *Requiem* (Verdi)

Shestopsalmie [Glory to God in the highest] from *Vespers* (Rachmaninov)

Slavoslovie Velikoe [Glory to God in the highest] from *Vespers* (Rachmaninov)

Tantum ergo (Webbe)

The heavens are telling from *The Creation* (Haydn)

The mirror of the Trinity from *Magnificat* (Praetorius)

Velichit Dousha Moya Gospoda [My soul doth magnify the Lord] from *Vespers* (Rachmaninov)

Worthy is the lamb that was slain from *Messiah* (Handel)

In each of these a sense of joy, awe and wonder bubbles up through the music, capturing the spirit in a way that words alone can never quite achieve. The music you would choose might, of course, be very different, but the important thing to recognise and act on is that using music can help involve our heart in worship as well as our mind.

There's also an increasingly wide selection of contemporary music written specifically to aid prayer and worship. Below are some tracks I've used on my various CDs:

Adoramus te, Domine Deus from *Fountain of Life* (Margaret Rizza)

All you nations from *Awakening in Love* (Margaret Rizza)

Be still from *Sacred Pathway* (Keith Duke)

Bless the Lord, my soul from *Light in Our Darkness* (Margaret Rizza)

Cantate Domino from *Awakening in Love* (Margaret Rizza)

Enfold me in your love from *Fire of Love* (Margaret Rizza)

I will bless the Lord from *Light in Our Darkness* (Margaret Rizza)

In God alone from *Light in Our Darkness* (Margaret Rizza)

In the Lord is my joy from *Fire of Love* (Margaret Rizza)

Magnificat from *Fountain of Life* (Margaret Rizza)

O magnum mysterium from *River of Peace* (Margaret Rizza)

Sanctum nomen from *Fire of Love* (Margaret Rizza)

Sanctus Dominus from *River of Peace* (Margaret Rizza)

Send forth your Spirit from *In God Alone* (Andrew Moore)

Send forth your Spirit, Lord from *Fountain of Life* (Margaret Rizza)

Thou art all things from *Fire of Love* (Margaret Rizza)

You are the maker from *Sacred Pathway* (Keith Duke)
You, Lord, are in this place from *Sacred Weave* (Keith Duke)

Many of the above have been included in the resources section (Part Four) of this book. A wealth of material is available from numerous contemporary artists and the following CDs may also be helpful:

Hillsong London: *Jesus Is*; *Look to You*; *Praise God*; *He Reigns*; *United We Stand*
Chris Tomlin: *Arriving*
Brian Littrell: *Welcome Home*
Delirious: *Access-D*; *Deeper*; *Glo*
Gaither: *Homecoming*
Kutless: *Hearts of the Innocent*; *Kutless*; *Strong Tower*
Nichole Nordeman: *Brave*; *The Mystery*; *To Know You*; *Woven and Spun*
Matt Redman: *Blessed Be Your Name*; *Facedown*; *The Father's Song*; *Where Angels Fear to Tread*
Abundant Life: *Divine Exchange*
Michael Smith: *Change Your World*; *Healing Rain*; *Worship Again*
CeCe Winans: *Alone in His Presence*; *Everlasting Love*
YFriday: *Open*; *Rain Maker*

Make a list of those that help you express your praise and worship, and make them an integral part of your prayer time.

Hymns and songs of praise

Praise, my soul, the King of heaven!
To his feet thy tribute bring;
ransomed, healed, restored, forgiven,
who like me his praise should sing?
Praise him! Praise him!
Praise him! Praise him!
Praise the everlasting King!

That well-loved hymn of H. F. Lyte (1793–1847), like so many others, perfectly captures the sense of awe, gratitude and joy that lies at the heart of worship. The list of possibilities that we could choose from is almost endless, many modern songs in particular tending to focus almost exclusively on praise and worship, but it's perhaps some of those which have stood the test of time that most stick in our minds. Take, for example, the unforgettable words of George Herbert (1593–1633):

King of glory, King of peace,
I will love thee;
and that love may never cease,
I will move thee.
Thou hast granted my appeal,
thou hast heard me;
thou didst note my ardent zeal,
thou hast spared me.

Wherefore with my utmost art,
I will sing thee,
and the cream of all my heart
I will bring thee.
Though my sins against me cried,
thou didst clear me,
and alone, when they replied,
thou didst hear me.

Seven whole days, not one in seven,
I will praise thee;
in my heart, though not in heaven,
I can raise thee.
Small it is, in this poor sort
to enrol thee:
e'en eternity's too short
to extol thee.

Or there's the well-loved hymn of Reginald Heber (1783–1826):

Holy, holy, holy! Lord God almighty!
Early in the morning our song shall rise to thee.
Holy, holy, holy, merciful and mighty!
God in three persons, blessèd Trinity!

Holy, holy, holy! Though the darkness hide thee,
though the eye of sinful man thy glory may not see,
only thou art holy, there is none beside thee,
perfect in power, in love, and purity.

And, of course, there's the rest of the hymn with which we started:

Praise him for his grace and favour
to our fathers in distress;
praise him, still the same for ever,
slow to chide and swift to bless.
Praise him! Praise him!
Praise him! Praise him!
Glorious in his faithfulness.

Father-like he tends and spares us;
well our feeble frame he knows;
in his hands he gently leads us,
rescues us from all our foes.
Praise him! Praise him!
Praise him! Praise him!
Widely as his mercy flows.

And so we could continue, a single hymn book able to offer numerous texts to express our worship. Any selection is, of course, hugely arbitrary, but what I look for in terms of personal devotion are ideally those hymns written in the first person – that is, in the form of a personal prayer. Here's are few suggestions:

Blessed assurance
Bless the Lord, O my soul
Father God, I wonder
Fill thou my life, O Lord my God
For the beauty of the earth
I am a new creation
Immortal, invisible, God only wise
Lord, you created a world full of splendour

My God, how wonderful you are
O God, you search me
O Lord, my God (How great thou art)
O Lord, we want to praise you
Praise God from whom all blessings flow
Sanctus, sanctus, sanctus
Send forth your Spirit, Lord
Teach me to dance
Tell out, my soul
When I feel the touch
You are the King of Glory
You laid aside your majesty

Many hymns are available as recordings.

Poetic worship

Besides the words of hymns, inspirational poetry comes in all shapes
and sizes, some poems written from a specifically Christian perspective
while others simply capture a sense of the sublime or spiritual. Most
that I have come across take the world of nature as their starting point,
celebrating glimpses of God in the wonder and beauty of creation.
Consider, for example, the following, by Anne Brontë (1820–49):

My soul is awakened, my spirit is soaring
And carried aloft on the wings of the breeze;
For above and around me the wild wind is roaring,
Arousing to rapture the earth and the seas.

The long withered grass in the sunshine is glancing,
The bare trees are tossing their branches on high;
The dead leaves, beneath them, are merrily dancing,
The white clouds are scudding across the blue sky.

I wish I could see how the ocean is lashing
The foam of its billows to whirlwinds of spray;
I wish I could see how its proud waves are dashing,
And hear the wild roar of their thunder today!

Compare that with words of William Wordsworth (1770–1850), taken from his 'Lines composed a few miles above Tintern Abbey':

> For I have learned
> To look on nature, not as in the hour
> Of thoughtless youth; but hearing oftentimes
> The still, sad music of humanity,
> Nor harsh nor grating, though of ample power
> To chasten and subdue. And I have felt
> A presence that disturbs me with the joy
> Of elevated thoughts; a sense sublime
> Of something far more deeply interfused,
> Whose dwelling is the light of setting suns,
> And the round ocean and the living air,
> And the blue sky, and in the mind of man:
> A motion and a spirit, that impels
> All thinking things, all objects of all thought,
> And rolls through all things. Therefore am I still
> A lover of the meadows and the woods,
> And mountains; and of all that we behold
> From this green earth; of all the mighty world
> Of eye, and ear – both what they half create,
> And what perceive; well pleased to recognise
> In nature and the language of the sense,
> The anchor of my purest thoughts, the nurse,
> The guide, the guardian of my heart, and soul
> Of all my moral being.

The first of those poems can speak *for* us, the second *to* us, both having a part in prayer, and, in this case, both expressing a sense of awe and wonder at creation. The celebrated poet Gerard Manley Hopkins (1844–89) wrote a well-loved poem, 'Pied Beauty', on the same theme:

> Glory be to God for dappled things –
>   For skies of couple-colour as a brinded cow;
>   For rose-moles all in stipple upon trout that swim;
> Fresh-firecoal chestnut-falls; finches' wings;
>   Landscape plotted and pieced—fold, fallow, and plough;
>   And áll trádes, their gear and tackle and trim.

All things counter, original, spare, strange;
    Whatever is fickle, freckled (who knows how?)
      With swift, slow; sweet, sour; adazzle, dim;
He fathers-forth whose beauty is past change:
               Praise him.

On the same theme again, is a beautiful poem by the American writer Edna St Vincent Millay (1892–1950), capturing again a sense of wonder at the loveliness of this world, at times almost too beautiful to bear:

God's World

O world, I cannot hold thee close enough!
Thy winds, thy wide gray skies!
Thy mists, that roll and rise!
Thy woods, this autumn day, that ache and sag
And all but cry with color! That gaunt crag
To crush! To lift the lean of that black bluff!
World, world, I cannot get thee close enough!

Long have I known a glory in it all
But never knew I this.
Here such a passion is
As stretcheth me apart. Lord, I do fear
Thou'st made the world too beautiful this year.
My soul is all but out of me – let fall
No burning leaf; prithee, let no bird call.

These are but some of the countless poems expressing praise and worship. Keep a store of any that speak for you, and use them as and when it feels right.

Reflective praise

I've found helpful many reflective prayers on the theme of praise, none more so than Michel Quoist's 'I would like to rise very high', found in *Prayers of Life*, or Peter Firth's 'First time' in his book *Lord of the Seasons*. Each speaks of discovering God in daily life and recognising his presence in the world around us, which, to me, is where worship most naturally flows from. I've tried to echo this in some of my own books, the following being one example of a prayer celebrating the beauty of creation:

The paint palette

It was a stunning selection:
    not just your run-of-the-mill colours,
    but every shade in between –
    a diverse array of reds, yellows, blues, greens
    and innumerable others besides,
    enough to paint almost any scene
    and capture every nuance –
    an artist's delight.

Yet for all its breadth, Lord,
    that palette is as nothing
    compared to the one you've used in creation,
    its range of colours being magnified there a million times over:
    in the splendour of a sunset and magic of a rainbow,
    the hues of the sea and glory of the sky;
    the tints of autumn and tapestry of a garden,
    the plumage of birds and loveliness of a meadow –
    an immeasurable spectrum that brightens every day,
    causing me to catch my breath in wonder
    and exult in spirit.
For the stamp of your hand on the canvas of life,
    breathtaking beyond words,
    receive my praise.
Amen.

Creation can be a fertile source of inspiration for reflective prayer, but it's by no means the only one. The following 'meditation' explores what King David might have been thinking as he wrote some of his great psalms of praise:

I want to sing to the Lord –
    to lift up my voice,
    lift up my soul,
    and sing his praises to the ends of the earth!

Yes, I know that may sound a bit clichéd,
    but I don't care, for it's true,
    the love he's shown,
    the goodness,
    the mercy,
    the faithfulness not just to me but to all his people,
    too special, too wonderful for anyone to keep silent.
I want to sing from the rooftops,
    let rip from the highest mountain!
And not just any old song,
    but something new,
    something different –
    a song which captures a little of the joy bubbling up within me,
    and which expresses, could it be possible, the majesty of our God!
It can't be done, of course –
    no words enough,
    no music sufficient to declare his greatness –
    but I'm going to try, despite that;
    I'm going to make a joyful noise,
    I'm going to pour out my heart and mind and soul,
    and I'm going to exalt the name of the Lord my God
    for all I'm worth!
Forgive me if it's not pretty, the song I sing –
    it may well not be –
    but I can promise you this:
    it will be real,
    welling up from deep within,
    a great fountain of celebration,
    irrepressible,
    inexhaustible;
    a spontaneous outpouring of praise,
    overflowing with thanksgiving,
    for he has blessed us beyond our deserving,
    he has done marvellous things for us, too many to number,
    he has heard our prayer and reached out in mercy –
    what more could anyone ask?
But enough of this,
    no time for talking;

come join me, my friends, in glad and grateful worship,
sing to the Lord a new song!

Finally, a prayer which suggests that we can all too easily lose a sense of
praise and worship in discipleship, allowing other concerns to crowd
it out:

I'd lost sight of what it is all about, Lord,
of your gift at the heart of the gospel –
a joy beyond words,
bubbling up within me,
brimful,
overflowing.
I brooded instead on faults and failings,
worrying about the weakness of my love,
wrestling with matters of doctrine,
and fretting over the cost of discipleship,
forgetting that though these are all part of commitment
they are not the whole,
and not finally what matters most.
But then you spoke again,
reminding me that you accept me as I am,
your love not earned but given;
emphasising that though I repeatedly let you down,
still you stay faithful,
nothing able to exhaust your grace;
The old self lives on,
yet I realise afresh that you are constantly making all things new,
offering life in abundance,
now and for all eternity.
Gracious God,
I pause,
I reflect,
I remember the wonder of your love,
and so once more I celebrate with heart and mind and soul.
This day, like all days, is your gift:
I will rejoice and be glad in it.
Amen.

Using our senses

One of the best decisions I've ever made, both in terms of my personal prayer life and my writing, has been, whenever possible, to take a lunch-time stroll. I'm lucky enough to live in a relatively quiet country town, so within a few minutes I can be out in the fields enjoying scenes of pastoral tranquillity, and I invariably find much there to inspire prayer and reflection. The sight of spring bulbs pushing their way through the bare earth in springtime, the warmth of summer sunshine, the rich tapestry of autumn colours, frost-covered branches in winter – all this and so much more fills me with a sense of joy and wonder, causing me instinctively to pour out my worship.

Not that we have to be out in the countryside to find inspiration. Take a walk at night, wherever you live, and gaze up at the starlit sky. Few things, for me at least, speak more eloquently than the vastness and grandeur of the universe, communicating a sense of the transcendent God, greater than we can begin to imagine. Walk down a busy city street, and there too you will find much to capture the imagination, the noise and bustle reminding us of God's gifts of life and human ingenuity.

So if you're looking to praise God but are not quite sure how, use your senses, take in the sights, sounds, scents, tastes and sensations of this amazing world we are so privileged to be a part of, and simply let your spirit soar to the one who is within, before and beyond it – the source and end of everything that is and has been and will be.

The following two prayers were both written while I was out walking, and express praise at the wonder of creation:

The beach

I ran the sand through my fingers,
    millions of grains,
    yet that one handful was just a fraction of what made up the beach,
    the beach one of thousands across the world,
    and the world itself merely a tiny speck in the vastness of space
    with its trillions of constellations and plethora of galaxies.

It leaves me reeling, Lord,
    such magnitude truly awesome,
    yet you brought it all into being,

sustaining it each day
and leading it towards fulfilment,
the universe and everything within it the work of your hands.
As you created the stars and the sand,
    so you have fashioned our lives –
    knowing us better than we know ourselves,
    calling us by name,
    loving us more than we can begin to fathom.
For the vastness of your purpose,
    the immensity of your creation
    and the mind-boggling wonder of your grace,
    Lord, I praise you.
Amen.

The sunglasses

They shielded my eyes from the worst of the glare,
    allowing me to gaze for a moment at the setting sun
    and glimpse its glory,
    a golden ball of light.
Without them I was dazzled,
    the light too much to bear,
    forcing me to look away.

Before you also, Lord, I must turn aside,
    your splendour too intense,
    your brightness too awesome,
    and yet, through Christ, I glimpse your grace and glory,
    wonderful beyond words.
For now it is partial,
    as though I look through darkened glasses,
    but it is enough and more than enough
    to lighten my path
    and illumine my soul.
Shine now,
    shine always,
    through his radiant love.
Amen.

Confession

Introduction

No forms of prayer are easy, but if you're anything like me, you'll find that confession comes more naturally than most. It's not that we've anything particularly shocking to get off our chest, but we all make our fair share of mistakes nonetheless. You know the sort of thing: outbursts of temper; unkind words and thoughtless deeds; displays of petulance or pride; greedy or selfish behaviour; the telling of lies or half-truths: little enough faults in themselves yet capable of causing so much hurt, disappointment, trouble or unhappiness. Most of us, most of the time, fall far short of the person we'd like to be, let alone the person we believe God has called us to be in Christ, and we feel the need to unburden ourselves; not just in order to escape our sense of guilt and shame but in the hope of starting again, being given a second chance with the slate wiped clean. Prayers of confession give us the opportunity to do just that. Whereas it's hard to admit our mistakes in public, let alone to say sorry to those we've directly wronged, with God it's a different matter. There's not the same face-to-face contact, and therefore neither the same feeling of embarrassment nor fear of reproach we have in our dealings with others.

So what do such prayers involve? First, they give us the opportunity to face up to the truth of who and what we are, acknowledging before God those faults and weaknesses we're reluctant to own up to before others. This should never degenerate into morbid introspection, dwelling on negatives, but, on the other hand, if it's to be meaningful and effective, it needs to be more than simply a vague apology for our faults and failings in general. True confession means facing up to our faults and seeing ourselves as we really are, so that, with God's help, we can start to change. Acknowledging a weakness can often be the first step in just that, so it's important to be specific, honest both to ourselves and God. To a point that's easy enough, most of us, as I've already said, being well aware of much wrong in our lives, but equally there are other things we may not be aware of and these, potentially, can be the most destructive of all, simply because we do not see them. In confession, then, we need to ask God's help in recognising our faults, whether this comes through sudden insight, words of Scripture, the message of a sermon, comments from a loved one, advice from friends or some other source.

All this is important, but if that were the sum total of confession, then it would do more harm than good, serving only to intensify our feelings of guilt, hopelessness and inadequacy. It's vital to remember that prayers of confession are not just about acknowledging our mistakes but also, and most of all, about finding forgiveness. If you confess your faults but leave it there, coming away from your prayer still feeling burdened rather than liberated, trapped rather than set free, then you have not finished praying or have failed to grasp what prayer and faith really mean. As the Psalms repeatedly remind us (86:15; 103:8; 145:8), ours is a God who is slow to anger, full of grace and mercy and over-flowing in love towards us. And so, as the first letter of John (1:9) puts it, 'If we confess our sins, God is faithful and just, and will not only forgive our sins but also cleanse us from all unworthiness.' That is the context in which we confess our sins to God – not in order to dwell on them but so that we might put them behind us and begin again. That, surely, is what the gospel is all about.

Old Testament confession

As well as the Psalms, which we will turn to in a moment, the Old Testament contains two great prayers relating to confession. The first is that of Solomon (found in 1 Kings chapter 8 and also recorded in 2 Chronicles 6) where, interceding for his people at the dedication of the temple, he also seeks God's forgiveness for the mistakes they have made and will continue to make:

> From your dwelling place in heaven, listen to us, and when you hear, forgive. Hear us in heaven and forgive the people of Israel, your servants, their sins, teaching them instead the true way they should walk. Forgive, act and deal with all appropriately, for you alone know what goes on in human hearts.
>
> *1 Kings 8:30b, 36a, 39*

The second prayer is that of Daniel:

> Lord God, great and awesome, faithful in your covenant and constant in love towards those who love you and honour your commandments, we have sinned and done wrong, wicked and rebellious in our actions, turning our backs on your commandments and instructions. To you, Lord, belongs righteousness, but to us humiliation, for we have sinned against you. Listen, though, to your servant's prayer, O God – to his pleas for mercy – and make your face shine, Lord, on your ruined sanctuary, for your name's sake. We plead for mercy not because we have any merit, but recognising your great mercy. Hear, O Lord, and forgive. Listen and act.
>
> *Daniel 9:4b, 5, 7a, 17, 18b, 19a*

Added to these we have the final words of Job as he recognises his unworthiness before God:

> I hate myself, and repent in dust and ashes.   *Job 42:6*

And, of course, there's confession in the Psalms. We've looked at some examples already , but others are equally memorable:

> Be merciful to me, O God. Through your constant love and overflowing mercy, obliterate my transgressions. Wash away my faults and purify me from my sins, for I am all too aware of my mistakes, and my weakness daily stares me in the face. I've sinned ultimately against you and you alone, doing what is evil in your sight, so your words are justified and your verdict is beyond reproach. Sprinkle me with hyssop, and I will be clean; wash me, and I will become whiter than snow.   *Psalm 51:1-4, 7*

> You know my folly, O God; there can be no hiding my wrongs from you. I have wandered astray like a lost sheep.
>
> *Psalm 69:5; 119:176a*

Search me, O God, and know my heart. Test me and know my thoughts. Look to see if there is any wickedness within me, and lead me in your everlasting way.   *Psalm 139:23, 24*

New Testament confession

There are only three examples of prayer in the New Testament relating directly to confession. The first is not strictly a prayer at all, but the response of Peter to the call of Christ: 'Get away from me, Lord, for I am a sinful man' (Luke 5:8b). The second is the familiar line from the Lord's Prayer: 'Forgive us our trespasses as we forgive those who trespass against us.' The third is the words of Jesus from the cross: 'Father, forgive them, for they don't understand what they're doing' (Luke 23:34). Not much to go on, you might think, but those three examples in fact tell us a massive amount about what we're doing in confession and why.

Take first the example of Peter. Confronted by the presence of Christ, his response was immediate and instinctive. He was overwhelmed by a sense of unworthiness, recognising that he and Jesus couldn't be more different. There was nothing forced or artificial about his words; they came straight from the heart. The words of the Lord's Prayer carry a different message: that God is ready to forgive our sins but that we should be ready to forgive others in turn. Finally, the simple prayer of Jesus on the cross reminds us of the extent of God's love; his willingness not just to surrender his own Son but his willingness to forgive and go on forgiving, making allowances for our folly. The message is summed up in those words from the first letter of John mentioned earlier:

If we claim that we do not sin, we are deceiving ourselves, and do not have the truth within us. If we confess our sins, God is faithful and just, and will not only forgive our sins but also cleanse us from all unworthiness.   *1 John 1:8, 9*

The New Testament, in other words, offers us a reminder that confession is not about dwelling on our mistakes or feeling bad about ourselves, but about acknowledging them before God so that we might find forgiveness, start again and, in time, put those mistakes behind us.

That is a truth wonderfully summed up in the words of Paul in Romans:

> I do not understand why I act as I do. For I end up doing the things I hate rather than the things I want to do. I do evil instead of the good I wish to do. What a wretched man I am! Who will deliver me from this body of death? Thanks be to God through Jesus Christ our Lord! *Romans 7:15, 24, 25*

Classic prayers of confession

A host of prayers have been written across the years on the theme of confession and forgiveness, far too many to number, but below are just a few, giving a feel of the kinds of resources we might turn to. First a classic from the *Book of Common Prayer*, which has spoken both *to* and *for* many across the years:

> Almighty and most merciful Father;
>   we have erred, and strayed from thy ways like lost sheep.
> We have followed too much
>   the devices and desires of our own hearts.
> We have offended against thy holy laws.
> We have left undone those things
>   which we ought to have done;
>   and we have done those things
>   which we ought not to have done;
>   and there is no health in us.
> But thou, O Lord, have mercy upon us, miserable offenders.
> Spare thou them, O God, who confess their faults.
> Restore thou them that are penitent;
>   according to thy promises declared unto mankind
>   in Christ Jesu our Lord.
> And grant, O most merciful Father, for his sake,
>   that we may hereafter live a godly, righteous, and sober life,
>   to the glory of thy holy Name.
> Amen.

No list of examples would be complete without one of the prayers of St Augustine of Hippo (354–430):

> O God, the Light of the heart that sees you,
>   the Life of the soul that loves you,
>   the Strength of the mind that seeks you:
>   may I ever continue to be steadfast in your love.
> Be the joy of my heart;
>   take all of me to yourself, and abide therein.
> The house of my soul is, I confess, too narrow for you.
> Enlarge it that you may enter.
> It is ruinous, but do repair it.
> It has within it what must offend your eyes;
>   I confess and know it,
>   but whose help shall I seek in cleansing it but yours alone?
> To you, O God, I cry urgently.
> Cleanse me from secret faults.
> Keep me from false pride and sensuality
>   that they may not get dominion over me.
> Amen.

The following prayer, written by Thomas Wilson (1663–1755), is another general confession, reminding us of those mistakes we're aware of and those we may, intentionally or otherwise, have pushed out of our consciousness:

> Forgive my sins, O Lord;
>   the sins of my present and sins of my past,
>   the sins which I have done to please myself,
>   and the sins which I have done to please others.
> Forgive my casual sins and my deliberate sins,
>   and those which I have tried so hard to hide
>   that I have hidden them even from myself.
> Forgive me, O Lord, for all of them,
>   for Jesus Christ's sake.
> Amen.

Another prayer, this one by Charles Kingsley (1819-75), is more specific, focusing on undue pride:

Take away from me, O God,
   all pride and vanity,
   all boasting and forwardness,
   and give me the true courage that shows itself in gentleness;
   the true wisdom that shows itself by simplicity;
   and the true power that shows itself by modesty.
Amen.

Next, part of a prayer by the theologian Karl Rahner (1904–84), which, as well as acknowledging faults, declares faith and hope in God's assurance of mercy:

I know that there is only one thing that I can say to you:
   have mercy on me.
I need your mercy, because I am a sinner.
I am unworthy of your mercy, because I am a sinner.
But I humbly desire your unfailing mercy,
   for I am a being of this world, not yet lost;
   one who still longs for the heavens of your goodness,
   who willingly and with tears of joy
   receives the inexhaustible gift of your mercy.
Amen.

The same theme of hope is even more in evidence in the following prayer, attributed to St Basil the Great (329–79):

O God and Lord of the Powers, and Maker of all creation,
   who, because of thy clemency and incomparable mercy,
   didst send your only-begotten Son and our Lord Jesus Christ
   for the salvation of mankind,
   and with his venerable cross
   didst tear asunder the record of our sins,
   and thereby didst conquer the rulers and powers of darkness;
   receive from us sinful people, O merciful Master,

these prayers of gratitude and supplication,
    and deliver us from every destructive and gloomy transgression,
    and from all visible and invisible enemies who seek to injure us.
Nail down our flesh with fear of you,
    and let not our hearts be inclined to words or thoughts of evil,
    but pierce our souls with thy love,
    that ever contemplating you,
    being enlightened by you,
    and discerning you,
    the unapproachable and everlasting Light,
    we may unceasingly render confession and gratitude to you:
    the eternal Father,
    with your only-begotten Son,
    and with your all-holy, gracious, and life-giving Spirit,
    now and ever, and unto ages of ages.
Amen.

Finally, one of the many prayers of St Francis of Assisi (1182–1226), this one moving from an acknowledgement of sin to a plea for renewal:

Almighty, eternal, just and merciful God,
    give us miserable ones the grace to do for you alone
    what we know you want us to do
    and always to desire what pleases you.
Inwardly cleansed,
    interiorly enlightened and inflamed by the fire of the Holy Spirit,
    may we be able to follow in the footprints of your beloved Son,
    our Lord Jesus Christ,
    and, by your grace alone,
    may we make our way to you,
    Most High,
    who live and rule in perfect Trinity and simple Unity,
    and are glorified
    God almighty,
    for ever and ever.
Amen.

Confession through music

Some of the loveliest music of all time was written as an expression of confession and celebration of God's forgiveness. Who having once heard it can ever forget the haunting harmonies of Allegri's *Miserere*, the pathos of Bach's 'Have mercy, Lord' or the majesty of Mozart's various renditions of the Kyrie? Any list of pieces suitable for confession will always be hopelessly arbitrary, but here are a few of my personal favourites:

All we, like sheep from *Messiah* (Handel)

And he shall purify from *Messiah* (Handel)

Have mercy, Lord from *St Matthew's Passion* (Bach)

Kyrie from *Coronation Mass* (Mozart)

Kyrie from *Credo Mass* (Mozart)

Kyrie from *Mass in C Minor* (Mozart)

Kyrie from *Mass No. 6 in E Flat* (Schubert)

Kyrie from *Missa aeterna Christa munera* (Palestrina)

Kyrie from *Missa O magnum mysterium* (Victoria)

Kyrie from *Missa O quam gloriosum* (Victoria)

Kyrie from *Missa Papae Marcelli* (Palestrina)

Kyrie from *Missa solemnis* (Mozart)

Kyrie from *Requiem* (Fauré)

Kyrie from *Requiem* (Mozart)

Lacrimosa from *Requiem* (Mozart)

Miserere (Allegri)

Miserere mei, Deus from *Cantiones sacrae* (Byrd)

O bone Jesu (Marc Antonio Ingegneri)

O divine Redeemer (Gounod)

Recordare from *Requiem* (Mozart)

Recordare from *Requiem* (Verdi)

Salvator mundi from *Mass for Four Voices* (Tallis)

Thou knowest, Lord, the secrets of our hearts (Purcell)

As well as the great classics there is once again a growing amount of contemporary music available, written expressly for personal and shared devotion. Below is a selection of pieces I have used in the resources section (Part Four):

Have mercy on me, O God from *In God Alone* (Andrew Moore)

Have mercy on us, Lord from *In God Alone* (Andrew Moore)

Kyrie eleison from *Fountain of Life* (Margaret Rizza)

Kyries from *Sacred Weave* (Keith Duke)

Life of Christ renew me from *River of Peace* (Margaret Rizza)

Misere nobis, Domine from *Awakening in Love* (Margaret Rizza)

O Lord, listen to my prayer from *Light in Our Darkness* (Margaret Rizza)

O Lord, my heart is not proud from *Fountain of Life* (Margaret Rizza)

Many of the above have been included in the resources section (Part Four) of this book. A wealth of material is available from numerous contemporary artists and the following CDs may also be helpful:

Hillsong London: *Jesus Is*; *Look to You*; *Praise God*; *He Reigns*; *United We Stand*

Chris Tomlin: *Arriving*

Brian Littrell: *Welcome Home*

Delirious: *Access-D*; *Deeper*; *Glo*

Gaither: *Homecoming*

Kutless: *Hearts of the Innocent*; *Kutless*; *Strong Tower*

Nichole Nordeman: *Brave*; *The Mystery*; *To Know You*; *Woven and Spun*

Matt Redman: *Blessed Be Your Name*; *Facedown*; *The Father's Song*; *Where Angels Fear to Tread*

Abundant Life: *Divine Exchange*

Michael Smith: *Change Your World*; *Healing Rain*; *Worship Again*

CeCe Winans: *Alone in His Presence*; *Everlasting Love*

YFriday: *Open*; *Rain Maker*

Make a list of those that you find helpful and make them an integral part of your prayer time.

Hymns of confession

There are many hymns on the theme of grace and forgiveness, but surprisingly few expressing sorrow and confession and fewer still written in the first person (singular or plural) and thus lending themselves to personal prayer. Of those that there are, though, many are memorable indeed, the words of hymns like 'Amazing grace', 'And can it be', 'Beneath the cross of Jesus', 'Dear Lord and Father of mankind', 'Rock of ages' and 'When I survey' having helped sum up the penitence and remorse of countless generations. If ever you find yourself searching for the right words, the words in hymns such as those listed below will help you to articulate your feelings.

Amazing grace
And can it be
Beneath the cross of Jesus
Blessed assurance
Dear Lord and Father of mankind
Dear Master, in whose life I see
Forgive our sins as we forgive
Have mercy on us, O Lord
I am trusting thee, Lord Jesus
I heard the voice of Jesus say
I know not why God's wondrous grace
Just as I am, without one plea
Lord, I was blind
O loving Lord, who art for ever seeking
Overwhelmed by love
Rock of ages, cleft for me
Saviour, thy dying love
We have not known thee as we ought
When I survey the wondrous cross

Poems of confession

Most of the devotional poetry I've come across focuses on praise and thanksgiving or personal needs, but a few poems relate to confession. The following, written centuries ago by the prolific devotional writer Francis Quarles (1592–1644), includes a touch of humour alongside an acknowledgement of sin and affirmation of faith in God's redemptive love:

The Authour's Dreame

My sinnes are like the haires upon my head,
And raise their Audit to as high a score:
In this they differ: these doe dayly shed;
But ah! my sinnes grow dayly more and more.
   If by my haires thou number out my sinnes;
   Heaven make me bald before the day begins.

My sinnes are like the sands upon the shore;
Which every ebbe layes open to the eye:
In this they differ: These are cover'd o'er
With every tide, my sinnes still open lye.
   If thou wilt make my head a sea of teares,
   O they will hide the sinnes of all my yeares.

My sinnes are like the Starres within the skies,
In view, in number, even as bright, as great:
In this they differ: these doe set and rise;
But ah! my sinnes doe rise, but never set.
   Shine Son of glory, and my sinnes are gone
   Like twinkling Starres before the rising Sunne.

Another old poem comes from the poet/hymn-writer John Donne (1573–1631). It sums up beautifully the sense of shame we feel at our repeated wrongdoing yet also wonder at God's unfailing grace:

A Hymn to God the Father

Wilt thou forgive that sin where I begun,
Which was my sin, though it were done before?
Wilt thou forgive that sin through which I run,

And do run still, though still I do deplore?
When thou hast done, thou hast not done;
   For I have more.

Wilt thou forgive that sin which I have won
Others to sin, and made my sins their door?
Wilt thou forgive that sin which I did shun
A year or two, but wallow'd in a score?
When thou hast done, thou hast not done;
   For I have more.

I have a sin of fear, that when I've spun
My last thread, I shall perish on the shore;
But swear by thyself that at my death thy Son
Shall shine as he shines now and heretofore:
And having done that, thou hast done;
   I fear no more.

Amongst Christian poets I was intrigued to find some of the greatest names in literary history, among them the Brontë sisters. The following is a prayer of confession written by Anne (1820–49):

A prayer

My God (oh, let me call thee mine,
Weak, wretched sinner though I be),
My trembling soul would fain be thine;
My feeble faith still clings to thee.

Not only for the past I grieve,
The future fills me with dismay;
Unless Thou hasten to relieve,
Thy suppliant is a castaway.

I cannot say my faith is strong,
I dare not hope my love is great;
But strength and love to thee belong;
Oh, do not leave me desolate!

I know I owe my all to thee;
Oh, take the heart I cannot give!
Do Thou my strength – my Saviour be,
And make me to thy glory live.

Perhaps one of the greatest names associated with religious poetry is
Gerard Manley Hopkins (1844–89), his work having touched a chord
for many. In the following poem he acknowledges how much he owes
to God's mercy, recognising that he is called in turn to show such mercy
towards others.

Thee, God, I come from

Thee, God, I come from, to thee go,
all day long I like fountain flow
from thy hand out, swayed about
mote-like in thy mighty glow.

What I know of thee I bless,
as acknowledging thy stress
on my being and as seeing
something of thy holiness.

Once I turned from thee and hid,
bound on what thou hadst forbid;
sow the wind I would; I sinned:
I repent of what I did.

Bad I am, but yet thy child.
Father, be thou reconciled.
Spare thou me, since I see
with thy might that thou art mild.

I have life before me still
and thy purpose to fulfil;
yea a debt to pay thee yet:
help me, sir, and so I will.

But thou bidst, and just thou art,
me shew mercy from my heart
towards my brother, every other
man my mate and counterpart.

In the resources section (Part Four) of this book I've included poetic prayers of my own, written expressly for personal devotion. Here are a couple of examples:

Amazing grace

Lord, I come to worship, not because I should,
not to claim I'm worthy, virtuous or good,
not because I'm special, different to the crowd,
having any merit, reason to be proud.
Rather, I come humbly, conscious of my need,
knowing I've been faithless, false in word and deed.
Day by day I stumble, miss the goals I seek;
though I mean to serve you, inwardly I'm weak.
Lord, I can't deceive you, hide what's deep inside,
yet you bid me welcome, arms extended wide.
Gratefully I worship, coming not in fear,
but responding gladly, thankful to be here.
I will *try* to follow, walk the Christian way,
not because I have to, but because I may.

Love divine

I have no claim on your love at all,
no grounds to seek clemency;
I mean to serve, but repeatedly fall,
my faithlessness plain to see.
The vows I've made, the faith I've professed
all seem to have been in vain,
as faults and flaws so often confessed
return to haunt me again.
You see the worst, all my ugliness,
all that poisons deep inside,

but still you love, always eager to bless,
refusing to be denied.
No words, O Lord, can begin to say
how much I will always owe;
no sacrifice even start to repay
the mercy and grace you show.
I give you thanks, bring my all to you,
amazed that such love can be –
so rich and full, so constant and true,
so priceless and yet so free.

Reflective confession

I've always found reflective prayers helpful, for they, perhaps above all others, are able to speak both *for* and *to* us, with the emphasis very often upon the latter. They bring home points I've never considered before, open up new horizons, deepening my understanding of life and faith, and when it comes to prayers of confession I find myself returning again to Michel Quoist, for his are surely some of the most powerful ever written. 'Lord, deliver me from myself', 'Agony: Lord, I am crushed', 'Temptation' and 'Sin' not only perfectly express the frustration and disappointment we feel at repeatedly failing God but also help us look more honestly at ourselves, recognising the full extent of that failure and the immense contrast between us and God. Yet alongside that dismay and despair there is also confidence in God's mercy, the assurance that we cannot begin to do what God has fully done for us in Christ.

I will never attain the lyricism of Quoist's prose, but in my own reflective prayers I've tried to get a similar balance between challenge and promise, articulating my thoughts while opening my heart to his. The following prayers give a few examples. First, a reflection inspired by Psalm 51 and echoing those words of Romans 7 quoted earlier (see page 123):

What can I say, Lord?
What *can* I say?
I've failed you again, haven't I?
Despite all my promises,
all my good intentions,
I've gone and let you down like so many times before.

And I'm sickened,
   crushed,
   disgusted with myself,
   ashamed I could be so pathetically weak,
   so hopelessly false.
I tried so hard, that's what gets me down.
I was determined to make up for the lapses of the past,
   to show you that I'm really serious
   about this business of discipleship,
   and to prove that the trust you've shown in me,
   your willingness to forgive and go on forgiving,
   actually means something to me, despite the way it may seem.
But could I do it?
No.
For a few hours,
   a few days, perhaps,
   but finally I fell as I always do
   back into the old familiar ways.
Why, Lord?
What's wrong with me?
What am I going to do?
I can't change,
   not by myself.
I've tried it,
   and it's just no good,
   the weaknesses running too deep,
   too much a part of me,
   for me to conquer them alone.
It's in your hands, Lord;
   only *you* have the power to help me.
I know I don't deserve it,
   that I've no claim on your love or mercy,
   but I'm begging you,
   pleading on bended knee,
   pardon my iniquities.
Deal kindly, despite my folly,
   cleanse my heart and renew my spirit.

Mould me,
    fashion me,
    forgive me,
    restore me,
    so that perhaps one day, by your grace, I may serve as I should.
Lord, in your mercy, hear my prayer.

The next prayer focuses on how hard we find it to forgive others:

I meant to forgive, Lord,
    to put the past behind me and start afresh . . .
    and I honestly thought I had.
But I see now that I was wrong,
    for I've raked things up again;
    mistakes long past,
    which we both thought were dead and buried,
    plucked from the ashes,
    rekindled,
    and hurled in white-hot accusation.
It was a shock, Lord,
    for I truly believed I'd dealt with the matter,
    any last flickering flame of anger finally extinguished,
    but somewhere, deep within, the embers were still smouldering,
    needing only a little more fuel to reignite them.
It's more complicated than I imagined,
    this business of offering real, unreserved pardon,
    for hurt and bitterness are hard to quench;
    but I need to douse the blaze once and for all,
    for it's consuming my relationships,
    not just with others
    but, worst of all, with you.
Have mercy, Lord,
    and by your grace replace the cinders of anger and resentment
    with the fire of love.
May your grace and mercy burn within me,
    so that I might learn to forgive
    as you have so faithfully forgiven,
    showing the same gracious and generous pardon

that you so freely offer all,
    through Jesus Christ my Lord.
Amen.

And finally, a prayer which explores how difficult we find it to say sorry
to those we've wronged:

Lord, teach me to say sorry –
    that's my prayer today.
Simple enough you might think,
    and it is,
    or it should be,
    yet it's a word I find so difficult.
Not with you, I've no problem there,
    nor myself either, that's the strange thing –
    I know my mistakes well enough,
    and am happy to admit them,
    to get them off my chest.
But with others it's a different story –
    I see my faults, all right, the hurt I've caused;
    I know I've acted falsely, unfairly wronged them;
    and yet, although I long to make amends,
    the word just will not come.
I mean to say it, I really do,
    and I look for the opportunity to make a move,
    yet when the moment comes,
    I back away and bite my tongue.
I'm ashamed, Lord,
    ashamed of all the needless pain so many bear,
    the broken trust and wounded hearts,
    because I will not bend.
But I know it's not you I should apologise to –
    it's them.

My child,
    are you serious?
I'd like to think so, but I'm not sure you are,
    for what then are you waiting for?

You've told me the answer along with the problem,
    so why still stand there talking?
It's as you say,
    down to the last detail.
    your apologies are due not to me but those you've wronged.
You may be sorry,
    but that means nothing, not unless you show it,
    and until you do,
    the heartache you've caused will go on growing
    and the rift you've created growing ever deeper.
It can only get harder, the longer you leave it,
    you know that, don't you? –
    the right moment you're waiting for,
    the perfect opportunity you hope to find always just out of reach.
So no more excuses,
    no more shirking the issue,
    it's time to grasp the nettle,
    to put this behind you once and for all,
    to make your peace and heal the wounds.
It's time to say sorry.

Further reflective prayers on confession and forgiveness can be found in the next section, 'Using our senses'.

Using our senses

In what ways, you might ask, could using our senses possibly relate to prayers of confession? The link, I agree, may not immediately be obvious, but it's there nonetheless. All kinds of sights, sounds, scents and so forth have the power to speak beyond themselves, presenting a powerful challenge concerning the integrity of our lifestyles in relation to our faith. In the following prayers, for example, the taste and scent of a meal, the sight of a charity collector, and the feel of loose change in my pocket prompted me to further reflection and confession.

The meal

They ate dutifully enough,
   smiling politely
   and making the odd appreciative noise,
   but I knew they were enjoying it no more than I was.
The meal was bland,
   all but tasteless,
   and with good reason,
   for I'd forgotten to add seasoning –
   so small an ingredient,
   so large an effect.

Forgive me, Lord, for the insipid fare I offer you,
   looking the part,
   and with so many of the components right,
   yet lacking the one thing needful:
   the savour of love.
Teach me that the poorest of dishes with that one vital ingredient
   is worth far more than the finest of feasts without it.
Amen.

The soup

We murmured appreciatively,
   licking our lips in anticipation,
   for the soup smelt good,
   a perfect way to start the meal.
And though it was soon finished,
   our bowls pushed aside,
   no matter,
   for it was just that –
   the first course –
   plenty more to come.

Only suddenly, Lord, I thought of the vagrant queuing at the hostel,
   his ladle of soup not a starter
   but the only meal he'd eat that day;
   nothing fine or fancy about it,
   yet to him a feast,

bringing a little succour to his ravaged body,
a respite from the winter's chill . . .
and I could eat no more,
my meal having lost its savour.
Teach me, Lord, in my plenty,
to remember those with so much less,
for should I forget them,
I forget you too.
Amen.

The charity collector

They were there outside the supermarket,
shaking their tins hopefully,
but I averted my eyes and shuffled past,
pretending I hadn't noticed their presence.
I'd no loose change to salve my conscience –
just a five-pound note, nothing smaller –
so I hurried by on the other side.

Lord, forgive me,
for I'd spent more on one treat for myself
than the fiver I begrudged to others.
I'd extolled the virtue of a generous heart
yet displayed the meanest of spirits,
my talk of concern and compassion
exposed for the sham it was.
Teach me, next time I'm asked to give,
to respond gladly,
and to offer not the least I can get away with
but more than I can truly afford.
Amen.

The loose change

I pocketed the coins with barely a glance,
the sum so small it seemed barely worth counting,
yet what I judged insignificant

others would have considered a fortune,
enough to spell the difference for them between life and death.
It could have bought food for the hungry,
    medicine for the sick
    or shelter for the homeless;
    but it did none of those,
    lying instead in my pocket
    until spent, not on others, but on myself.

Forgive me, Lord,
    for I have received so much yet give so little,
    frittering away money on trivia and luxuries I do not need,
    while a multitude suffer and die for want of a pittance.
Remind me of how fortunate I am
    and of all I can do for others at such little cost,
    and teach me to respond,
    ready to give not just my small change but sacrificially,
    just as you gave your all for me.
Amen.

Open your senses, then, to the world around you, and you'll be amazed at how much brings God's challenge, calling you to examine your life and acknowledge the ways you fall short of his call.

Thanksgiving

Introduction

One of the first things we're taught as children is to say please and thank you, considered by most people to be essentials of social etiquette. We need, in other words, not only to be able to ask for things in the right way but also to express appropriate gratitude for what we're given. But if most of us learn that more or less successfully in our relations with others, it can be a very different matter when it comes to God. All of us will, I suspect, have pleaded many times for certain things in prayer, but how many times when such prayers were answered did we make a point of saying thank you? If you're anything like me, then the answer, sadly, is not very often. When the need is met, crisis over, problem resolved, challenge faced, somehow the incentive to pray is not so strong, included, if remembered at all, as an afterthought. Is God offended by this neglect? I don't think so, for he knows and understands our human weakness, but he wants us to give thanks nonetheless, not for his benefit but for ours.

Negative aspects of life can too easily crowd out the positive, dwelt upon to the point that our perception is out of all proportion to reality. It's only when we stop to count our blessings that we realise sometimes how lucky we are, how many reasons we have to celebrate. Pausing to consider and acknowledge such things can help us to see all of life in a different light, such that we approach it with hope instead of resignation, as half-full rather than half-empty. The list of good things, if we only stop to look, is endless: the warmth of the sun, caress of a breeze, refreshment of rain or beauty of a snowfall; the love of a child, reassurance of an embrace, closeness of a friend or camaraderie of the workplace; the sound of laughter, song of birds, rhythm of a pop song or chords of a symphony; the taste of food, scent of a flower, grandeur of a view, or touch of a feather; and so we could continue, *ad infinitum*.

When you stop to think about it, it's a wonder we don't spend all our lives thanking God, and yet, of course, we don't. Much of the time, quite rightly and as God intends, we're simply too busy getting on with the business of enjoying what he's given. Don't take it for granted, though, assuming it's yours by right. Make a point of acknowledging the countless good things you receive each day, and you will find that prayer changes the way you feel, speak and act; in short, changes the person you are.

Old Testament thanksgiving

Look at the pages of the Old Testament, the Psalms in particular, and the theme of thanksgiving is never far from the surface, for at the heart of the Jewish nation's life was a sense of gratitude for all God had done for them, seen supremely in his delivering them from slavery in Egypt and leading them into the Promised Land. Here was a message to be taught to one's children and one's children's children; to be learned and relearned so that it would never be forgotten. God had taken a rootless wandering people and had given them a sense of purpose that shaped every part of life. Moreover, of course, he was the one who had brought the universe into being; the giver of life in all its richness and variety. Thanks was given also for the way God faithfully provided help, comfort, strength and protection.

Below are just some of the verses in the Psalms that give expression to this all-pervading sense of gratitude:

I will give you thanks always, because of the things you have done. In the presence of your people I will honour your name, for it is good. *Psalm 52:9*

I will offer you thanks, Lord, with all my heart; I will tell everyone of your mighty acts; I will exult and be glad in you. *Psalm 9:1, 2a*

The Lord is my strength and shield; I trust in him with all my heart and so am sustained. My heart sings for joy within me as I give thanks to him. *Psalm 28:7*

You have turned my tears into dancing; you have removed sackcloth from me and clothed me instead with joy, such that I sing your praise and cannot be silent. Lord God, I will always thank you. *Psalm 30:11, 12*

I thank you, Lord God, with my whole heart, and will give glory to your name for ever, for great is the constancy of your love to me. *Psalm 86:12, 13a*

It is good to give thanks to you, Lord, to sing praises to your name, O Most High, to declare your steadfast love in the morning, and your faithfulness at night. For you, O Lord, have made me glad by your work; at the works of your hands I sing for joy.

Psalm 92:1, 2, 4

You are my God, and I thank you for it; you are my God; I will acclaim you. *Psalm 118:28*

Everything you have made and done will offer you thanks, Lord, and all your faithful people will bless you! *Psalm 145:10*

New Testament thanksgiving

Although we find few direct prayers of thanksgiving in the New Testament, there are innumerable expressions of gratitude to God and repeated calls to give thanks in turn. And that thankfulness is not just for those blessings celebrated in the Old Testament but, above all, for the life, death and resurrection of Christ – the supreme expression of God's love. So Philippians 4:6 urges, 'Do not brood over anything, but bring all your needs thankfully to God through your prayers and petitions.' Colossians 3:17 puts it like this: 'Whatever you do, whether in word or deed, do it in the name of the Lord Jesus, offering thanks to God the Father through him.' It's the same idea in 1 Thessalonians 5:18: 'Whatever situation you're in, give thanks, for that's what God wants for you in Jesus Christ.' And so also in Ephesians 5:19, 20: 'Sing psalms, hymns and spiritual songs among yourselves, singing and making music in your hearts to the Lord and in everything giving thanks to God the Father, in the name of our Lord Jesus Christ.'

We may not, of course, always feel thankful, gratitude sometimes being the last thing on our minds, but these words of the New Testament remind us that whatever we may go through, nothing can take away what God has done for us, or the assurance of his love and mercy, now and for evermore.

Classic prayers of thanksgiving

There are surprisingly few ancient prayers of thanksgiving, a reflection perhaps of the difficulty in distinguishing thanks from praise. The following, written by the prolific St Augustine of Hippo (354–430), is short but to the point:

> Thanks be to you, O Creator and governor of the universe,
> for my well-being through the years since I arrived at birth.
> Thanks be to you, my joy, my confidence, my God,
> for the gifts by which you have preserved me
> and enabled me to grow.
> Amen.

One of the best-known early prayers of thanksgiving is that of St Richard of Chichester (1197–1253):

> Thanks be to you, my Lord Jesus Christ,
> for all the benefits you have won for me,
> for all the pains and insults you have borne for me,
> O most merciful redeemer, friend and brother.
> May I know you more clearly,
> love you more dearly
> and follow you more nearly,
> day by day.
> Amen.

An example of thanksgiving spilling over into praise, though with the emphasis on the former, can be seen in the following prayer of Lancelot Andrewes (1555–1626):

> For all these, and also for all other mercies,
> known and unknown,
> open and secret,
> remembered by us or now forgotten,
> kindnesses received by us willingly or even against our will,
> we praise you,
> we bless you,
> we thank you,
> and will praise and bless and thank you
> all the days of our life,
> through Jesus Christ our Lord.
> Amen.

A classic prayer, known as the General Thanksgiving, dates back to Tudor times and reflects the genius of Thomas Cranmer, to whom, in large part, we owe the *Book of Common Prayer*. Cranmer, in turn, drew on Catholic monastic tradition, this prayer being part of the ancient order of Compline.

> Almighty God, Father of all mercies,
>> we your unworthy servants
>> give you most humble and hearty thanks
>> for all your goodness and loving-kindness to us and to all people.
> We bless you for our creation, preservation,
>> and all the blessings of this life;
>> but above all for your inestimable love
>> in the redemption of the world by our Lord Jesus Christ,
>> for the means of grace,
>> and for the hope of glory.
> And we beseech you, give us that due sense of all your mercies,
>> that our hearts may be unfeignedly thankful,
>> and that we show forth your praise,
>> not only with our lips, but in our lives;
>> by giving up ourselves to your service,
>> and by walking before you in holiness and righteousness
>> all our days;
>> through Jesus Christ our Lord,
>> to whom with you and the Holy Ghost be all honour and glory,
>> world without end.
> Amen.

Finally, a prayer of George Herbert (1593–1633), simple but special:

> You, Lord, have given so much to me;
>> give me one thing more,
>> a grateful heart.
> Amen.

Music of thanksgiving

As with classic prayers, there's less music relating specifically to the theme of thanksgiving than you might expect. The following, though, are some possibilities you might like to make use of. First, from the world of classical music:

Confitebor from *Solemn Vespers* (Mozart)
Gratias from *Mass in C Minor* (Mozart)
Gratias agimus tibi from *Gloria*, RV 588 or RV 589 (Vivaldi)
Gratias agimus tibi from *Mass in B Minor* (Bach)
Ode to joy from *Symphony No. 9* (Beethoven)
On wings of song (Mendelssohn)

Second, some more contemporary music suggestions which are also included in the resources section (Part Four) of this book:

I give my work to you, Lord from *Awakening in Love*
　(Margaret Rizza)
In God alone is my soul at rest from *In God Alone* (Andrew Moore)
Kyries from *Sacred Weave* (Keith Duke)
O give thanks to the Lord from *Light in Our Darkness*
　(Margaret Rizza)
The Lord is my light and my salvation from *Light in Our Darkness*
　(Margaret Rizza)
The Lord is my shepherd from *In God Alone* (Andrew Moore)

Many of the above have been included in the resources section (Part Four) of this book. A wealth of material is available from numerous contemporary artists and the following CDs may also be helpful:

Hillsong London: *Jesus Is*; *Look to You*; *Praise God*; *He Reigns*;
　United We Stand
Chris Tomlin: *Arriving*
Brian Littrell: *Welcome Home*
Delirious: *Access-D*; *Deeper*; *Glo*
Gaither: *Homecoming*
Kutless: *Hearts of the Innocent*; *Kutless*; *Strong Tower*
Nichole Nordeman: *Brave*; *The Mystery*; *To Know You*; *Woven
　and Spun*; *Gratitude Trax*

Matt Redman: *Blessed Be Your Name*; *Facedown*; *The Father's Song*; *Where Angels Fear to Tread*
Abundant Life: *Divine Exchange*
Michael Smith: *Change Your World*; *Healing Rain*; *Worship Again*
CeCe Winans: *Alone in His Presence*; *Everlasting Love*
YFriday: *Open*; *Rain Maker*

Make a list of any pieces that help you express your thanksgiving, and make them an integral part of your prayer time.

Hymns of thanksgiving

As with prayers and music, there are fewer great hymns of thanksgiving around than I expected. The following – an old Latin hymn, translated by Edward Caswall (1814–78) – captures well the spirit in which thanksgiving should be offered: not seeking any reward or out of a sense of duty, but in response to what God has done in Christ.

My God, I love thee; not because
I hope for heaven thereby,
nor yet because who love thee not
are lost eternally.
Thou, O my Jesus, thou didst me
upon the Cross embrace;
for me didst bear the nails and spear
and manifold disgrace.

And griefs and torments numberless,
and sweat of agony;
yea, death itself – and all for me
who was thine enemy.
Then why, O blessed Jesu Christ,
should I not love thee well?
Not for the sake of winning heaven,
nor of escaping hell.

Not from the hope of gaining aught,
not seeking a reward;

but as thyself hast loved me,
O ever-loving Lord.
So would I love thee, dearest Lord,
and in thy praise will sing;
solely because thou art my God,
and my most loving King.

One of the best-known hymns of thanksgiving must surely be that written by Martin Rinkart (1586–1649) and later translated by Catherine Winkworth (1827–78). The first verse brims over with gratitude:

Now thank we all our God,
with hearts and hands and voices,
who wondrous things hath done,
in whom his world rejoices;
who, from our mother's arms,
hath blessed us on our way
with countless gifts of love,
and still is ours today.

Then, of course, there's the often-quoted hymn of Johnson Oatman Jr, first published in 1897, and reminding us of the importance of counting our blessings:

When upon life's billows you are tempest tossed,
when you are discouraged, thinking all is lost,
count your many blessings, name them one by one,
and it will surprise you what the Lord hath done.

Refrain
Count your blessings, name them one by one,
count your blessings, see what God hath done!
count your blessings, name them one by one,
and it will surprise you what the Lord hath done.

Are you ever burdened with a load of care?
Does the cross seem heavy you are called to bear?
Count your many blessings, every doubt will fly,
and you will keep singing as the days go by.

When you look at others with their lands and gold,
think that Christ has promised you his wealth untold.
Count your many blessings. Wealth can never buy
your reward in heaven, nor your home on high.

So, amid the conflict whether great or small,
do not be disheartened, God is over all;
count your many blessings, angels will attend,
help and comfort give you to your journey's end.

A lesser-known hymn, but one of my personal favourites, is that by
T. W. Jex-Blake (1832–1915). In two verses it covers just about everything we could think of, before going on to showing our gratitude in
word as well as deed.

Lord, we thank thee for the pleasure
that our happy lifetime gives,
for the boundless worth and treasure
of a soul that ever lives;
mind that looks before and after,
lifting eyes to things above;
human tears, and human laughter,
and the depths of human love.

For the thrill, the leap, the gladness
of our pulses flowing free;
e'en for every touch of sadness
that may bring us nearer thee;
but, above all other kindness,
thine unutterable love,
which, to heal our sin and blindness
sent thy dear Son from above.

Teach us so our days to number
that we may be early wise;
dreamy mist, or cloud, or slumber,
never dull our heavenward eyes.
Hearty be our work and willing,
as to thee, and not to men:
for we know our souls' fulfilling
is in heaven, and not till then.

The following hymns may be helpful, though, of course, you will probably be able to think of many more.

All that I am
Count your blessings
Every minute of every day
Faithful one, so unchanging
Great is thy faithfulness
I give my hands
I lift my eyes to the quiet hills
In heavenly love abiding
My God, I love thee
My heart will sing to you
Now thank we all our God
O Love that wilt not let me go
Such love
Thanks be to God
Thank you for saving me
Thank you for the summer morning
Thank you, Lord
The God of love my shepherd is
The King of love my shepherd is
The Lord's my shepherd
To God be the glory!
What a friend we have in Jesus
What a wonderful change
When I survey the wondrous cross
Why should I feel discouraged

Poetic thanksgiving

In the poetry I've come across, thanksgiving frequently stems from the natural world, where God's goodness and faithfulness are glimpsed. The following, taken from a 1922 book of American poetry, is a good example:

A song of thanks

For the sun that shone at the dawn of spring,
    for the flowers which bloom and the birds that sing,
for the verdant robe of the gray old earth,
    for her coffers filled with their countless worth,
for the flocks which feed on a thousand hills,
    for the rippling streams which turn the mills,
for the lowing herds in the lovely vale,
    for the songs of gladness on the gale –
from the Gulf and the Lakes to the Oceans' banks –
    Lord God of Hosts, we give thee thanks!

For the farmer reaping his whitened fields,
    for the bounty which the rich soil yields,
for the cooling dews and refreshing rains,
    for the sun which ripens the golden grains,
for the bearded wheat and the fattened swine,
    for the stalled ox and the fruitful vine,
for the tubers large and cotton white,
    for the kid and the lambkin frisk and blithe,
for the swan which floats near the river-banks –
    Lord God of Hosts, we give thee thanks!

For the pumpkin sweet and the yellow yam,
    for the corn and beans and the sugared ham,
for the plum and the peach and the apple red,
    for the dear old press where the wine is tread,
for the cock which crows at the breaking dawn,
    and the proud old 'turk' of the farmer's barn,
for the fish which swim in the babbling brooks,
    for the game which hide in the shady nooks –
from the Gulf and the Lakes to the Oceans' banks –
    Lord God of Hosts, we give thee thanks!

For the sturdy oaks and the stately pines,
    for the lead and the coal from the deep, dark mines,
for the silver ores of a thousand fold,
    for the diamond bright and the yellow gold,

for the river boat and the flying train,
    for the fleecy sail of the rolling main,
for the velvet sponge and the glossy pearl,
    for the flag of peace which we now unfurl –
from the Gulf and the Lakes to the Oceans' banks –
    Lord God of Hosts, we give thee thanks!

For the lowly cot and the mansion fair,
    for the peace and plenty together share,
for the Hand which guides us from above,
    for thy tender mercies, abiding love,
for the blessed home with its children gay,
    for returnings of Thanksgiving Day,
for the bearing toils and the sharing cares,
    we lift up our hearts in our songs and our prayers –
from the Gulf and the Lakes to the Oceans' banks –
    Lord God of Hosts, we give thee thanks!

Edward Smyth Jones

The following poem focuses specifically on the beauty of sunrise:

The lattice at sunrise

As on my bed at dawn I mus'd and pray'd,
I saw my lattice prank'd upon the wall,
The flaunting leaves and flitting birds withal –
A sunny phantom interlaced with shade;
'Thanks be to heaven,' in happy mood I said,
'What sweeter aid my matins could befall
Than the fair glory from the East hath made?

What holy sleights hath God, the Lord of all,
To bid us feel and see! we are not free
To say we see not, for the glory comes
Nightly and daily, like the flowing sea;
His lustre pierceth through the midnight glooms
And, at prime hour, behold! He follows me
With golden shadows to my secret rooms.'

Charles Tennyson Turner (1808–79)

The poet William Wordsworth (1770–1850), in his poem 'September 1819', gives thanks of a different sort, inspired by listening to a hymn to reflect on the loving provision of God:

> This, this is holy – while I hear
> These vespers of another year,
> This hymn of thanks and praise,
> My spirit seems to mount above
> The anxieties of human love,
> And earth's precarious days.
> But list! – though winter storms be nigh,
> Unchecked is that soft harmony:
> There lives Who can provide
> For all his creatures; and in Him,
> Even like the radiant Seraphim,
> These choristers confide.

Finally, a poem by Anne Brontë (1820–49) in which, despite sharing in a loved one's sorrow, she celebrates also God's promise of life beyond death:

> I mourn with thee, and yet rejoice
> That thou shouldst sorrow so;
> With angel choirs I join my voice
> To bless the sinner's woe.
> Though friends and kindred turn away,
> And laugh thy grief to scorn;
> I hear the great Redeemer say,
> Blessed are ye that mourn.
> Hold on thy course, nor deem it strange
> That earthly cords are riven:
> Man may lament the wondrous change,
> But there is joy in Heaven!

Reflective thanksgiving

We have so much to be thankful for, don't we, yet all too often we fail to count our blessings. Reflective prayers can help us do just that, reminding us of the many things we so often and easily overlook. Michel Quoist, for example, in a prayer titled simply 'Thank you', gives thanks for just about anything and everything, ranging from 'the toothpaste that refreshes', 'the street-cleaning lorry and the men who run it', 'the wind that caressed my face and . . . the trees that nodded to me on the way' to 'the tranquil night . . . the stars . . . the silence'.

Sadly most of us are good at asking God for things but poor at thanking him for what he's given – a point explored in the following reflection:

Lord, I sent a card today.
Nothing out of the ordinary,
   just a simple thank-you note for a special gift.
There was no need to send it,
   for it wasn't expected,
   and I very nearly didn't,
   time, as always, being short.
But that present had meant something to me,
   touched my heart,
   and I wanted to show my appreciation,
   to make it plain it wasn't just taken for granted,
   but that I was truly grateful.
Yet it struck me, Lord,
   as I popped that card into the post-box,
   that while I'm good on the whole
   at saying thank you to others,
   I'm pretty hopeless when it comes to you.
I'd never considered it before,
   the thought simply not occurring to me,
   but suddenly I realised
   my prayers are all too often 'please'
   and all too rarely 'thank you'.
It's true, isn't it, Lord?
I'm always after something –
   another problem to solve,
   another request,
   another need,
   another desire,
   and I bring them to you without a second thought,

almost automatically,
confident you'll help.
But when the crisis is over,
your answer given,
it's all forgotten,
nothing more said until the next time.
There's no excuse, Lord, I know that –
so today, quite simply, I want to say thank you,
thank you, for everything.

My child,
thank *you*.
It's good to hear you,
for, believe me, you're not the only one who fails to thank me.
I'm inundated each day by a multitude of people
with a multitude of requests,
a myriad of problems –
yet a modicum of gratitude.
'Do this,' they tell me.
'Do that.'
'Give me strength.'
'Hear my prayer.'
And I do,
willingly,
only too glad to grant my blessing.
I don't demand a response or even expect one,
love bringing its own reward,
but to know I've touched a life and given joy
means as much to me as it would to anyone.
In fact, there's only one thing more special,
and that's when someone not only says thank you
but shows they mean it –
responding when I offer guidance,
trusting when I offer strength,
risking when I offer freedom,
rejoicing when I offer life.
Do that, my child –
show gratitude in action –

and words no longer matter,
for it's all the thanks I need.

As we've already noted, the Psalms offer time and again a reminder and example of the thanks we ought to offer each day. The following reflection was inspired by Psalm 16 and seeks to echo that burning sense of gratitude:

I'm a lucky man –
    so much to be thankful for,
    so much to celebrate,
    my life running over with good things!
All right, I've not got everything, admittedly,
    and yes, perhaps I would change the odd detail given the chance,
    but nothing major,
    certainly nothing to fret over,
    for when I stop to count my blessings,
    weigh things up in the balance,
    I realise how truly fortunate I am.
I should never have forgotten, of course,
    but I did,
    and I do,
    time after time,
    to my shame not only failing to be thankful
    but actually complaining,
    bemoaning my lot,
    dwelling on the bad rather than the good.
It's crazy, I know,
    but we all do it, don't we? –
    so much taken for granted,
    unrecognised,
    unappreciated;
    so feeble a response to so vast a treasure.
Probably it will always be the same, despite my best intentions,
    the gratitude I feel now evaporating yet again before I know it.
Probably I'll still end up feeling sorry for myself,
    looking enviously at my neighbour,

muttering that life's not fair.
But today at least I want to give thanks,
  I want to celebrate everything in life that is good and special,
  and, above all, I want to praise God, to whom I owe it all.

Using our senses

It's hard sometimes to separate praise and thanksgiving, for in many ways they're two sides of the same coin, gratitude so often leading us to worship and vice versa. When I'm out on a country walk I find that more than ever, what moves me to praise moving me equally to thankfulness. It may be the sight of a buzzard soaring overhead, a kingfisher darting into a stream, rabbits scampering across a field, snowdrops dancing in the breeze, cows quietly grazing or trees bursting into life. Or it may be the sound of schoolchildren playing during their lunchtime break, the song of birds, the scent of bluebells, the softness of a feather or the crunch of leaves beneath my feet. Confronted by these and so much more, I cannot but help give thanks, prayer arising as naturally as breathing – not always in the form of words but often simply through grateful thoughts offered up to God. And, of course, we don't need to be out in the countryside to find reasons to give thanks: in the home, at work, and in our leisure there's likewise so much to celebrate – family, friends, food, clothing, health, hobbies, love, laughter, to name but some. Wherever you are, whenever it might be, make a point of focusing on those things you have cause to be grateful for, and you will find your prayers of thanksgiving taking on a vitality and spontaneity greater than anything you've known before.

Praying for ourselves

Introduction

If there's one thing most of us find it relatively easy to pray about, it's ourselves. Each of us, after all, is faced day after day with a host of pressures, problems, demands and decisions, concerning which we feel in need of support, so what could be more natural than to bring all this to God in prayer, seeking his help and guidance? We cannot help doing so, simply because they matter to us, each being an integral part of who and what we are. But, as I said earlier, that doesn't mean prayer is merely a list of requests to God. It does not guarantee every hope will be realised, every desire met, every difficulty taken away and every sorrow lifted, life for the Christian bringing as many trials and temptations as for anyone else – each being a part of what it means to be human. Faith offers no immunity, but what it does give us is the assurance of God's presence with us in whatever we face; his joy, peace, love and strength able to see us through it all. That is why, as we shall see, so many petitionary prayers, hymns, poems and reflections focus not on specific requests but on a yearning to know and love God better, grasping more fully who and what he is and offering more faithful service in return. The closer we grow to him, the more we will find every part of life transformed by the touch of his hand, our prayers not perhaps answered as we expected, but answered nonetheless.

In short, then, petitionary prayer has two angles, on the one hand focusing on our daily concerns and on the other seeking deeper faith and understanding. Instinctively we will bring the first before God, asking for strength and guidance to face what life may throw at us, but for this to happen we need also to know him more nearly and dearly. Seek that, and you *will* find.

Old Testament petition

If you're looking for a broad sweep of concerns in prayer, then the Psalms have them in plenty, ranging from the distinctly down to earth to the unmistakably spiritual. As we've seen already, some speak of fear, others of despair, others again of doubt, and others still of gratitude, awe, repentance or commitment, and so we could go on. The following give just a flavour of this diversity:

> Give ear to me, Lord, and answer, for I'm vulnerable and in need. Deal kindly with me, for I call to you, Lord, throughout the day. Hear my prayer; listen to my appeal for favour. I know you answer me, so in this time of trouble I call to you.   *Psalm 86:1, 3, 6, 7*

> In the morning, Lord, meet our needs through your unfailing love so that we may celebrate and exult every day.   *Psalm 90:14*

> Lord, hear my prayer, let my cry reach you! Do not abandon me in my hour of need, but give ear to my call and respond quickly.
> *Psalm 102:1, 2*

> Safeguard my mouth, Lord, and shield the gateway of my lips! Prevent my heart from veering towards evil, being drawn into the shady activities of evildoers and indulging in their delights.
> *Psalm 141:3, 4*

> Remind me each morning of your constant love, for my trust is in you. Help me to understand the path I should take, for I lift my soul to you.   *Psalm 143:8*

> Reveal your ways to me, Lord, instruct me in your paths. Guide and teach me in your truth, for you are the God who saves me; I wait for you all day long.   *Psalm 25:4, 5*

> O God, listen to my prayer, and do not keep your distance when I appeal for your mercy. Attend to me, and answer me; I am agitated, whinging and grumbling. My heart is tormented, crushed by the fear of death, all manner of anxiety and dread having come over me to the point that I'm overwhelmed by terror.
> *Psalm 55:1, 2a, 4, 5*

> Lord, hear me when I call out to you, deal kindly and answer me. You have instructed us, 'Seek my face', and my heart responds, 'I do seek it, Lord', so please don't hide your face from me. Do not reject me in your anger, you who have so often been my help. Saving God, do not discard or abandon me!   *Psalm 27:7-9*

Pour out your light and truth and let them guide me; let them lead
me to your holy hill and your dwelling place.   *Psalm 43:3*

New Testament petition

I've spoken of the two prongs of petitionary prayer, and we see both of
these reflected in the New Testament. Thus we have the advice of Paul,
already mentioned, to pray about anything and everything: 'Do not
brood about anything, but thankfully bring all your needs to God
through your prayers and petitions' (Philippians 4:6). This, however, is
counterbalanced by the words of Jesus in the Lord's Prayer: 'Give us
this day our daily bread', and alongside his words we have his example,
notably in those celebrated words in Gethsemane: 'not my will but
yours be done'. Of course we will have much to pray for, all kinds of
concerns and needs that we want to bring before God, but ultimately
our request should always echo that supreme expression of trust,
prayer not about *us* having *our* way but *God* having *his*.

Classic prayers of petition

When it comes to prayers of petition we really do have a plethora of
riches, there being enough to fill this book several times over. Almost
all take as their theme a longing to know and love God better. Below
are just a few examples. More can be found in the resources section
(Part Four) of this book.

> Lord, you know what is best;
>   let this be done or that be done as you please.
> Give what you will,
>   as much as you will,
>   when you will.
> Do with me as you know best,
>   as will most please you,
>   and will be for your greater honour.

Place me where you will and deal with me freely in all things.
I am in your hands;
    turn me about whichever way you will.
Behold, I am your servant, ready to obey in all things.
Not for myself do I desire to live, but for you –
    would that I could do this worthily and perfectly!
Amen.

Thomas à Kempis (1379–1471)

O Lord,
    teach me to seek you,
    and reveal yourself to me
    when I seek you.
For I cannot seek you unless you first teach me,
    nor find you unless you first reveal yourself to me.
Let me seek you in longing,
    and long for you in seeking.
Let me find you in love,
    and love you in finding.
Amen.

St Ambrose of Milan (c. 340–97)

Wise, merciful, loving God, do not cast me from your presence.
Keep me in your service all the days of my life.
Ask of me what you will.
Only grant what you command of me.
Even if I tire in your service,
    you in your patience will not tire of me.
You will come to help,
    you will give me the strength
    to make a fresh start again and again;
    to hope against hope;
    in all my defeats to have faith in victory
    and in your triumph within me.
Amen.

Karl Rahner (1904–84) (extract)

Lord, I know not what I ought to ask of you,
　　you only know what I need;
　　you love me better than I know how to love myself.
Father, give to your child
　　that which he himself knows not how to ask.
I dare not ask either for crosses or consolations;
　　I simply present myself before you.
I open my heart to you.
Behold my need, which I know not myself;
　　see and do according to your tender mercy.
Smile or heal,
　　depress me or raise me up;
　　I adore all your purposes without knowing them:
　　I am silent;
　　I offer myself in sacrifice;
　　I yield myself to you;
　　I would have no other desire than to accomplish your will.
Teach me to pray.
Pray yourself in me.
Amen.

François Fénelon (1651–1715)

Petitionary music

Compared to praise and confession there are only a few classic pieces
I'm aware of that directly relate to prayers of petition. These include
the following:

Cum Sancto Spiritu from *Gloria* (Vivaldi)
Cum Sancto Spiritu from *Mass in B Minor* (Bach)
Cum Sancto Spiritu from *Mass in C Minor* (Mozart)
Libera me from *Requiem* (Verdi)
O for the wings of a dove (Mendelssohn)
Pilgrim's Chorus from *Tannhäuser* (Wagner)

With contemporary composers, though, it's a different story. The
following pieces, for example, are just some of those currently available

on CD. Many of these have been included in the resources section (Part Four) and on the CDs accompanying this book.

Calm me, Lord from *Fire of Love* (Margaret Rizza)
Christ be near from *Sacred Pathway* (Keith Duke)
Come, Holy Dove from *Sacred Pathway* (Keith Duke)
Come, my Lord, my light, my way from *Sacred Weave* (Keith Duke)
Come, my way from *River of Peace* (Margaret Rizza)
Desert waters from *Sacred Pathway* (Keith Duke)
Evening dedication from *Sacred Weave* (Keith Duke)
Hymn of St Patrick from *River of Peace* (Margaret Rizza)
Let your beauty from *Awakening in Love* (Margaret Rizza)
Life of Christ, renew me from *River of Peace* (Margaret Rizza)
Lighten our darkness from *Sacred Pathway* (Keith Duke)
Like the deer that yearns from *In God Alone* (Andrew Moore)
O God, be gracious and bless us from *Awakening in Love* (Margaret Rizza)
O Lord, listen to my prayer from *Light in Our Darkness* (Margaret Rizza)
Oculi mei from *Awakening in Love* (Margaret Rizza)
Prayer of St Patrick from *Fire of Love* (Margaret Rizza)
Saviour of my soul from *Sacred Pathway* (Keith Duke)
Silent, surrendered from *Fountain of Life* (Margaret Rizza)
Take, Lord from *Awakening in Love* (Margaret Rizza)
Take my life, Lord from *Fire of Love* (Margaret Rizza)
The Grail prayer from *Fire of Love* (Margaret Rizza)
The Lord is my light from *Fire of Love* (Margaret Rizza)
Traveller's prayer from *Sacred Pathway* (Keith Duke)
You are the centre from *Fountain of Life* (Margaret Rizza)

Many of the above have been included in the resources section (Part Four) of this book. A wealth of material is available from numerous contemporary artists and the following CDs may also be helpful:

Hillsong: *Jesus Is*; *Look to You*; *Praise God*; *He Reigns*; *United We Stand*

Chris Tomlin: *Arriving*

Brian Littrell: *Welcome Home*

Delirious: *Access-D*; *Deeper*; *Glo*

Gaither: *Homecoming*

Kutless: *Hearts of the Innocent*; *Kutless*; *Strong Tower*

Nichole Nordeman: *Brave*; *The Mystery*; *To Know You*; *Woven and Spun*

Matt Redman: *Blessed Be Your Name*; *Facedown*; *The Father's Song*; *Where Angels Fear to Tread*

Abundant Life: *Divine Exchange*

Michael Smith: *Change Your World*; *Healing Rain*; *Worship Again*

CeCe Winans: *Alone in His Presence*; *Everlasting Love*

YFriday: *Open*; *Rain Maker*

Petitionary hymns

Unsurprisingly, as with prayers and music, numerous hymns give expression to a longing to know and serve God better. The following, written by W. J. Mathams (1853–1931), is a personal favourite:

Christ of the upward way,
my guide divine,
where thou hast set thy feet
may I place mine:
and move and march wherever thou hast trod,
keeping face forward up the hill of God.

Give me the heart to hear
thy voice and will,
that without fault or fear
I may fulfil
thy holy purpose with a glad and holy zest,
like one who would not bring less than his best.

Give me the eye to see
each chance to serve,
then send me strength to rise
with steady nerve,

and leap at once with kind and helpful deed
to the sure succour of a soul in need.

Give me the good stout arm
to shield the right,
and wield thy sword of truth
with all my might,
that, in the warfare I must wage for thee,
more than I victor I may ever be.

Christ of the upward way,
my guide divine,
where thou hast set thy feet
may I place mine:
and when thy last call comes serene and clear,
calm may my answer be, 'Lord, I am here.'

Equally memorable is the lovely translation of the ancient Irish hymn, 'Be thou my vision', by Mary Byrne (1880–1931) and Eleanor Hull (1860–1935):

Be thou my vision, O Lord of my heart,
be all else but naught to me, save that thou art;
thou my best thought in the day and the night,
both waking and sleeping, thy presence my light.

Be thou my wisdom, be thou my true word,
be thou ever with me, and I with thee, Lord;
be thou my great Father, and I thy true son;
be thou in me dwelling, and I with thee one.

Be thou my breastplate, my sword for the fight,
be thou my whole armour, be thou my true might,
be thou my soul's shelter, be thou my strong tower,
O raise thou me heavenward, great power of my power.

Riches I heed not, nor man's empty praise,
be thou mine inheritance now and always;
be thou and thou only the first in my heart,
O sovereign of heaven, my treasure thou art!

High King of heaven, thou heaven's bright sun,
O grant me its joys, after victory is won;
great heart of my own heart, whatever befall,
still be thou my vision, O ruler of all.

Another lovely old hymn is that by George Herbert (1593–1633):

Come, my Way, my Truth, my Life:
such a way as gives us breath;
such a truth as ends all strife;
such a life as killeth death.

Come, my Light, my Feast, my Strength:
such a light as shows a feast;
such a feast as mends in length;
such a strength as makes his guest.

Come, my Joy, my Love, my Heart:
such a joy as none can move;
such a love as none can part;
such a heart as joys in love.

More recent by comparison is the great hymn by Edwin Hatch (1835–89):

Breathe on me, Breath of God,
fill me with life anew,
that as you love, so may I love,
and do what you would do.

Breathe on me, Breath of God,
until my heart is pure:
until my will is one with yours
to do and to endure.

Breathe on me, Breath of God,
fulfil my heart's desire,
until this earthly part of me
glows with your heavenly fire.

Breathe on me, Breath of God,
so shall I never die,
but live with you the perfect life
of your eternity.

In some of my own hymns, I've tried to express the confusion we feel at times in the face of life's traumas, and our longing for help in making sense of it all:

Lord, there are times when I have to ask, 'Why?' –
times when catastrophe gives faith the lie.
Innocents suffer and evil holds sway;
grant me some answers, Lord, teach me your way.

Lord, there are times when I have to ask, 'Where?' –
times when it seems that you simply don't care.
Though I call out, you seem distant, aloof,
grant me some answers, Lord, show me some proof.

Lord, there are times when I have to ask, 'What?' –
times when your love isn't easy to spot.
What is life's purpose and what of me here?
Grant me some answers, Lord, make your will clear.

Lord, there are times when I have to ask, 'How?' –
times when what's preached doesn't square with life now.
Wrestling with doubt I ask, 'How can this be?'
Grant me some answers, Lord, help me to see.

Lord, there are times when the questions run fast –
times when I fear that my faith may not last.
Help me, support me, Lord, help me get through.
Lead me through darkness till light shines anew.

You may find the words of many other hymns of help when it comes to prayer. Listed below are just a few of the possibilities, some being included in the resources section (Part Four) of this book:

Abba, Father, let me be

As pants the hart

As the deer pants for the water

Be the centre of my life

Be thou my guardian and guide

Be thou my vision

Breathe on me, Breath of God

Christ be with me

Christ of the upward way

Come down, O Love divine

Come, my Way, my Truth, my Life

Father, hear the prayer we offer

Father, I place into your hands

Forth in thy name, O Lord, I go

Give me joy in my heart

Glory to thee, my God, this night

Guide me, O thou great Redeemer

I am trusting thee, Lord Jesus

I bind unto myself today

I need thee every hour

It's me, O Lord

Jesus, be the centre

Lead us, heavenly Father, lead us

Like a dove come to me

Lord, I come to you

Lord, I lift my hands to you in prayer

Lord of all hopefulness

Lord, speak to me, that I may speak

Lord, there are times

Lord, when I turn my back on you

Love divine, all loves excelling

May the mind of Christ my Saviour

My faith looks up to thee

O Jesus Christ, grow thou in me

O Jesus, I have promised

O thou who camest from above
One more step along the world I go
Open our eyes, Lord
Rock of ages, cleft for me
Spirit of God
Spirit of the living God
Sun of my soul, thou Saviour dear
Take me, Lord
Take my hands, Lord
Take my life, and let it be
Take this day
Take this moment
Thy way, not mine, O Lord
When days are touched with sadness

Poetic petitions

It's impossible to give an idea of the breadth of themes covered in
poetry, but below are a few examples. First a poem by Anne Brontë
(1820–49) seeking help and strength in a time of emotional exhaustion:

Oh, I am very weary,
though tears no longer flow;
my eyes are tired of weeping,
my heart is sick of woe;
my life is very lonely,
my days pass heavily,
I'm wearying of repining,
wilt thou not come to me?
Oh, didst thou know my longings
for thee, from day to day,
my hopes, so often blighted,
thou wouldst not thus delay!
God! if this indeed be all
that Life can show to me;
if on my aching brow may fall

no freshening dew from thee –
if with no brighter light than this
the lamp of hope may glow,
and I may only dream of bliss,
and wake to weary woe;
if friendship's solace must decay,
when other joys are gone,
and love must keep so far away,
while I go wandering on –
wandering and toiling without gain,
the slave of others' will,
with constant care, and frequent pain,
despised, forgotten still;
grieving to look on vice and sin,
yet powerless to quell
the silent current from within,
the outward torrent's swell:
while all the good I would impart,
the feelings I would share,
are driven backward to my heart,
and turned to wormwood, there;
if clouds must ever keep from sight
the glories of the Sun,
and I must suffer Winter's blight,
'ere Summer is begun;
if Life must be so full of care,
then call me soon to thee;
or give me strength enough to bear
my load of misery.

Next, an extract from a poem called 'Temptation' by William Cowper (1731–1800) in which he too cries out for help in the face of personal turmoil:

The billows swell, the winds are high,
Clouds overcast my wintry sky;
Out of the depths to thee I call –
My fears are great, my strength is small.

O Lord, the pilot's part perform
And guard and guide me through the storm;
Defend me from each threatening ill,
Control the waves – say, 'Peace! be still.'

Amidst the roaring of the sea
My soul still hangs her hope on thee;
Thy constant love, thy faithful care,
Is all that saves me from despair.

Another of Cowper's poems, 'Peace after a Storm', celebrates the fact that God is with us in times of trouble, even when we do not see it, and asks for greater faith in the future:

When darkness long has veil'd my mind,
And smiling day once more appears,
Then, my Redeemer, then I find
The folly of my doubts and fears.

Straight I upbraid my wandering heart,
And blush that I should ever be
Thus prone to act so base a part,
Or harbour one hard thought of thee!

Oh! let me then at length be taught
What I am still so slow to learn,
That God is love, and changes not,
Nor knows the shadow of a turn.

Another poem, this time by John Norris (1657–1711), again asks for deeper faith and trust, as the following extract illustrates:

In vain, great God, in vain I try
To escape thy quick all-searching eye:
Thou with one undivided view
Dost look the whole creation through.

My private walks to thee are known;
In solitude I'm not alone:
Thou round my bed a guard dost keep;
Thine eyes are open while mine sleep.

Thou art the light by which I see;
Be it my joy to live in thee:
Beset me, Lord, behind, before;
And draw my heart to love thee more.

Similar sentiments are expressed by John Henry Newman (1801–90) in his poem 'The soul before God':

Take me away, and in the lowest deep
   there let me be,
     and there in hope the lone night-watches keep,
   told out for me.
There, motionless and happy in my pain,
   lone, not forlorn –
     there will I sing my sad perpetual strain,
   until the morn.
There will I sing, and soothe my stricken breast,
   which ne'er can cease
     to throb, and pine, and languish, till possess'd
   of its Sole Peace.
There will I sing my absent Lord and Love –
   take me away,
     that sooner I may rise, and go above,
   and see him in the truth of everlasting day.

Finally a simple poem by George Herbert (1593–1633) through which he commits all of life to God:

Enrich my heart, mouth, hands in me,
   with faith, with hope, with charity,
   that I may run, rise, rest with thee.

Reflective petitions

The strength of reflective prayers is that they not only express our thoughts but also shape them. Michel Quoist, for example, in his beautiful prayers 'I would like to rise very high', 'Lord, deliver me from myself', 'Lord, why did you tell me to love?' and 'Help me to say "Yes"', articulates what we might want to say so much better than we could do ourselves, yet at the same time opens up aspects of life and faith we've probably never even considered before.

In my own book, *Are You Listening?*, I explore issues of daily life – anxiety, fear, anger, lust, impatience and so forth – bringing these before God and seeking to discover what he might say about them. Here are a couple of examples:

God, I'm scared!
Don't tell anyone I told you, for there's no knowing what they'll think,
    but I'm petrified,
      more frightened than I can ever say,
      and the terrible thing is, I don't know why.
You think that sounds stupid?
Well, yes, it probably is,
    but you see there's no single factor I can put my finger on,
    no simple explanation for how I'm feeling.
It's more a combination of everything –
    all the little anxieties,
    the nagging doubts,
    the constant demands,
    all coming together to overwhelm me.
I can feel it now, fear beavering away within,
    gnawing into my very soul,
    and I'm powerless to stop it;
    the harder I try, the more tenaciously it clings,
    the more I resist, the more I wake up and it's there to greet me.
I walk down the street, and it's there by my side.
I meet a stranger, even a friend,
    and it leers out at me.
I look longingly to the future but it's there too waiting for me.
Lord, is there nowhere I can escape,
    nowhere I can be free?

My child,
   don't be afraid,
   I'm here,
   no need to panic.
Let's look at these fears of yours, slowly and sensibly.
You tell me you're not afraid of one thing in particular,
   and you're right,
     for if you were you'd have come to terms with it by now,
    sorted it out once and for all.
No, it's a deeper problem you're suffering from –
   the fear of fear itself,
    and that's something much harder to deal with,
    a dilemma only you finally can resolve.
You need to stop running,
   stop looking over your shoulder,
   and face your fear head on.
You need to stop brooding,
   stop struggling,
   and let it do its worst.
When you do that you'll realise this monster of your imagination
   is just an empty phantom,
   powerless to touch you,
   still less to hurt.
It won't be easy at first, for you must change the habit of a lifetime,
   but trust me,
   remember I am with you,
   pay heed to my words,
   and before you know it, your fears will be fleeing from you,
   rather than *you* from *them*.

This prayer deals with our inability to stop worrying:

I'm worried, Lord,
   more than I've ever been in my life.
I know I shouldn't be –
   there are enough people telling me that –
   but I just can't help it,
   the more I struggle to stay calm, the more worried I become.

It just adds another anxiety to all the rest,
and there's enough of those already, aren't there? –
health,
money,
work,
family –
never allowing a moment's peace.
Time and again, despite my efforts, I catch myself brooding,
haunted by a multitude of questions about the future
and all the time the spectre grows –
of life spinning crazily out of control,
taking all I value with it.
It's easy to say, 'Don't worry',
that everything will be all right,
but what if it isn't,
what if my fears come true?
What then, Lord?

My child,
you know what I'm going to say, don't you?
That's right: don't worry!
But before you jump down my throat,
stop and hear me out.
I'm not pretending everything will come good,
for I know it doesn't sometimes,
all too rarely for my liking.
And I'm not saying your fears are unfounded,
for sadly some of them probably aren't.
But what I *am* telling you is this:
that the only thing worry will change is you – for the worst.
It won't make you feel any better,
that somehow you will have everything sorted.
It won't stop your fears coming true,
still less help you face them if they do.
On the contrary, it will suck you dry,
sap you of energy,
rob you of the very strength you will need should crisis come.

That's one reason I tell you not to worry –
 because I see what it does to you and know it achieves nothing.
But there's another reason, more important still,
 for the main thing is that I love you
 and understand your needs,
 and care about your welfare more than you would ever imagine.
No, I can't promise you a bed of roses –
 that's not the way I work –
 but I do guarantee this:
 whatever you face,
 however many nightmares come true,
 I'll be there with you always,
 come what may,
 to see you through.

This next prayer speaks of Christ's call to do as we would be done by:

Nice one, Lord!
You've hit the nail on the head,
 your summary of the law and prophets
 encapsulating all I try to live by:
 doing to others as I've had done to me.
That's right, isn't it?
Of course it is . . .
 what else could you mean?
If someone wrongs me, I'll look to get even,
 simply a question of justice.
If someone picks a fight,
 starts a quarrel,
 then of course they get what's coming to them.
All right,
 so perhaps occasionally I'm the transgressor –
 acting unkindly,
 doing what you'd rather I didn't –
 but if so, there'll be good reason, you can be sure of that,
 such behaviour the exception rather than the norm.
It's a matter of give and take, I suppose –
 I'll scratch their back if they scratch mine:
 that's what you're after, Lord, isn't it?

What's that?
I've got it wrong?
Surely not!
You can't mean do to others what I'd *have* done to me
    instead of what I've *had* done!
You *do*, don't you!
You really want me to put others first and self second!
But that's such a huge gamble,
    such a massive leap of faith!
And who can say where it all might lead?
I thought I'd understood,
    but I hadn't;
    I *still* haven't –
    my head's in a spin as I struggle to take it in,
    let alone accept and follow.
I need help, Lord,
    your Spirit within me
    for I can't do it alone,
    even should I wish to.
Give me the strength I need,
    the courage and commitment to deal with others your way;
    as you say,
    recognising that, costly though it may seem,
    it is no more so –
    indeed, far less –
    than the way you have dealt with me in Christ.
Amen.

Inspired by words from the Lord's Prayer, the following prayer touches again on apparently unanswered prayer, and the sort of things we should actually ask for:

'Lord, save me!' I cried.
'Protect me!'
'Deliver me!'
But disaster struck nonetheless,
    bringing heartbreak,

hurt,
confusion.
'Lord, bring healing!' we begged.
'Bring wholeness!
'Make well!'
But there was no happy ending,
no sudden and miraculous recovery –
just the harrowing and lingering death of one we loved.
And I threw up my hands in anger,
asking, 'Why?'
'How?'
'Where were you when we needed you?
It shook me to the core,
my faith buckling,
all but broken,
until I remembered that those words, 'rescue us from evil',
were spoken by your Son who went on to face evil at its fiercest,
his suffering and sorrow as great as anyone's,
and I realised that the brokenness of this world
grieved you as much as me.
You were there all along, sharing the hurt,
weeping over everything that denies your love
and frustrates your purpose,
but you were there also to support and strengthen,
reaching through the pain to share it and bear it,
and finally to lead us through.
Remind me of that whenever life is hard and days are dark,
and teach me, then above all times,
to pray from the heart:
'rescue me from evil'.
Amen.

Using our senses

If the prayers that come most easily to us are for ourselves, then using our senses provides an important counterbalance, for, in my experience at least, personal concerns in this form of prayer tend to take second place to praise, thanksgiving, confession and intercession. Looking around at the natural world or those around us somehow helps us to get a different perspective on life, our own needs seeming smaller, our worries trivial, our grievances petty and many of our desires misplaced. That may, finally, lead us to petitionary prayers, but, if so, they tend to be of a different sort to 'Lord, do this' or 'Lord, give that', being more in the nature of 'Lord, teach me always to see things as clearly as I do now' or 'Help me to keep my focus on the things that really matter'. As we rush about from one thing to the next we too easily let problems grow out of proportion, resentments fester, fears become magnified and disappointments rankle until we can see nothing else. To get out into the world is so often to get outside ourselves and thus to see things in a new light; this not merely shaping our prayers but almost being an answer to them in itself.

The following reflection emphasises the importance of getting the bigger picture.

The window cleaner

I was ashamed when he'd finished,
    appalled that so much dirt could have built up
    without me noticing,
    clouding my vision and obscuring the view.
Suddenly the sun seemed brighter,
    colours enriched,
    little details previously hidden now noticed,
    everything fresh,
    made new.

Wipe clear, Lord, the windows of my soul,
    so that, seeing you better,
    I may know you more fully.
Grant me a clearer picture of you
    that sheds new light on every aspect of life,
    each part transformed by your sanctifying touch.
Amen.

Intercession

Introduction

Of all the forms of prayer, I find intercession the hardest. Why? Not because I can't find the words or because I don't care about others, but for two simple reasons. First, I find it hard to come to terms with any idea that the well-being or fortune of others is in some way dependent upon my remembering them, with the implicit thought within this that if nobody prays for them, then God will withhold his blessing. That would make God dependent on us, and do so in a way that denies his love, justice and purpose. The second problem arises from the first, for if praying for others somehow helps to release God's power or blessing, then how can we ever stop, for there is always someone or something that needs praying for, the list of human need, even among our nearest and dearest, vast, let alone in the world as a whole.

Intercession, then, perplexes me in terms of the questions it raises, and yet praying for others comes almost instinctively to us. Never mind that we don't understand how such prayers work or precisely what impact they may have – the fact is that we care about people, deeply and passionately, and cannot but help express our love and concern for them before God. Whether it's a loved one in need, a sick friend or relative, the future or safety of our children, or an acquaintance facing difficulties, we instinctively commend that person to God's care. Similarly, when we see pictures on television of starving children; or lands ravaged by war, famine or natural disaster; or victims of brutality; or refugees, the unemployed, poor, disadvantaged and so on; our heart goes out to them and we long for God to offer them help just as we wish we could ourselves. And perhaps here is the key to at least partially understanding what intercession is all about: above all, I suspect, it involves identifying ourselves with God's compassion, sharing with him in his love and concern for others. It implies, then, a desire to respond, not just in words but in actions, helping, so far as we're able, to translate our prayers into deeds, our hopes into reality. What we can do, of course, is limited, severely so. We cannot heal the person with terminal illness, restore broken relationships, take away the agony of bereavement, overcome world poverty, or eradicate injustice. And for reasons we don't understand,

God can't always do so either, his hands seemingly tied. Yet we *can* respond, whether through showing our care, being there to listen, offering our money, signing a petition, supporting a campaign or giving our time. And the testimony of countless generations is that God responds time and again, innumerable people having felt themselves supported in prayer and finding strength and help in their time of need.

So what should we pray for, and how? Obviously we can't pray for everyone and everything. And if we attempt to do so, we will turn prayer into a burden, a ploughing day after day through an ever-lengthening list from which we are afraid of leaving somebody off. Better by far to focus on a few particular needs known to us, or even on a single concern; perhaps our family and friends, perhaps those we know to be depressed or mourning loved ones, perhaps a recent tragedy in the news, perhaps the ongoing problems of hunger, war, hatred and violence. Bring those quietly to God, not expecting all the answers, still less to change the world by a single prayer, but identifying with his love and compassion for all.

As well as more formal times of intercession, such prayers may also arise naturally out of daily life, as we will explore later under the heading 'Reflective intercessions'. Such prayers may take the form of a single sentence or even merely a thought, committing a person or situation into God's keeping. Again the emphasis is on specific needs rather than covering all the world's ills.

Remember though, once again, that if we are to avoid the trap of well-meant platitudes, we need always to be open to what God may be saying to us as we pray – open, in other words, to the possibility that he's asking *us* to respond to the needs we identify, *us* to be his hands and feet, his eyes and mouth, ministering in word and deed his love to all. Prayer is not a substitute for action but a complement to it, the two belonging together.

Intercession and the Old Testament

The Old Testament doesn't have much to say on the subject of intercession, but it's clear nonetheless that praying for others was both accepted and expected. In Numbers 21:7, for example, we read that 'Moses prayed for the people'. In 1 Samuel 12:19 the people of Israel ask Samuel to pray for them so that they might be spared God's anger, to which Samuel reponds, 'For my part, far be it from me to fail the Lord by failing to pray for you' (1 Samuel 12:23a). And in Psalm 122 listeners are urged to pray for the peace of Jerusalem, seeking the good and peace of those within it.

Many other passages emphasise God's concern for the poor and those in need, a concern we are called to share. Below are just a few examples:

Whoever exploits the poor insults their Maker, whereas those who deal kindly with the needy honour him. Those who close their ears to the cry of the poor will not be heard when they themselves call out. *Proverbs 14:31; 21:13*

When the poor and those in need look for water but can't find any, so that their tongues are shrivelled with thirst, I the Lord God of Israel will answer them; I will not abandon them. *Isaiah 41:17*

Those in need will not be overlooked for ever, nor will the dreams of the poor be allowed to die. *Psalm 9:18*

Learn to do good; look to deal fairly, put right exploitation; ensure justice to the orphan, and support the cause of the widowed. *Isaiah 1:17*

In the Psalms we find several instances of the psalm writer interceding on behalf of his people, including the following:

May the Lord strengthen his people; may he bless them with peace. *Psalm 29:11*

The Lord is his people's strength; the safe haven of his anointed. Rescue your people and bless your heritage! Be a shepherd to them and bear them always in your arms. *Psalm 28:8, 9*

A careful look at the Old Testament, then, will provide material for intercessory prayer as well as an appreciation of the concerns closest to God's heart; concerns that inevitably will shape our words and thoughts.

Intercession and the New Testament

In the New Testament it's the same story as with the Old: intercession is clearly integral to the life of the early Church. Paul, for example, writes to the Colossians (1:3): 'We continually thank God, the Father of our Lord Jesus Christ, whenever we pray for you', continuing, a few verses later (v. 9): 'from the day we heard, we haven't stopped praying for you, asking that you will be filled with understanding of his will in complete spiritual perception and discernment'. Similarly, he tells the Thessalonians, 'With this goal in mind we constantly pray for you: namely that our God might help you live up to his calling so that you can honour all your resolutions to do good and work in faith by his power' (2 Thessalonians 1:11). And if he prayed for others, Paul clearly expected others to do the same for him: 'Pray too for us,' he asked the Colossians (4:3), 'at the same time, asking God to open to us a door for the word, so that we may proclaim the mystery of Christ, on whose account I'm currently incarcerated.' In his first letter to Timothy (2:1), Paul is even more explicit about the importance of praying for others: 'Above all, therefore, I would advocate that you offer requests, intercessions and thanksgiving in your prayers for everyone.' The letter of James urges us in turn to 'Pray for one another' (James 5:16).

In all this the New Testament writers are faithful to the words of Jesus, who, for example, urged that we pray for those who persecute us (Matthew 5:44) and who, in his great prayer for the Church and world; recorded in Johns Gospel, asked: 'that they may be one just as we are one, I in them and you in me, that they may become completely one, in order that the world may know you sent me and love them even as you love me' (John 17:22a, 23).

Finally, if you struggle when praying for others to find the right words, wondering sometimes just who and what to pray for or feeling almost overwhelmed by the amount of human need around you, don't despair, for the New Testament offers an assurance that intercession finally is not simply down to us. Hebrews 7:25 tells us that Jesus 'lives to intercede constantly' for all who approach God in faith, while Romans 8:26 speaks of the Spirit who intercedes for us in a way that no words can quite express. Intercession is about us expressing our concern for others; the rest is down to God.

Classic prayers

Were you to compile a list of favourite prayers, one would almost certainly come top of the pile, and that is the prayer of St Francis (1182–1226). It's not strictly an intercession, but in its desire to reach out to the needs of the world, it explores classic intercessory themes:

> Lord, make me an instrument of your peace:
>> where there is hatred, let me sow love,
>> where there is injury, pardon,
>> where there is doubt, faith,
>> where there is darkness, light,
>> where there is despair, hope,
>> and where these is sadness, joy.
>
> Divine Master,
>> grant that I may not so much seek to be consoled as to console,
>> to be understood as to understand,
>> to be loved as to love.
> For it is in giving that we receive,
>> it is in pardoning that we are pardoned,
>> and in dying that we are born to eternal life.
> Amen.

The following prayer of St Augustine of Hippo (354–430) commits to God all who sorrow or suffer:

> Watch, dear Lord,
>> with those who wake, or watch, or weep tonight,
>> and give your angels charge over those who sleep.
> Tend you sick ones, O Lord Christ,
>> rest your weary ones,
>> bless your dying ones,
>> soothe your suffering ones,
>> pity your afflicted ones,
>> shield your joyous ones,
>> all for your love's sake.
> Amen.

The next prayer, that of St Anselm (1033–1109), casts the net wider:

> I bring before you, O Lord,
>> the troubles and perils of people and nations,
>> the pain of prisoners and captives,
>> the sorrows of the bereaved,
>> the needs of strangers,
>> the vulnerability of the weak,
>> the downheartedness of the weary,
>> the diminishing powers of the aged.
> O Lord, draw near to each,
>> for the sake of Jesus Christ our Lord.
> Amen.

In similar vein is the following ancient prayer, coming from the fourth-century Liturgy of St Basil:

> Lord,
>> the help of the helpless,
>> the hope of those past hope,
>> the rescuer of the storm-tossed,
>> the harbour of the voyagers,
>> the healer of the sick:
>> I ask you to become all things to all people,
>> for you know the needs of each one.
> Accept us all into your kingdom,
>> making us children of light;
>> and give us your peace and love,
>> Lord our God.
> Amen.

A more recent prayer, written by William Angus Knight (1836–1916), covers a similarly wide range of concerns:

> Almighty and most merciful Father,
>> who has taught us not to think only of ourselves
>> but also of the needs of others,

I remember before you all who are burdened and oppressed,
   those whose hopes have been crushed
   and whose plans have come to nothing.
I remember also those who are afflicted by poverty,
   or worn down by sickness and disease,
   those who are in darkness or despair,
   or who are suffering for righteousness' sake.
Help them all, O God,
   to rest in you for comfort and strength.
Amen.

Many intercessory prayers focus specifically on peace, that of St Dionysius (sixth century) being one of many:

O God the Father,
   source of all that is good and true,
   in whom is calmness, peace and harmony,
   heal the dissensions which divide people from each other,
   and bring us back to a unity of love
   which may bear some likeness to your divine nature.
And as you are above all things,
   make us one by unity of thought,
   that through the bonds of love we may be one,
   both with ourselves and with each other;
   through that peace of yours which makes all things peaceful,
   and through the grace, mercy and love of your Son,
   Jesus Christ.
Amen.

Another well-known prayer for peace is that by Francis Paget (1851–1911), one-time Bishop of Oxford:

Almighty God,
   from whom all thoughts of truth and peace proceed:
   kindle, we pray you, in the hearts of all people
   the true love of peace;

and guide with your pure and peaceable wisdom
those who take counsel for the nations of the earth;
that in tranquillity your kingdom may go forward,
till the earth be filled with the knowledge of your love,
through Jesus Christ our Lord.
Amen.

Focusing on peace more generally is an Indian prayer, taken from ancient Hindu texts known as the Vedas:

May there be peace in the higher regions;
may there be peace in the firmament;
may there be peace on earth.
May the waters flow peacefully;
may the herbs and plants grow peacefully;
may all the divine powers bring unto us peace.
The supreme Lord is peace.
May we all be in peace, peace, and only peace;
and may that peace come unto each of us.

The prayer of St Edmund of Abingdon (c. 1175–1240) brings us closer to home, commending into God's care our nearest and dearest:

Into your hands, O Father and Lord,
I commend my soul and body,
my parents and home,
my family, friends and neighbours,
all people of faith and love,
and all who stand in special need.
Lighten our lives with your holy grace,
and the knowledge of your constant presence,
O Lord in Trinity, God everlasting.
Amen.

Finally, the celebrated prayer of William Laud (1573–1645), focusing on the Church:

Gracious Father, I pray for your holy Christian Church.
Fill it with all truth, in all truth with all peace.
Where it is corrupt, cleanse it.
Where it is in error, direct it.
Where it is superstitious, rectify it.
Where anything is amiss, reform it.
Where it is right, strengthen and confirm it.
Where it is in want, supply its need.
Where it is divided and torn apart, heal the divisions,
    O Holy One of Israel.
Amen.

Intercessory music

I've found it harder to find intercessory music than any other form. In the classical realm, nothing suggests itself as immediately suitable, though much may provoke reflection leading on to prayers for others. Contemporary church music yields a little more, including the following, many of which have been included in the resources section (Part Four) of this book:

Come, Lord from *Fountain of Life* (Margaret Rizza)
Creator Spirit, come from *Sacred Weave* (Keith Duke)
Exaudi nos, Domine from *Fire of Love* (Margaret Rizza)
Judge eternal (Malcom Archer) from *Festival of Anthems*
Kum ba yah from *Our Favourite Hymns 3*
O God be gracious from *Awakening in Love* (Margaret Rizza)
Oh Lord, listen to our prayer from *Light in Our Darkness*
    (Margaret Rizza)
Prayer for peace from *River of Peace* (Margaret Rizza)
Send forth your Spirit from *In God Alone* (Andrew Moore)
Send forth your Spirit, Lord from *Fountain of Life*
    (Margaret Rizza)

Many of the above have been included in the resources section (Part Four) of this book. A wealth of material is available from numerous contemporary artists and the following CDs may also be helpful:

Hillsong London: *Jesus Is*; *Look to You*; *Praise God*; *He Reigns*; *United We Stand*

Chris Tomlin: *Arriving*

Brian Littrell: *Welcome Home*

Delirious: *Access-D*; *Deeper*; *Glo*; *The Mission Bell*

Gaither: *Homecoming*

Kutless: *Hearts of the Innocent*; *Kutless*; *Strong Tower*

Nichole Nordeman: *Brave*; *The Mystery*; *To Know You*; *Woven and Spun*

Matt Redman: *Blessed Be Your Name*; *Facedown*; *The Father's Song*; *Where Angels Fear to Tread*

Abundant Life: *Divine Exchange*; *Let the World See Jesus*

Michael Smith: *Change Your World*; *Healing Rain*; *Worship Again*

CeCe Winans: *Alone in His Presence*; *Everlasting Love*

YFriday: *Open*; *Rain Maker*

Andrew Mitchell: *Let Your Kingdom Come*

Weeping Willows: *Lift Up Your Eyes*; *His Manifest Presence*

Caedmon's Call: *In the Company of Angels II*; *The World Will Sing*; *40 Acres*; *Share the Well*

Intercessory hymns

As with music, there is a dearth of good intercessory hymns, though recently this has begun to change, not least with the excellent and thought-provoking offerings of John Bell and the Iona Community. An increasing awareness of social and environmental awareness has sparked an upsurge in creative hymnody, many of the words, in my view, being better read as poems than sung as hymns. If you're looking, then, for words to articulate your intercessions, take time to thumb through some modern hymn books, and make a note of whatever you find to be helpful.

Most older hymns on intercessory themes tend to feel dated, either due to their language or the concepts they use, but a few nonetheless caught my eye. Take the following, written by J. H. B. Masterman (1867–1933):

Almighty Father, who dost give
the gift of life to all who live,
look down on all earth's sin and strife,
and lift us to a nobler life.

Lift up our hearts, O King of kings,
to brighter hopes and kindlier things,
to visions of a larger good,
and holier dreams of brotherhood.

The world is weary of its pain,
of selfish greed and fruitless gain,
of tarnished honour, falsely strong,
and all its ancient deeds of wrong.

Hear thou the prayer thy servants pray,
uprising from all lands today,
and o'er the vanquished powers of sin
O bring thy great salvation in.

Another of Masterman's hymns seems as relevant today as when it was
first written:

Grant us thy peace; for thou alone canst bend
our faltering purpose to a nobler end;
thy love alone can teach our hearts to see
the fellowship that binds all lives in thee.

Grant us thy peace; for men have filled the years
with greed and envy and with foolish fears,
with squandered treasures and ignoble gain,
and fruitless harvests that we reap in vain.

Grant us thy peace; till all our strife shall seem
the hateful memory of some evil dream;
till that new song ring out that shall not cease,
'In heaven thy glory and on earth thy peace!'

Next, a hymn by Thomas Curtis Clark (1877–1953):

Where restless crowds are thronging along the city ways,
where pride and greed and turmoil consume the fevered days,
where vain ambitions banish all thoughts of praise and prayer,
the people's spirits waver: but thou, O Christ, art there.

In scenes of want and sorrow and haunts of flagrant wrong,
in homes where kindness falters, and strife and fear are strong,
in busy street of barter, in lonely thoroughfare,
the people's spirits languish: but thou, O Christ, art there.

O Christ, behold thy people – they press on every hand!
Bring light to all the cities of our beloved land.
May all our bitter striving give way to visions fair
of righteousness and justice: for thou, O Christ, art there.

I've written a few intercessory hymns, including the following – an adapted version of a hymn I wrote for the new millennium:

An urgent voice is calling, a voice from far away;
it's crying out for justice, and yearning for that day
when no one need go hungry, despair will be no more –
a day at last that heralds a new start for the poor.

An urgent voice is calling, a voice from somewhere near;
it's crying out with longing, yet no one seems to hear;
despite long years of witness, a multitude still search –
forgive us, Lord, and grant now a new start for the Church.

An urgent voice is calling, a voice from all around;
it's crying out in anguish, the grim and tragic sound
of God's creation groaning, stripped bare, denied her worth –
Lord, curb our greed, and bring now a new start for the earth.

An urgent voice is calling, a voice from close at hand;
it's crying out in anger, campaigning for a land
where all will be respected, and war will find no place –
a world of peace and friendship, a new start for our race.

An urgent voice is calling, the voice of God above;
it's crying out in sorrow, and urging us to love,
for still a world lies bleeding, the weak go to the wall –
Lord, help us build together a new start for us all.

Below are listed a few other hymns you may find useful:

Born in the night
Brother, sister, let me serve you
Compassion walks the city street
Cry 'Freedom!'
Eternal Father, strong to save
For the healing of the nations
Inspired by love and anger
Jesus Christ is waiting
Kum ba yah
Make me a channel of your peace
We call to mind the needs
When I needed a neighbour
Will you come and follow me

Intercessory poems

As with hymns and music, there is little poetry on intercessory themes, still less any couched in the form of prayer. The following, though, written by William Blake (1757–1827), asks the all-important question of whether we can be aware of need and not in some way respond. The poem is called 'On Another's Sorrow':

Can I see another's woe,
And not be in sorrow too?
Can I see another's grief,
And not seek for kind relief?

Can I see a falling tear,
And not feel my sorrow's share?
Can a father see his child
Weep, nor be with sorrow filled?

Can a mother sit and hear
An infant groan, an infant fear?
No, no! never can it be!
Never, never can it be!

And can he who smiles on all
Hear the wren with sorrows small,
Hear the small bird's grief and care,
Hear the woes that infants bear –

And not sit beside the next,
Pouring pity in their breast,
And not sit the cradle near,
Weeping tear on infant's tear?

And not sit both night and day,
Wiping all our tears away?
Oh no! never can it be!
Never, never can it be!

He doth give his joy to all:
He becomes an infant small,
He becomes a man of woe,
He doth feel the sorrow too.

Think not thou canst sigh a sigh,
And thy Maker is not by:
Think not thou canst weep a tear,
And thy Maker is not near.

Oh! He gives to us his joy,
That our grief he may destroy:
Till our grief is fled and gone
He doth sit by us and moan.

Recognising the dearth of intercessory poems, I decided to write some myself. Below are a few examples.

The first focuses on those who strive to change this world for the better:

> For those who fight injustice
> and make a stand for good,
> who strive to give the poor a chance
> to live life as they should,
> for all who labour, heart and soul,
> to make our world more fair,
> I ask your courage, succour, strength –
> Lord, answer, hear my prayer.
>
> For those who show compassion,
> who work to heal and mend,
> who nurse the sick, support the weak,
> encourage and befriend,
> for all who reach out in your name
> to offer love and care,
> I ask your blessing, power, help –
> Lord, answer, hear my prayer.
>
> For those who tackle conflict,
> where wounds run red and raw,
> who strive to conquer hatred
> and put a stop to war,
> who work to foster dialogue
> despite the scars we bear;
> I ask your guidance, vision, faith –
> Lord, answer, hear my prayer.
>
> For those who try to witness
> to Christ through word and deed,
> to show his love embraces
> each colour, culture, creed;
> who point to light and life and hope
> in which we all can share,
> I ask your wisdom, grace and truth –
> Lord, answer, hear my prayer.

Second, a poem for those facing ill health or the infirmity associated with old age:

> When days are filled with struggle and nights are racked by pain,
> when faculties are failing and health is on the wane,
> when living seems an effort, past vigour long since gone,
> and darkness starts encroaching where once the sun had shone,
> Lord, teach me you'll be with me, to comfort and console –
> that, though time wastes the body, it cannot touch the soul.
>
> When youth seems but a memory and limbs are stiff and sore,
> when daily I'm reminded of things I'll do no more,
> when inwardly I'm willing but outwardly I'm weak,
> and succour proves elusive, no matter how I seek,
> Lord, teach me you'll be with me, to cherish and to mend –
> that though this life is passing, the grave is not the end.
>
> When treasures start to tarnish, as all things surely must,
> when childhood dreams have faded and hopes lie in the dust,
> when life no longer sparkles quite as it used to shine
> and nothing can recapture the joys that once were mine,
> Lord, teach me you'll be with me, to strengthen and sustain –
> that, though the night is falling, your light will shine again.

Next a poem that wrestles with questions of faith posed by recent world events:

> Where were you, Lord, when the planes struck
> and the towers came crashing down?
> What did you do to stop it?
> Why were you out of town?
> Where were you in the Balkans
> when the streets ran red with blood?
> And how about the shanty town
> engulfed by streams of mud?
> Why don't you end the famine?
> Why don't you stop the war?
> How can you let these happen?
> What can it all be for?

Lord, is it wrong to ask you,
faithless to speak my mind?
Shouldn't I look for answers?
Don't you say 'seek and find'?
Yes, I know much is beyond me,
truth often hard to discern,
but I'm ready and willing to listen,
eager and hungry to learn.
Don't think I'm daring to judge you,
set myself up in your place –
some things, I know, must stay hidden,
at least till we meet face to face –
yet in a world where so many
feel faith and hope are in vain,
give us some sign, Lord, I beg you
to prove you are here in our pain.

Finally, a general intercession for all those facing hard times:

Where love is met with hatred, and dreams have been snuffed out,
where days are full of suffering and faith has turned to doubt,
where evil conquers goodness and life is full of care,
grant through it all the knowledge that you, O Lord, are there.

Where joy has turned to sorrow and hope gives way to fear,
where peace is cruelly shattered as sudden storms appear,
where life belies convictions on which we once relied,
grant through it all the knowledge you're always by our side.

Where darkness like a shadow extinguishes the light,
where plans are brought to ruin and nothing quite goes right,
where health begins to falter and life begins to fade,
grant through it all the knowledge we need not be afraid.

To those enduring trouble with which they cannot cope,
to those for whom disaster has put an end to hope,
to those who carry burdens too difficult to bear,
grant through it all the knowledge that you, O Lord, are there.

Reflective intercessions

When it comes to intercessions the prayers of Michel Quoist (1921–2000) come into their own, covering such diverse topics as 'The Delinquent', 'The Funeral', 'Hunger', 'Housing' and 'The Hospital'. For me these bring both challenge and inspiration, opening my eyes to the needs of those around me. I've attempted to do something similar in some of my own recent prayers, of which the following are examples:

The alien

It was inhuman,
    literally,
    a monstrous creature from another world,
    with no scruples, compassion or feeling,
    mutilating bodies and destroying lives
    without even a shred of compunction.
But, of course, it wasn't real –
    just a figment of the author's imagination:
    an extraterrestrial dreamt up in the mind
    and brought to life on the screen.
I saw *more* inhumanity,
    more suffering and slaughter,
    only this time it was all too real and part of this world –
    pictures on the television and in the papers
    of unspeakable carnage,
    lives cruelly shattered with equal lack of compunction.
And it was no alien to blame, but ordinary people,
    fellow human beings
    who somehow saw murder as their mission,
    killing as their calling.

Heal, Lord, our broken world,
    and put an end to its madness,
    so that, whatever divides,
    and whatever our colour, creed or culture,
    we may see beyond cause or grievance
    to the common humanity that unites us all.
Amen.

The test-tube

It reminded me of childhood experiments –
    cocktails of chemicals simmering over a Bunsen burner,
    and litmus paper testing strange solutions –
    but it spoke also of complex research,
    of scientists unravelling the mysteries of life,
    creating new drugs,
    fertilising eggs
    and identifying genes –
    unlocking secrets undreamt of in years gone by.

Such powers, Lord, scare but excite me,
    for they have potential for both good and evil,
    able to enrich life or undermine it,
    to transform yet destroy.
Give wisdom to all scientists and researchers
    and to those who set laws regulating their activities,
    so that the skills you have given may be used responsibly
    and to the good of all.
Amen.

The frayed rope

It had been strong once,
    easily able to bear the load and take the strain,
    but the rope now was frayed –
    just about serviceable,
    but *only* just:
    the question not *if* it would snap,
    but *when*.

It reminded me, Lord, of people,
    so many worn to breaking point,
    ground down by sickness, hurt, worry and fear,
    or the ravages of time,
    and uncertain how much longer they can cope.
Reach out to strengthen and restore,
    from the tangled threads of their lives
    weaving cords that will not be broken.
Amen.

The injury

It was a painstaking business,
    the bones shattered by the impact,
    needing to be pieced together like a jigsaw,
    then carefully supported while the breaks began to knit.
Would the injury heal,
    the body mend?
We could only hope and pray.

Lord, our world lies equally broken,
    fractured by prejudice,
    splintered by hate,
    scarred by fear,
    and for all our efforts we cannot make it whole.
Pick up the pieces and bind them together,
    bring healing where there is hurt
    and unity where there is division.
Hear our prayer
    and honour our hopes.
Amen.

The cancer patient

The treatment was hard enough to bear –
    the hair loss, nausea and pain –
    and worse still was the fear,
    not just of suffering and slow decline,
    but of being separated from loved ones,
    and of saying goodbye.
Yet hardest of all were the awkward silences,
    forced smiles
    and well-meant platitudes,
    the being seen not as a person but a patient,
    no longer an individual but a disease.

Lord, to all wrestling with terminal illness,
    give the assurance that you will always value them for who they are;
    help their families, friends and colleagues

as they struggle to come to terms with their feelings
to do the same,
seeing not the illness but the individual underneath.
Whatever else may be lost,
    may *that* continue,
    to the end,
    and beyond.
Amen.

Using our senses

If looking at the world around us can move us to praise and thanksgiving,
it can just as easily inspire intercession, for if there is much joy around,
there is also much sorrow; as well as beauty, much ugliness; and as well as
pleasure, much pain. We see this especially in a busy town or city, those
teeming people we pass on our way to work or the shops all having
their own hidden needs and problems. Some places speak more obviously than others: walk past a hospital, benefit office, charity shop or
hostel for the homeless, and human need cries out at you. So also with
the elderly and infirm, the profoundly disabled, the down-and-out in a
shop doorway or the drunk lying face down in the gutter. We cannot
pretend to pray for these in any depth, for we know little about what
they experience or have been through, but we can consciously commit
each one to God and in so doing hear his voice calling through them.
So also with much else: the people we meet, relax, work or worship with,
each facing their own trials and traumas, joys and sorrows. Interceding
for others need only be a thought offered to God. Even that can help
change us and them more than we might imagine.

Part Four

RESOURCES FOR GROUP AND PERSONAL DEVOTION

Introduction

We've considered the various ingredients of prayer, but how do we put them together into a cohesive whole? We won't always attempt to do so, for all we're able to manage sometimes is a few words or moments of quiet snatched amid the hurly-burly of the day. Most of us, however, crave for more meaningful times of devotion; times that nurture and nourish us deep within. We want to come away from prayer feeling we've spoken to God and heard his voice; in other words, that we've made contact. No one can guarantee this for you, but building some structure into your prayer life, if only on occasions, can help bring it closer.

The sessions that follow provide examples of how various aspects of prayer can be combined. They are arranged under themes – praise, confession, thanksgiving, petition and intercession respectively – but you could just as easily interweave these so that your prayer time involves elements of all. The sessions are intended not simply as examples but as a resource for group or personal use, so that – with a few friends or alone – you can dedicate a few moments to God. Each session generally comprises the following:

- music suggestions (you may prefer to substitute your own choices here)

- verses from Scripture

- silence

- one or more classic prayers from the past

- a poem, hymn-text or reflective prayer

- a personal prayer, with responses for group use.

As well as illustrating how material cited earlier in this book can be used, you'll find much more here, some drawn from our rich Christian heritage, the rest new. All one hundred sessions are available on double CDs published by Kevin Mayhew.

EXPRESSING OUR WORSHIP

1
Glimpsing God in daily life

Music   You, Lord, are in this place from *Sacred Weave*
(Keith Duke)

Scripture   See how the wild flowers grow, pay heed to them.
They do not labour or weave, yet I can assure you that
not even Solomon in all his grandeur was decked out
like one of these. *Matthew 6:28b, 29*

Surely the Lord is in this place and I didn't know it.
How awe-inspiring it is . . . nothing less than the
house of God, the very gate of heaven.
Genesis 28:16, 17

Prayer   O splendour of God's glory bright,
who bringest forth the light from light;
O Light of lights, the fountain spring;
O day our days illumining;
come very sun of truth and love,
come in thy radiance from above,
and shed the Holy Spirit's ray
on all we think or do today.

Silence

Those lovely words of St Ambrose remind us that
God touches every part of life, anything and everything
able to speak of his love and presence. Look around
you with the eye of faith and you'll find that to be
true. The following prayer, for example, was inspired
by some particularly untidy handwriting.

It was barely legible,
    an indecipherable scrawl,
    yet to the trained eye it was far more,
    every dot, squiggle, line and curve
    saying as much as the words,
    if not more,
    revealing the quirks, traits, strengths and weaknesses
    of the one who wrote it.

Teach me, Lord, to glimpse you in the daily round of life
    and the wonder of this world.
Where others look and see nothing,
    help me to observe with the eye of faith,
    perceiving your glory beneath the surface.
Open my heart as well as my eyes,
    that I may look and truly see.
Amen.

Silence

Look around you now at the everyday things that surround you. What do they say of God? Look out of the window at the trees, sky, birds, houses. What do *they* say? Pause for a moment and recognise everything you have reason to praise God for.

Silence

Final prayer

For everything that highlights your power
and testifies to your mercy,
    God of all,
    I praise you.

For everything that illustrates your mercy
and demonstrates your grace,
    God of all,
    I praise you.

For everything that confirms your care
and displays your love,
God of all,
I praise you.

For everything that imparts your peace
and brings us joy,
God of all,
I praise you.

For everything you are and all you have given,
God of all,
I praise you.
Amen.

Music   You, Lord, are in this place from *Sacred Weave*
(Keith Duke)

2
The wonder of creation

Music   You are the maker from *Sacred Pathway* (Keith Duke)

Scripture The heavens proclaim the glory of God; the firmament
testifies to his handiwork. Each day witnesses to it
eloquently and each night communicates knowledge,
without need of speech, language or any other voice.
Their music pervades all the earth; the words of their
mouth reach out to the furthest parts of the world.

Psalm 19:1-4

Prayer   Lord, you created a world rich in splendour,
touched with a beauty no words can express,
able to move us to outbursts of wonder,
so much to thrill us and so much to bless.

Mountains and moorlands rise up to the heavens,
rivers and streams tumble down to the sea,
gifts that amaze in profusion surround us,
each a reflection of your majesty.

Promise of springtime and harvest of autumn,
cold winter mornings and warm summer days,
season by season brings new joys to greet us,
reason to thank you and reason to praise.

Deep in the forest, remote in the desert,
down in the ocean or high in the air;
life in abundance is everywhere round us,
proof of your power and sign of your care.

Lord, you have given a world rich in splendour,
touched with a beauty that fills us with awe;
hear now our praises, we bring you our worship,
with all creation we kneel and adore.

Silence

Next, a prayer by an anonymous writer dating from between the third and sixth centuries:

May none of God's wonderful works keep silence,
   night or morning.
Bright stars,
   high mountains,
   the depths of the seas,
   sources of rushing rivers:
   may all these break into song
   as we sing to the Father, Son and Holy Spirit.
May all the angels in the heavens reply:
Amen, Amen, Amen.
Power, praise, honour, eternal glory to God,
   the only giver of grace.
Amen, Amen, Amen.

Silence

Final prayer   Sovereign God,
   creator of the ends of the earth,
   source of all that is and has been and will be,
   giver of life –
   in grateful praise
   I bring you my worship.

For the wonder of our world
   and vastness of the universe;
   its complexity, grandeur, beauty and design –
   in grateful praise
   I bring you my worship.

For everything that lifts the spirit,
   inspiring awe, fascination, delight and contentment –
   in grateful praise
   I bring you my worship.

For bringing light out of darkness,
   life out of death,
   everything out of nothing –
   in grateful praise
   I bring you my worship.
Amen.

Music   You are the maker from *Sacred Pathway* (Keith Duke)

3
The God both far and near

Music   Sanctus, Dominus from *River of Peace* (Margaret Rizza)

Scripture   The Word took on our flesh and blood and lived among us, such that we have seen his glory – the glory of a father's only son – full of grace and truth.

John 1:14

When I gaze at the heavens, your handiwork, the moon and stars that you brought into being, what are human beings, such that you bother with them, mortals that they matter to you? Yet, you have made them scarcely lower than God and crowned them with glory and honour. You have given them authority over your creation and put all things under their feet.

Psalm 8:3-6

Prayer   Gaze up at the stars at night and, like the Psalm writer, you can't help being struck by how small we are compared to the vastness of space. Yet the God who created all this is concerned about each of us, intimately involved in our daily lives. The following prayer picks up that theme, inspired in this case by the grains of sand on a beach:

I ran the sand through my fingers, Lord,
millions of grains,
yet that one handful was just a fraction
of what made up the beach,
the beach one of thousands across the world,
and the world itself merely a tiny speck
in the vastness of space
with its trillions of constellations
and plethora of galaxies.

It leaves me reeling, Lord,
    such magnitude truly awesome,
    yet you brought it all into being,
    sustaining it each day
    and leading it towards fulfilment,
    the universe and everything within it
    the work of your hands.
As you created the stars and the sand,
    so you have fashioned our lives –
    knowing us better than we know ourselves,
    calling us by name,
    loving us more than we can begin to fathom.
For the vastness of your purpose,
    the immensity of your creation
    and the mind-boggling wonder of your grace,
    Lord, I praise you.
Amen.

Silence

Few prayers I've come across quite capture a sense of
the God who is both near and far, as well as that by
the celebrated German theologian Karl Rahner
(1904–84). The following is just a small extract taken
from it:

Almighty, holy God, to you I come, to you I pray.
I acknowledge you, Father, Son and Holy Spirit,
    I praise, glorify and adore you.
I give you thanks for your great glory.
What can I say to you, my God?
Shall I collect together
    all the words which praise your holy Name,
    shall I give you all the names of this world,
    you, the Unnameable?
Shall I call you God of my life,
    meaning of my existence,

hallowing of my acts,
  my journey's end,
  you my most treasured happiness?
Shall I say: Creator, Sustainer, Pardoner,
  Near One, Distant One, Incomprehensible One,
  God both of flowers and stars,
  God of the gentle wind and of terrible battles,
  Wisdom, Power, Loyalty, and Truthfulness,
  Eternity and Infinity,
  you the All-merciful,
  you the Just One,
  you Love itself?
What can I say to you, my God?
Should I consecrate myself to you?
Should I say that I belong to you
  with all that I have and am?
O my God, how can I give myself to you,
  unless your grace accepts me?
How can I devote myself to your service,
  unless you call me?
Amen.

Silence

Final prayer   Higher than my highest thoughts,
  yet always close by my side;
  greater than I can ever imagine,
  yet made known to me in Christ;
  more powerful than words can express
  yet having a special concern for everyone.
Sovereign God,
  I worship you.

Though I wander far from you,
  always you seek me out.
Though you sometimes seem distant,
  always you are near.

Though you reign over all,
    you are here by my side,
    your hand reaching out to bless.
Sovereign God,
  I worship you.

Whatever I face,
    wherever I am,
    you are there,
    always at work,
    your love sure,
    your goodness constant,
    whether I see it or not.
Sovereign God,
  I worship you.
Amen.

Music   Sanctus, Dominus from *River of Peace* (Margaret Rizza)

4
The God who does more than we can ask or imagine

Music   Enfold me in your love from *Fire of Love*
(Margaret Rizza)

Scripture   I realise now you can do anything, and that nothing is
able to frustrate your purpose. I have spoken of mysteries I do not understand, things so wonderful they
are beyond my comprehension.

Job 42:2, 3b

Prayer   Gracious God, you grant to me
more than I can ever need –
joy to last me all my days,
love that makes me blessed indeed.
Though I'm poor, you make me rich;
though I'm weak, in you I'm strong.
Lord, I lift my heart in praise,
lift my voice in joyful song.

Gracious God, you give to me
more than I could ever ask –
light to point the way ahead,
endless sun in which to bask,
life beyond my wildest dreams,
hope that will not ever die.
Lord, once more I sing your praise,
lift your holy name on high!

Silence

Next, words by Lancelot Andrewes (1555–1626). Written in the sixteenth century, they remind us of the God whose love across the years goes beyond our highest expectations:

Blessing and honour, thanksgiving and praise,
    more than I can utter,
    more than I can understand,
    be yours, O most glorious Trinity,
    Father, Son and Holy Spirit,
    by all angels, all people, all creatures,
    now and for ever.
Amen.

Silence

Mighty God,
    I can do so little
    but *you* can do so much,
    nothing beyond your sovereign power.
For that knowledge
    I praise you.

When life is dark,
    the future uncertain,
    problems insurmountable
    and my resources to meet them all too few,
    you are able to see me through.
For that knowledge
    I praise you.

When life is good,
    full of promise
    and overflowing with special things,
    you offer yet more blessings,
    constantly able to surprise me
    with the wonder of your love.

For that knowledge
   I praise you.

Time and again you meet not only my *needs*
   but so much more,
   transforming each moment of every day;
   and you are able to go on doing so for all eternity.
For that knowledge
   I praise you.
   Amen.

Silence

Final prayer   To him who by his power at work within us is able to achieve inestimably more than anything we can ask or even dream of, to him be glory in the Church and in Christ Jesus in this and every generation, now and always. Amen.

Ephesians 3:20, 21

Music   Enfold me in your love from *Fire of Love* (Margaret Rizza)

5
The wonder of God's love

Music   Adoramus te, Domine Deus from *Fountain of Life*
(Margaret Rizza)

Scripture   I will sing unceasingly of your unfailing love, O Lord;
I will declare your faithfulness to all generations.
Your constant love is unchanged from the beginning
of time, and your faithfulness is as permanent as the
heavens.   *Psalm 89:1, 2*

How precious, O God, is your unfailing love.
Psalm 36:7a

Prayer   For love so rich and special –
like nothing else on earth –
that found me, lost and hopeless,
and brought new life to birth;
that sees my many failings
yet loves me just the same,
and though it meets rejection
still seeks me out by name;
that knows my faith can waver,
enough at times to break,
yet gave itself completely –
faced anguish for my sake –
for love like this, so precious,
I give you, Lord, my praise,
my heart alight with wonder,
my spirit set ablaze.
Receive my grateful worship
and help me show, I pray,
a fraction of the ardour
you show to me each day.

Silence

O God the Eternal,
    the refuge and help of all your children,
    in our weakness you are strength,
    in our darkness you are light,
    in our sorrow you are comfort and peace.
We cannot number your blessings,
    we cannot declare your love.
For all your goodness we bless you.
May we ever live in your presence,
    and love the things you love,
    and serve you with the service of our daily lives,
    through Jesus Christ our Lord.
Amen.   *St Boniface*

Silence

Final prayer

Gracious God,
    you bless me beyond my imagining,
    love me beyond my dreaming,
    forgive me beyond my deserving
    and use me beyond my hoping.
To you belong praise and thanksgiving,
    honour and adoration,
    now and always.
Amen.

Music

Adoramus te, Domine Deus from *Fountain of Life*
(Margaret Rizza)

6
The otherness of God

Music

O magnum mysterium from *River of Peace*
(Margaret Rizza)

Scripture

O Lord, I do not let my heart get above itself or raise
my eyes too high; nor do I fret over those things that
are too wonderful and awesome for me to understand.
Psalm 131:1

Oh how deep are the riches, wisdom and understanding
of God – how far beyond us are his judgements and
unfathomable his ways! 'Who has figured out the
Lord's mind, or been his advisor?' 'Who has offered
him gifts deserving repayment?' All things are from
him, through him and to him. Glory be to him for
ever. Amen. *Romans 11:33-36*

Prayer

Immortal, invisible, God only wise,
in light inaccessible hid from our eyes,
most blessed, most glorious, the Ancient of Days,
almighty, victorious, thy great name we praise.

Unresting, unhasting, and silent as night,
nor wanting, nor wasting, thou rulest in might;
thy justice like mountains high soaring above
thy clouds which are fountains of goodness and love.

To all life thou givest, to both great and small;
in all life thou livest, the true life of all;
we blossom and flourish as leaves on the tree,
and wither and perish, but naught changeth thee.

Great Father of glory, pure Father of Light,
thine angels adore thee, all veiling their sight;
all laud we would render, O help us to see
'tis only the splendour of light hideth thee.

Silence

The sense of God's awesomeness expressed in that
celebrated hymn by Walter Chalmers Smith (1824–
1908) is articulated yet more powerfully in the ancient
prayer of St Gregory of Nazianzen:

O all-transcendent God –
    and what other name could describe you?
    what words can hymn your praises?
No word does you justice.
What mind can probe your secrets?
No mind can encompass you.
You are alone beyond the power of speech,
    yet all that we speak stems from you.
You are alone beyond the power of thought,
    yet all that we can conceive springs from you.
All things proclaim you,
    those endowed with reason and those bereft of it.
All the expectation and pain of the world
    coalesce in you.
All things utter a prayer to you,
    a silent hymn composed by you.
You sustain everything that exists,
    and all things move together to your orders.
You are the goal of all that exists.
You are one and you are all,
    yet you are none of the things that exist,
    neither a part nor the whole.
You can avail yourself of any name;

how shall I call you,
the only unnameable?
All-transcendent God!

Silence

Final prayer   God of all,
you are greater than my highest thoughts,
mightier than I can ever comprehend,
before all, in all, and beyond all.
To you, O Lord,
be praise and honour,
glory, adoration and worship.

In awe and wonder I acknowledge your greatness,
marvel at your love,
rejoice in your mercy
and celebrate your many blessings.
To you, O Lord,
be praise and honour,
glory, adoration and worship.

Accept the words of my prayer,
thoughts of my heart
and offering of my life,
for I give it all from the heart.
To you, O Lord,
be praise and honour,
glory, adoration and worship.
Amen.

Music   O magnum mysterium from *River of Peace*
(Margaret Rizza)

7
God's awesome devotion

Music   Bless the Lord my soul from *Light in Our Darkness*
              (Margaret Rizza)

Scripture God loved the world so passionately that he sacrificed
              his only Son, in order that those who believe in him
              will not die but will instead enjoy eternal life.
                                                          John 3:16

              Lord, my heart does not get above itself nor do I lift
              my eyes higher than I can hope to see. I do not dwell
              on matters beyond my comprehension, too wonderful
              for me to fathom. No, I see myself instead as a weaned
              child, as one whose mother has set my soul at rest.
              That's what my soul's like: a child gently soothed by a
              mother's love.   *Psalm 131:1, 2*

Prayer   In the passionate care of a mother
              and the heartfelt concern of a friend,
              in the tender embrace of a lover,
              in a love that nothing can end,
              I glimpse, gracious God, just a fraction
              of the place I enjoy in your heart,
              of your love shown so clearly in action,
              breaking down all that keeps us apart:
              your sacrifice – suffering and dying –
              to draw us once more to your side,
              your mercy that never stops trying,
              your purpose that won't be denied.
              Such wonderful love leaves me reeling,
              amazed it can really be true.
              Lord, grant me the same depth of feeling
              in all of my dealings with you.

              Silence

May you be blessed for ever, Lord,
   for not abandoning me when I abandoned you.
May you be blessed for ever, Lord,
   for offering your hand of love in my darkest,
   most lonely moments.
May you be blessed for ever, Lord,
   for putting up with such a stubborn soul as mine.
May you be blessed for ever, Lord,
   for loving me more than I love myself.
May you be blessed for ever, Lord,
   for continuing to pour out your blessings upon me,
   even though I respond so poorly.
May you be blessed for ever, Lord,
   for drawing out the goodness in all people,
   even including me.
May you be blessed for ever, Lord,
   for repaying my sin with your love.
May you be blessed for ever, Lord,
   for being constant and unchanging
   amidst all the changes of this world.
May you be blessed for ever, Lord,
   for your countless blessings on me
   and on all your creatures.
Amen.

St Teresa of Avila (1515–82)

Silence

Final prayer   Gracious God,
   I praise you that, above all else,
   you are a God of love –
   not of judgement, anger or vengeance,
   but of constant and total love.
For that truth
   I worship you.

Though I repeatedly fail you,
   turning my back on your goodness,
   still you continue to love me,
   fiercely and wholeheartedly.
For that truth
I worship you.

Though I turn away from you,
   wilfully rejecting your guidance
   and repeatedly betraying your trust,
   still you long to take me back,
   to restore a living, loving relationship with you.
For that truth
I worship you.

For this awesome love,
   greater than words can express,
   deeper than I can begin to understand
   and more passionate
   than anything else I shall ever experience,
   receive my praise and worship.
Amen.

Music   Bless the Lord my soul from *Light in Our Darkness*
(Margaret Rizza)

8
God's faithful guidance

Music   Speak, Lord from *The New Dawn* (Margaret Rizza)

Scripture   The Lord's my shepherd, I want for nothing. He makes me lie down in fertile pastures, he leads me beside tranquil waters, he restores my soul. He leads me in right paths for his name's sake.   *Psalm 23:1-3*

When I thought, 'My foot is starting to slip', your love, O Lord, supported me. I am constantly with you; you hold my right hand. I will acclaim you, O Lord, for I was at rock bottom and you lifted me up.
Psalm 94:18; 73:23; 30:1

Prayer   **Why dost thou shade thy lovely face?**

My light thou art; without thy glorious sight
Mine eyes are darken'd with perpetual night.
My God, thou art my way, my life, my light.

Thou art my way; I wander if thou fly:
Thou art my light; if hid, how blind am I!
Thou art my life; if thou withdraw, I die.

Mine eyes are blind and dark, I cannot see;
To whom or whither should my darkness flee,
But to the light? And who's that light but thee?

My path is lost, my wand'ring steps do stray;
I cannot safely go, nor safely stay;
Whom should I seek but thee, my path, my way?
Francis Quarles (1592–1644)

Silence

We pray to you, O Lord,
   who are the supreme Truth,
   and all truth is from you.
We beseech you, O Lord,
   who are the highest Wisdom,
   and all the wise depend on you for their wisdom.
You are the supreme Joy,
   and all who are happy owe it to you.
You are the Light of minds,
   and all receive their understanding from you.
We love, we love you above all.
We seek you, we follow you,
   and we are ready to serve you.
We desire to dwell under your power
   for you are the King of all.
Amen.   *St Albert the Great*

Final prayer   Loving God,
      for your constant guidance throughout my life –
      the way you have so faithfully been there to lead me,
      through hopes and fears,
      joy and sorrow,
      pleasure and pain –
      I praise you.

     For the ways you have spoken –
      through your Word,
      your Son,
      your Spirit,
      your Church
      and your Creation –
      I praise you.

     For the knowledge that you will be with me
      now and for all eternity –
      watching over me,
      directing my steps,

prompting, inspiring,
teaching, equipping,
forgiving, renewing –
I praise you.
Amen.

Music   Speak, Lord from *The New Dawn* (Margaret Rizza)

9
God's acceptance of our flawed worship

Music   In God alone from *Light in Our Darkness*
(Margaret Rizza)

Scripture   I am filled with anguish and surely lost, for I am an unworthy person living among unworthy people, yet with my own eyes I have glimpsed the sovereign God, the Lord of all. Holy, holy, holy is the Lord of hosts; his glory fills the whole world! *Isaiah 6:5, 3b*

I do not understand why I act as I do. For I end up doing the things I hate rather than the things I want to do. I do evil instead of the good I wish to do. What a wretched man I am! Who will deliver me from this body of death? Thanks be to God through Jesus Christ our Lord! *Romans 7:15, 24, 25*

Prayer   O Lord, I want to praise you,
your holy name confess,
your mighty deeds acknowledge,
your awesome love express.
I want to give you worship,
to lift your name on high,
yet somehow words are lacking
however hard I try.

O Lord, I want to praise you,
through all I say and do,
to so live out the gospel
that all may know it's true.
I want to bring you glory,
to help your kingdom grow,
yet though I strive to serve you,
it rarely seems to show.

O Lord, I want to praise you,
to celebrate your love,
to thank you for the blessings
you pour down from above.
I want to bring you honour,
respond with all my heart,
yet sacrifice is costly –
I rarely even start.

O Lord, I want to praise you,
poor though my words may be;
although my faults are many
I come still, joyfully.
For though I often fail you
and know you but in part,
you look beneath the surface
and see what's in my heart.

Silence

The following prayer, written by John Hoyland
(1887–1957), powerfully, almost shockingly, captures
the contrast between the holiness of God and our human
weakness. Make it your own:

From man's unfaithfulness,
    our hearts turn longingly to you,
    O love eternal and unchanging.

From man's weak fickleness,
    our hearts turn longingly to you,
    O will inimitable.

From man's exceeding feebleness
    our hearts turn longingly to you,
    O might omnipotent.

From man's gross filth
our hearts turn longingly to you,
O purity divine and absolute.

From man's deformity
our hearts turn longingly to you,
O beauty perfect and ineffable.
Amen.

Final prayer

Mighty God,
for your grace that thrills our hearts,
your wonder that fills our minds,
your peace that stills our souls
and your love that fulfils our lives,
receive my praise.
Amen.

Music

In God alone from *Light in Our Darkness*
(Margaret Rizza)

10
Celebrating what God has done

Music
Cantate Domino from *Awakening in Love*
(Margaret Rizza)

Scripture
Lord God, you have piled high your marvellous deeds and thoughtfulness towards us; none can begin to compare with you! I will make known what you have done to all, speaking of your blessings beyond number. You, O Lord, are my God. I will acclaim you and praise your name, for you have done marvellous things, fulfilling your age-old purpose, dependable and certain.   *Psalm 40:5; Isaiah 25:1*

My soul magnifies the Lord, and my spirit exults within me in God my Saviour, for . . . he has done great things for me. Holy is his name!'
Luke 1:46, 47, 49

Prayer
God has done so much for us, but we so easily forget it, as illustrated by the following prayer, inspired by an out-of-date newspaper:

I glimpsed the headline
   emblazoned over the front page –
   sensational stuff! –
   but shrugged indifferently
   and turned aside,
   for it was old hat,
   yesterday's paper,
   news no longer.
What excited once, bores now,
   what was fresh then, is stale now.

I glimpsed the message running through the pages,
    the Word made flesh,
    Christ crucified and risen –
    sensational stuff! –
    but once more I shrugged and turned aside,
    for it was again old hat,
    news no longer.
Only I was wrong,
    for it's as much today's news as yesterday's,
    as alive now as it will ever be,
    news for you,
    for me,
    for everyone.
Lord, keep me ever-enthused,
    ever-excited,
    by what you have done and continue to do,
    through Christ my Lord.
Amen.

Silence

The words of one of our best-loved hymns, written by Frances van Alstyne (1820–1915), celebrates the same truth:

To God be the glory! great things he hath done;
so loved he the world that he gave us his Son;
who yielded his life an atonement for sin,
and opened the life-gate that all may go in.
Praise the Lord, praise the Lord!
Let the earth hear his voice!
Praise the Lord, praise the Lord!
Let the people rejoice!
O come to the Father, through Jesus the Son,
and give him the glory; great things he hath done.

O perfect redemption, the purchase of blood!
To every believer the promise of God;
the vilest offender who truly believes,
that moment from Jesus a pardon receives.
Praise the Lord, praise the Lord!
Let the earth hear his voice!
Praise the Lord, praise the Lord!
Let the people rejoice!
O come to the Father, through Jesus the Son,
and give him the glory; great things he hath done.

Great things he hath taught us,
great things he hath done,
and great our rejoicing through Jesus the Son;
but purer, and higher, and greater will be
our wonder, our rapture, when Jesus we see.
Praise the Lord, praise the Lord!
Let the earth hear his voice!
Praise the Lord, praise the Lord!
Let the people rejoice!
O come to the Father, through Jesus the Son,
and give him the glory; great things he hath done.

Final prayer   Lord of all,
for the wonder of this world,
and for health and strength to enjoy it;
for family and friends,
a home, food and clothing;
for the great things you have done in my life
and that of so many others –
for all this and so much more,
gladly I praise you.

For the wonder of your love in Christ,
and your gift of life through him;
for the constancy of your mercy
and faithfulness of your guidance;
for the hope you have given

and the joy, peace and blessing
you daily shower upon us;
for the great things you have done
and continue to do –
for all this and so much more,
gladly I praise you.
Amen.

Music   Cantate Domino from *Awakening in Love*
(Margaret Rizza)

11
God's constant strength and support

Music   Rock of ages from *Our Favourite Hymns 2*

Scripture   The Lord is my rock, fortress and deliverer. He is my
                   rock, the one in whom I take refuge, my shield and
                   source of salvation, a stronghold, refuge and saviour.
                                                        2 Samuel 22:2, 3a

                   God is our sanctuary and stronghold, always close by
                   to help us in times of trouble.
                                                              Psalm 46:1

Prayer   For the knowledge day by day
                   you'll be with me, come what may;
                   for the fact my whole life through
                   you've been faithful, ever true;
                   for the many ways you bless,
                   more than words can quite express;
                   living Lord, with heart ablaze,
                   full of joy, I bring you praise.

                   Silence

                   If prayer can be poetic, it can also be inspired by and
                   find expression in the most ordinary things around
                   us. I wrote the following prayer, for example, after
                   spotting a group of people huddled in a run-down
                   shelter during a thunderstorm:

They'd hardly noticed it before,
    passing it by with barely a glance,
    but when the storm broke and the rain lashed down,
    they noticed it *then*,
    and huddled hurriedly inside,
    grateful for its cover.

I'm forgetful of *you* Lord, much of the time,
    paying you scant heed until trouble strikes,
    only then remembering your love
    and running for shelter in your protective arms,
    a refuge in time of need.
Yet though I ignore you for so long
    always you are ready to welcome,
    as faithful as I am fickle.
For being there, Lord, come what may,
    receive my praise.
Amen.

Final prayer

O God, the deathless hope of all,
    we rejoice that you support us
    both when little and even to grey hairs.
When our strength is of you, it is strength indeed;
    but when our own only, it is feebleness.
With you are refreshment and true strength.
Amen.

St Augustine of Hippo (354–430)

Music

Rock of ages from *Our Favourite Hymns 2*

12
Responding to God's love

Music   I will bless the Lord from *Light in Our Darkness* (Margaret Rizza)

Scripture   I will sing of your power; each morning I will sing unashamedly of your unswerving love, for in my time of need you showed yourself to be a stronghold and sanctuary. You are my fortress and my strength, a God of unfailing love, so I will sing praises to you.
Psalm 59:16, 17

Open my lips, Lord, and my mouth will proclaim your praise. *Psalm 51:15*

Prayer   Warm as the sun,
fresh as the breeze,
fair as a flower,
tall as the trees,
clear as the dew,
pure as the dove,
so unto me,
Lord, is your love.

Lovely as dawn,
welcome as light,
peaceful as dusk,
restful as night,
high as the clouds,
deep as the sea,
so is your love,
Lord, unto me.

Swift as a stream,
free as a bird,
firm as a rock,
sure as your word,
bright as the stars,
shining above,
so unto me,
Lord, is your love.

Bursting with joy,
leaping with praise,
glowing with thanks,
heart set ablaze,
Lord, I would serve,
always be true –
such is my love,
Jesus, for you.

Silence

Of all the prayers expressing a response to God's love, few can be more powerful than the following of St Francis de Sales (1567–1662). Make his prayer your own:

Lord, I am yours,
    and I must belong to no one but you.
My soul is yours,
    and must live only by you.
My will is yours,
    and must love only for you.
I must love you as my first cause,
    since I am from you.
I must love you as my end and rest,
    since I am for you.

I must love you more than my own being,
  since my being subsists by you.
I must love you more than myself,
  since I am all yours and all in you.
Amen.

Silence

Final prayer God is as much present in daily life as in times of quiet
devotion, so much of what we see around us speaking
of him and calling for a response. The following
reflective prayer was inspired by the renovation of an
old building featured on the BBC television series
Restoration:

It had cost a fortune,
  involving innumerable appeals
  and funding applications,
and there had been plenty to question
  the wisdom of continuing,
  convinced the money could have been spent
  better elsewhere,
  but at last the project was complete,
  the building restored to its former glory,
  and as the crowds filed through,
  marvelling at its splendour,
  all the time and effort seemed more than worth it,
  a small price for such a spectacular jewel.

Remind me, Lord, of what it cost you
  to restore your broken world,
  the price you so freely paid to make us whole.
Remind me of the immensity of your love,
  the awesome sacrifice
  through which you have made all things new.

I can never repay such goodness,
   whatever I offer in return,
   but I give you my praise,
   in grateful thanks
   and joyful worship.
Amen.

Music   I will bless the Lord from *Light in Our Darkness*
(Margaret Rizza)

13
God's amazing grace

Music Worthy is the lamb from *Messiah* (Handel)

Scripture You are worthy, Lord, to take the scroll and unseal it, since you were slaughtered, ransoming people for God from every culture, language, race and continent, and transforming them into a kingdom and priests to our God, who will reign on the earth. Worthy is the Lamb that was slain to receive dominion, riches, wisdom, power, veneration, glory and praise! To the one who sits on the throne and to the Lamb be blessing, homage, glory and might, now and always!
Revelation 5:9, 10, 12, 13b

Prayer For the message I've believed,
all the mercy I've received,
heavy burdens you've relieved,
hear my praise.

For the life you've helped me start,
untold treasures you impart,
gift of joy within my heart,
hear my praise.

For the constant love you show,
priceless truth I've come to know,
living faith you've caused to grow,
hear my praise.

For your grace that makes me whole,
perfect peace within my soul,
precious prize you've made my goal,
hear my praise.

For the blessings that you share,
countless pointers that you care,
certain knowledge you are there,
hear my praise.

For the life you hold in store,
lived with you for evermore,
giving hope so strong, so sure,
hear my praise.

Silence

An old prayer of Thomas Ken (1637–1711) reminds
us likewise of the new life won for us through Christ's
suffering and sacrifice:

To God the Father who first loved us,
   and made us accepted in the beloved Son;
   to God the Son,
   who loved us
   and washed us from our sins in his own blood;
   to God the Holy Spirit,
   who sheds abroad the love of God in our hearts;
   to the one true God
   be all love and all glory for time and eternity.
Amen.

Silence

Next, a prayer celebrating God's forgiveness:

For your awesome love and unfailing grace,
   the way, day after day, you show mercy,
   accepting my feeble faith and hesitant discipleship,
   understanding my weakness,
   putting my faults behind me
   and helping me to start again,

Merciful God,
I praise you.

For the knowledge that however often I fail you,
    your patience is never exhausted,
    that however often I go astray,
    you will seek me out,
    that though I obstruct and deny your will,
    nothing will stop you loving me;
    Merciful God,
    I praise you.

I deserve so little, yet you give so much.
My love is so weak, yet you respond so richly.
My faith is so small, yet you bless me so constantly;
    Merciful God,
    I praise you.
Amen.

Silence

Final prayer   To him, our only Saviour,
    who is able to keep our feet from slipping,
    and to present us faultless
    and brimming over with joy
    into the glorious presence of God –
    to him be glory and sovereignty,
    dominion and authority,
    now and always.
    Amen.   *Jude, verse 24*

Music   Worthy is the lamb from *Messiah* (Handel)

14
Glimpsing God's greatness

Music   Sanctum nomen from *Fire of Love* (Margaret Rizza)

Scripture   Who has gauged the waters in the palm of his hand and
                   set the boundary between heaven and earth? Who has
                   weighed up the raw materials for this planet, calculating
                   the proportions of hills and mountains? Who advised
                   the Lord's Spirit, offering counsel and instruction? Who
                   did he confer with for guidance, and who showed him
                   the way of justice? Who educated him and gave him
                   wisdom? Whole countries and cultures are like a drop
                   in a bucket compared to him, little more than dust
                   when weighed in the balance.   *Isaiah 40:12-15a*

Prayer   We talk often of God's greatness, but it's only occasion-
                   ally that we're reminded of how truly awesome he is. I
                   wrote the following reflective prayer after watching a
                   news report concerning a space probe sent to explore
                   the planet and moons of Jupiter:

                   They were exciting pictures –
                       fascinating glimpses of swirling gas,
                       soaring mountains,
                       massive craters
                       and rocky wastes.
                   At last we knew a little more about the universe beyond,
                       but it was simply a single planet,
                       one of trillions spiralling away into infinity;
                       in terms of our solar system,
                       let alone space,
                       just a stone's throw away.
                   For all it taught us,
                       the lesson relearned was how vast are the heavens
                       and how small is the earth.

Thank you, Lord, for the capacity of humankind
   to explore profound mysteries,
   our ability constantly to push back
   the boundaries of comprehension.
But thank you also for your incomparable greatness –
   the unfathomable immensity of your love,
   awesome breadth of your purpose
   and staggering scale of your power.
You are higher than our highest thoughts,
   above all, before all and beyond all.
Receive my praise.
Amen.

Silence

Lord, put your hands on my eyes,
   that I shall be able to see
   not only that which is visible
   but also that which is invisible.
Let my eyes be focused not only on that which is present
   but also that which is to come.
Unseal my heart's visions,
   that I may gaze on you in your glory.
Amen.

Origen of Alexandria (185–254)

Silence

Final prayer   Father God,
   all good,
   all true,
   all powerful,
   almighty,
   in awe and wonder
   I praise you.

Gracious God,
    all loving,
    all merciful,
    all faithful,
    all compassionate,
    in awe and wonder
    I praise you.

Mighty God,
    always active,
    always leading,
    always calling,
    always knowing,
    in awe and wonder
    I praise you.

Saving God,
    always forgiving,
    always restoring,
    always teaching,
    always encouraging,
    in awe and wonder
    I praise you.

Sovereign God,
    above and below,
    before and after,
    here and everywhere,
    all in all,
    in awe and wonder
    I praise you.
Amen.

Music   Sanctum nomen from *Fire of Love* (Margaret Rizza)

15
The unchanging God

Music O God, our help in ages past from *Our Favourite Hymns 2*

Scripture I, the Lord, do not change. *Malachi 3:6a*

Jesus Christ remains the same, yesterday, today, tomorrow. *Hebrews 13:8*

Prayer So much in life, Lord, has shifted,
so much is different and strange;
everything somehow has drifted –
only your love does not change.

So much around me is fleeting,
here for a moment then gone.
Old Father Time brooks no cheating –
only your love carries on.

So much I loved, Lord, has vanished,
now just a memory or name;
into posterity banished –
only your love stays the same.

So much I think to be certain,
proves in the end to be frail,
history brings down the curtain –
only your love will not fail.

Silence

The older we get, the more we recognise that the world around us is changing, even those things that seem to have been here for ever. The following prayer was inspired by a sea stack off the Pembrokeshire coastline:

It looked so solid,
   so permanent,
   standing tall and proud against the waves,
   certain to be there still when I am long gone,
   defying the march of time.
But all was not as it seemed,
   for that rock –
   once a cliff,
   once a mountain –
   was destined to become a boulder,
   pebble,
   stone,
   and, finally, a grain of sand,
   before, who could say, being thrust up again
   in aeons to come,
   the whole process beginning again.

Only you, Lord, do not change,
   your love eternal,
   your mercy constant,
   your purpose enduring.
Teach me in this shifting world,
   here today and gone tomorrow,
   to trust in you,
   the same now and always.
Amen.

Silence

Final prayer   Eternal God,
   I praise you
   that in a world of constant change and upheaval,

you remain the same;
that though so much is swept away
by the relentless march of time,
your light continues to shine in the darkness.
Heaven and earth may pass away,
but your love endures for ever.

I praise you for the knowledge
that whatever today may hold or tomorrow bring,
the future is secure,
for you are with me,
always the same.
Heaven and earth may pass away,
but your love endures for ever.

I praise you that
though so much which seems permanent
proves to be shadow,
unable truly to satisfy or bring lasting fulfilment;
that though beauty fades and pleasures tarnish;
you remain unchanged and unchangeable.
Heaven and earth may pass away,
but your love endures for ever.
Amen.

Music   O God, our help in ages past from *Our Favourite Hymns 2*

16
The God who loves us as we are

Music　　　Just as I am, without one plea from *Our Favourite Hymns 2*

Scripture　　The Lord does not see as people see. They look at appearances, but he sees into the heart.

1 Samuel 16:7b

Prayer　　　You see me as no one else starts to,
the person concealed deep inside,
the weaknesses, faults and temptations,
the defects I'd much rather hide.
You see me laid bare of pretension,
the surface veneer stripped away,
the failings I cannot quite conquer
exposed to the cold light of day.
And yet you continue to love me,
your mercy and grace shining through;
despite all the times that I fail you,
you carry on making me new.
Such love is too awesome to credit,
like no other love that I know,
but though, Lord, I can't quite believe it,
you show me each day it is so.

Silence

Sometimes God can speak to us in the most unexpected of places. The seeds of the following prayer, for example, were sown on a visit to my local barber:

What a strange job,
    cutting all that hair,
    head after head,
    day after day.
Does he get bored, I wonder?
He must do,
    but he doesn't show it,
    just makes casual conversation as he snips away.
He's passing the time of day, of course,
    for he doesn't know me,
    not *really* –
    doesn't know most of his customers, come to that.

But *you* do, Lord,
    every hair of my head,
    every thought of my mind,
    every aspect of my character –
    nothing hidden from your gaze.
Inside out and back to front,
    you know each one of us
    and yearn that we might know you too.
For that great truth,
    Lord, I praise you.
Amen.

Silence

Ours then, is a God who welcomes us not for what we might become but as we are, with all our faults and weaknesses, all our failure and ugliness. The point is beautifully made by George Herbert (1593–1633) in his lovely poem-cum-prayer: 'Love Bade Me Welcome':

Love bade me welcome; yet my soul drew back,
guilty of dust and sin.
But quick-eyed Love, observing me grow slack
from my first entrance in,

drew nearer to me, sweetly questioning
if I lack'd any thing.
A guest, I answer'd, worthy to be here:
Love said, You shall be he.
I the unkind, ungrateful? Ah, my dear,
I cannot look on thee.
Love took my hand, and smiling did reply,
who made the eyes but I?
Truth, Lord, but I have marr'd them: let my shame
go where it doth deserve.
And know you not, says Love, who bore the blame?
My dear, then I will serve.
You must sit down, says Love, and taste my meat:
so I did sit and eat.

Silence

Final prayer Living God,
for your greatness beyond imagining,
your grace beyond deserving,
your goodness beyond measuring
and your love beyond comparing,
I give you my praise in awe and wonder.
Amen.

Music Just as I am, without one plea from *Our Favourite Hymns 2*

17
God's faithfulness

Music   Great is thy faithfulness from *Our Favourite Hymns 1*

Scripture Lord, I entrust myself into your care, confident you
               will save me, for you are a faithful God. You, Lord, are
               a forgiving and loving God, unfailingly patient, habit-
               ually compassionate and constant. No one, almighty
               God, is as great as you; you are faithful, Lord, in
               everything.   *Psalm 31:5; 86:15; 89:8*

               In whatever he does, God is faithful and fair; reliable
               in whatever he commands.   *Psalm 111:7*

Prayer   Great is thy faithfulness, O God my Father,
               there is no shadow of turning with thee;
               thou changest not, thy compassions they fail not;
               as thou hast been thou for ever wilt be.
               Great is thy faithfulness! Great is thy faithfulness!
               Morning by morning new mercies I see;
               all I have needed thy hand hath provided,
               great is thy faithfulness, Lord, unto me.

               Summer and winter, and springtime and harvest,
               sea, moon and stars in their courses above,
               join with all nature in manifold witness
               to thy great faithfulness, mercy and love.
               Great is thy faithfulness! Great is thy faithfulness!
               Morning by morning new mercies I see;
               all I have needed thy hand hath provided,
               great is thy faithfulness, Lord, unto me.

Pardon for sin and a peace that endureth,
thine own dear presence to cheer and to guide;
strength for today and bright hope for tomorrow,
blessing all mine, with ten thousand beside!
Great is thy faithfulness! Great is thy faithfulness!
Morning by morning new mercies I see;
all I have needed thy hand hath provided,
great is thy faithfulness, Lord, unto me.

As those celebrated words of the hymn-writer Obadiah
Chisholm (1866–1960) so beautifully remind us, many
things can speak to us of God's faithfulness, including
much in the world around us. The following prayer
was inspired by the sight of a river in full flow:

It surged past me,
   a mighty torrent,
   and I marvelled at the flow of water,
   at how, year in, year out,
   century after century,
   despite days without rain,
   even weeks of drought,
   it never ran dry.

It spoke of you, Lord:
   your faithful provision and constant love.
Through sunshine and storm,
   summer or winter,
   it remains the same –
   a stream of living water,
   refreshing and reviving,
   unfailing, come what may.
For the constancy of that provision,
   receive my praise.
Amen.

Silence

Final prayer   Though I repeatedly disobey your commandments
and lose sight of your goodness,
still you love me.
Faithful God,
I praise you.

Though I reject your guidance,
betray my convictions
and deny my calling,
still you care for me.
Faithful God,
I praise you.

Always you are there,
watching over me,
calling me back,
welcoming me home.
Faithful God,
I praise you.

Day after day I receive fresh blessings, new joys,
from your loving hands,
your grace inexhaustible,
your love too awesome for words.
Faithful God,
I praise you.
Amen.

Music   Great is thy faithfulness from *Our Favourite Hymns 1*

18
Expressing our joy

Music

In the Lord is my joy from *Fire of Love* (Margaret Rizza)

Scripture

Praise the Lord! Let my soul praise the Lord! I will extol the Lord all my days; I will honour him my whole life long with songs of worship. What a joy it is and how appropriate to sing praises to our God.

Psalm 146:1, 2; 147:1b

I am contented deep within, like someone who has enjoyed a sumptuous meal. When I lie awake at night, reflecting during the hours of darkness over all you have done, my mouth worships you, songs of joy on my lips, for you have helped me, encircling me in the shadow of your wings.

Psalm 63:5-7

Prayer

Lord, with a heart that leaps for sheer delight,
I bring the worship which is yours by right;
year after year you've blessed this life of mine,
turning what once was water into wine.

Lord, with a tongue that cries in joyful song,
gladly I praise you for your love so strong,
each day you bless me, always by my side,
come rain or sunshine you are there to guide.

Lord, with a mind that soars in grateful praise,
I will acclaim you, now and all my days;
you bring me hope, unbounded joy and love,
life in abundance streaming from above.

Silence

The joy of faith can be overshadowed sometimes by the tragedies and trials of daily life, but there is much equally to remind us of that joy which God seeks to pour into our hearts. I wrote the following prayer after a fountain in my local park caught my eye:

It danced in the breeze,
    a cascade of water leaping and cavorting,
    like a newborn lamb,
    a playful kitten,
    exuberant,
    free,
    full of life.
Restless and vivacious,
    it spoke of unquenchable energy,
    an irrepressible vitality bubbling deep within.

May your Spirit, Lord,
    course through me with similar energy,
    your joy with comparable verve,
    your love with equal spontaneity,
    and your peace with matching abandon.
So fill me with your presence
    that my soul may dance each day
    in jubilant praise and exultant gratitude.
Amen.

Silence

Final prayer   I'd lost sight of what it is all about, Lord,
    of your gift at the heart of the gospel –
a joy beyond words,
bubbling up within me,
brimful,
overflowing.
I brooded instead on faults and failings,
    worrying about the weakness of my love,

wrestling with matters of doctrine
and fretting over the cost of discipleship,
forgetting that though these are all part
of commitment
they are not the whole,
and not finally what matters most.
But then you spoke again,
  reminding me that you accept me as I am,
  your love not earned but given;
  emphasising that though I repeatedly let you down,
  still you stay faithful,
  nothing able to exhaust your grace.
The old self lives on,
  yet I realise afresh
  that you are constantly making all things new,
  offering life in abundance,
  now and for all eternity.
Gracious God,
  I pause,
  I reflect,
  I remember the wonder of your love,
  and so once more I celebrate
  with heart and mind and soul.
This day, like all days, is your gift:
  I will rejoice and be glad in it.
Amen.

Music   In the Lord is my joy from *Fire of Love* (Margaret Rizza)

19
Heartfelt worship

Music   Papillon (Kronke) from *Champagne Classics*

Scripture   My heart is constant, O God, resolute within me. I will
sing and make music. I will publicly give you thanks,
Lord, and sing praise among the nations, for your
unfailing love reaches up to the heavens, and your
constancy extends beyond the clouds. Let your name
be honoured, O God, above the heavens, and your
glory known across the earth!   *Psalm 57:7, 9-11*

I give thanks to the Lord with all my heart. I offer
thanks in your name for your unfailing love and
constancy; your name and your love are exalted
above everything.   *Psalm 138:1a, 2b*

Prayer   I'm a great believer in using music in worship, for it stirs
the heart as well as the mind, and that should be true of
worship. It's not just about intellectual assent but an
emotional response. I tried to capture that in the following prayer written after listening to a piece of music:

It stirred my heart,
     bringing a lump to my throat;
     the emotions it aroused so powerful,
     almost overwhelming,
     that my spirit soared with the melody,
     transported to new heights,
     an ecstasy of delight.

May the same be true, Lord, of knowing you,
     your presence causing me

to catch my breath in wonder,
to exult and marvel.
Instead of being an arid issue of the mind –
an intellectual assent to truth –
may faith be an affair of the heart,
capturing my imagination,
lifting me up and transporting me
into your presence,
so that, overwhelmed with joy and filled with awe,
my spirit may rise to you each day
in rapturous praise and grateful worship.
Amen.

Silence

The hymn-writer George Herbert (1593–1633) well understood how important the heart is in worship, as can be seen from one of his best-known hymns:

King of glory, King of peace,
I will love thee;
and, that love may never cease,
I will move thee.
Thou hast granted my appeal,
thou hast heard me;
thou didst note my ardent zeal,
thou hast spared me.

Wherefore with my utmost art,
I will sing thee,
and the cream of all my heart
I will bring thee.
Though my sins against me cried,
thou didst clear me,
and alone, when they replied,
thou didst hear me.

Seven whole days, not one in seven,
I will praise thee;
in my heart, though not in heaven,
I can raise thee.
Small it is, in this poor sort
to enrol thee:
e'en eternity's too short
to extol thee.

Silence

Final prayer   Finally, an adaptation of a prayer by the twelfth-century monk, philosopher and theologian Isaac of Stella (c. 1100–69). Respond to God in worship through his memorable words:

You yourself are my contemplation,
    my delight.
I seek you, for your own sake, above all else.
From you yourself I feed within.
You are the field *in* which I labour,
    the food *for* which I labour.
You are my cause,
    my goal,
    my beginning,
    and my end without end.
You, for me, are eternity.
Amen.

Music   Papillon (Kronke) from *Champagne Classics*

20
The beauty of God's creation

Music   How great thou art from *Our Favourite Hymns 2*

Scripture   Lord, let the wonder of the universe give you praise,
                testifying among the assembly of your holy people to
                your great faithfulness.   *Psalm 89:5*

Prayer   The beauty of dew in the morning
                and the chorus of birds in the trees,
                the thrill of a new day dawning,
                the hum of life on the breeze,
                so much within creation
                enthuses and uplifts.
                O Lord, you bring elation
                through all your many gifts.

                Through the peace of twilight falling,
                the sun setting low in the sky,
                the sound of a blackbird calling,
                the sparkling stars on high;
                through these, O Lord, you bless us,
                your power in each displayed.
                Receive my praise and worship
                for all that you have made.

                Silence

                The theme of praise for the beauty of this world and
                grandeur of the universe is taken up in a prayer by
                Walter Rauschenbusch (1861–1918):

O God, I thank you for this universe;
    for its vastness and its riches,
    and for the variety of life which teems within it
    and of which I am a part.
I praise you for the sky and the winds,
    for the clouds
    and for the constellation of the heavens.
I praise you for seas and rivers,
    for mountains and trees,
    and the grass beneath my feet.
I thank you for the senses which enable me
    to see the splendour of the morning,
    to hear the song of the birds,
    and to enjoy the scents of springtime.
Open my heart, I pray,
    to all this joy and beauty,
    and save me from being so burdened by care
    or blinded by greed
    that I fail to notice when even the thornbushes
    are aflame with your glory.
Amen.

Silence

Final prayer For the wonder of this world
    and vastness of the universe,
    for all that you have made,
    uplifting the spirit and moving us to wonder,
    Creator God,
    I worship you.

For bringing order out of chaos,
    an order that we can see throughout the cosmos;
    that we can depend on, explore and understand;
    that reflects your sovereign purpose and constant love,
    Creator God,
    I worship you.

For the incredible beauty, diversity
   and fascination of all you have made,
   for the countless blessings and untold riches
   you have so freely given,
   and for the delicate balance of life
   you so wonderfully sustain,
   Creator God,
   I worship you.
Amen.

Music   How great thou art from *Our Favourite Hymns 2*

EXPRESSING OUR SORROW

1
Passing judgement on others

Music   Have mercy on me, O God from *In God Alone*
(Andrew Moore)

Scripture Do not judge, and you in turn will escape judgement;
do not condemn, and you avoid being condemned;
forgive, and you will find forgiveness.   *Luke 6:37*

Avoid judging by appearances, but judge wisely instead.
John 7:24

Prayer   Judging others is wrong for a host of reasons, not least
that the judgements we make are usually based upon
outward appearances rather than the person underneath. The following reflective prayer, inspired by the
unearthing of a Saxon burial chamber near my boy-
hood home in Southend-on-Sea, explores that theme:

Who would have thought it? –
    so special a find,
    so rare an artefact,
    hidden so near
    for so long,
    a nondescript patch of earth
    yielding hidden treasure.

Forgive me, Lord,
    for I judge people by what I see,
    too often failing to delve deeper,
    and, in consequence, I miss hidden gems,
    the jewels beneath the surface.

Teach me never to dismiss anyone,
   however ordinary they may seem.
Open my heart instead to the value in all.
Amen.

Silence

Why *do* we pass judgement on others? Often it stems
from a narrow view of God, in which we assume that
our judgements reflect his own, but, as the words of
the following hymn written by F. W. Faber (1814–63)
make clear, God is far less ready to judge than we are:

There's a wideness in God's mercy,
like the wideness of the sea;
there's a kindness in his justice,
which is more than liberty.

There is no place where earth's sorrows
are more felt than up in heaven;
there is no place where earth's failings
have such kindly judgement given.

For the love of God is broader
than the measures of man's mind;
and the heart of the Eternal
is most wonderfully kind.

But we make his love too narrow
by false limits of our own;
and we magnify his strictness
with a zeal he will not own.

There is plentiful redemption
in the blood that has been shed;
there is joy for all the members
in the sorrows of the Head.

If our love were but more simple,
we should take him at his word;
and our lives be filled with gladness,
from the presence of the Lord.

Silence

Final prayer   Almighty God,
so often I have set myself up in your place,
presuming I have a right to judge others.
Lord,
forgive me, and help me to change.

I know it is wrong,
and I try to stop myself,
yet I repeatedly fall into the same trap,
pointing the accusing finger in condemnation.
Lord,
forgive me, and help me to change.

I jump to conclusions
that say more about me than anyone;
I see faults in others
yet am blind to my own innumerable failings.
Instead of seeing the best I see the worst;
instead of looking for good I dwell on evil,
instead of building up I destroy.
Lord,
forgive me, and help me to change.

Teach me to forgive as you have forgiven me,
and to leave final judgement where it belongs:
with you.
Amen.

Music   Have mercy on me, O God from *In God Alone*
(Andrew Moore)

2
Unfulfilled intentions

Music   Kyrie, eleison from *Fountain of Life* (Margaret Rizza)

Scripture   It almost seems to be a law that whenever I intend to
do good, evil is there as well, for while inwardly I
delight in God's law, I see a different law in my body
battling with the law of my mind, enslaving me to the
law of sin that dwells in my members.
Romans 7:21-23

I do not understand why I act as I do. For I end up
doing the things I hate rather than the things I want
to do. I do evil instead of the good I wish to do. What
a wretched man I am! Who will deliver me from this
body of death? Thanks be to God through Jesus
Christ our Lord!   *Romans 7:15, 24, 25*

Prayer   Dear Master, in whose life I see
all that I long, but fail to be,
let thy clear light for ever shine,
to shame and guide this life of mine.

Though what I dream and what I do
in my poor days are always two,
help me, oppressed by things undone,
O thou, whose deeds and dreams were one.

Silence

That lovely hymn by John Hunter (1848–1917)
perfectly captures the frustration we feel at failing to

honour our intentions. We mean well, but so often fail to produce the goods. The following poem-cum-prayer expresses the same dismay:

Where are the vows of long ago,
the promises I made,
the faith and trust I used to show,
the vision I displayed?
Where is the eagerness I knew
to follow day by day;
though all else failed to still stay true
and serve you, come what may?
Where is the life I swore to lead,
the love I aimed to share,
the gentle word and thoughtful deed
that showed how much I care?
Lord, for all my lofty dreams
I've fallen so far short –
to walk the way of Christ, it seems,
much harder than I thought.
Make up in me the strength I lack
to stay true to your call,
for I would offer something back
to you who gave your all.

Silence

Next a prayer of St Augustine (354-430), through his words seeking God's forgiveness:

Lord Jesus, my Saviour,
   let me now come to you.
My heart is cold:
   warm it by your selfless love.
My heart is sinful:
   cleanse it by your precious blood.

My heart is weak:
    strengthen it by your joyous Spirit.
My heart is empty:
    fill it with your divine presence.
Lord Jesus, my heart is yours:
    possess it always and only for yourself.
Amen.

Silence

Final prayer   Gracious God,
    forgive those things I should have done
    and intended to do
    but somehow left undone nonetheless:
    the acts of kindness I never found time for,
    the thoughtful word never spoken,
    the message of encouragement or concern never sent,
    the helpful deed never attempted.
Lord, in your mercy,
    hear my prayer.

Forgive me the opportunities I have missed:
    the plans I never made,
    dreams I never brought to reality,
    possibilities I never imagined,
    gifts I never used.
Lord, in your mercy,
    hear my prayer.

Forgive my failure to serve you as I once promised:
    the prayers never offered,
    sacrifices never made,
    faith never shown,
    commitment never given.
Lord, in your mercy,
    hear my prayer.

Forgive my neglect of my calling:
    my forgetfulness of my loved ones,
    of my friends,
    of my neighbour,
    of you.
Lord, in your mercy,
    hear my prayer.

Forgive me all my unfulfilled intentions,
    and help me to translate thoughts into actions,
    preaching into practice,
    fine ideals into meaningful deeds –
    to walk, in other words, the way of Christ.
Lord, in your mercy,
    hear my prayer.
Amen.

Music   Kyrie, eleison from *Fountain of Life* (Margaret Rizza)

3
Pride goes before a fall

Music   O Lord, my heart is not proud from *Fountain of Life* (Margaret Rizza)

Scripture   Pride goes before a fall, and an arrogant spirit before one's undoing. It is better to take a seat among the poor than to divide the spoil of the proud. Let someone else flatter you, not your own mouth – someone you don't know rather than your own lips.

Proverbs 16:18, 19; 27:2

In humility, count others better than yourselves.

Philippians 2:4

Prayer   For the foolishness of pride
and the hurt to which it leads;
for the value I've denied
to my neighbours' words and deeds;
for the failings I condemn,
and the flaws I'm swift to see,
and those faults I find with them
yet can never spot in me;
for dismissing every view
running counter to my own,
overlooking people's gifts,
having time for mine alone,
grant your pardon, God, I pray;
call me back, before I fall;
help me take the Saviour's way
and respect the worth of all.

Silence

Take away from me, O God,
   all pride and vanity,
   all boasting and forwardness,
   and give me the true courage
   that shows itself by gentleness;
   the true wisdom that shows itself by simplicity;
   and the true power that shows itself by modesty.
Amen.

Charles Kingsley (1819–75)

Silence

If we are to boast in anything, then, as Paul reminds us, it should be in the cross of Christ. The same idea is taken up by Isaac Watts in his celebrated hymn:

When I survey the wondrous cross
on which the Prince of Glory died,
my richest gain I count but loss,
and pour contempt on all my pride.

Forbid it, Lord, that I should boast,
save in the death of Christ, my God;
all the vain things that charm me most,
I sacrifice them to his blood.

Silence

Final prayer   Merciful God,
   I have been guilty of the sin of pride,
   thinking of myself more highly than I should,
   boasting of my own achievements
   and looking down on those around me.
Forgive me,
   and grant me true humility.

I have not listened to your voice
  or the voice of others,
    believing instead that I know best,
    imagining I have all the answers,
    assuming that I can go it alone.
Forgive me,
  and grant me true humility.

I have been guilty of pride in more subtle ways,
    hiding my frailties behind a mask of self-sufficiency,
    denying my weaknesses,
    refusing support when it has been offered.
Forgive me,
  and grant me true humility.

Teach me to listen to your voice,
    recognise my weaknesses
    and acknowledge my need of others,
    so that I may be ready to put you and others first
    and self second,
    walking the way of Jesus Christ my Lord.
Amen.

Music   O Lord, my heart is not proud from *Fountain of Life*
(Margaret Rizza)

4
Failure to admit our mistakes

Music   Just as I am from *Our Favourite Hymns 2*

Scripture   Those who conceal their wrongdoings will never flourish, but those who acknowledge and turn away from them will find forgiveness.   *Proverbs 28:13*

I will get up and go to my father, and I will say to him, 'Father, I have sinned against heaven and against you; I no longer deserve to be called your son.'
Luke 15:18, 19a

Prayer   Admitting our mistakes is hard, isn't it; hardest of all to admit them to others, but difficult also to be truly honest with ourselves and God. As the following reflective prayer explores, it's tempting to try to hide them, but the only way to deal with our faults is to acknowledge them before God and so find forgiveness. The prayer was inspired by the sight of a decorator whitewashing walls.

It was basic, true,
    plain to the point of stark,
    but it did the job,
    covering over a multitude of sins –
    cracks, hollows, stains and mould
    all neatly hidden –
    but, of course, it was no real answer,
    the problems merely being masked
    rather than tackled,
    and it would be only a matter of time
    before they surfaced again,
    as bad as they were before.

There are as many faults in my life, Lord,
    and I try the same trick,
    attempting to whitewash over them,
    hide them from view.
But only *you* can do that,
    your love covering what I can never hope to conceal.
Come now,
    and though my sins are as scarlet,
    make me whiter than snow.
Amen.

Silence

Forgive my sins, O Lord;
    the sins of my present and sins of my past,
    the sins which I have done to please myself,
    and the sins which I have done to please others.
Forgive my casual sins and my deliberate sins,
    and those which I have tried so hard to hide
    that I have hidden them even from myself.
Forgive me, O Lord, for all of them,
    for Jesus Christ's sake.
Amen.   *Thomas Wilson (1663–1755)*

Silence

Final prayer   Merciful God,
    it's not easy being honest with myself,
    for I prefer to keep some things hidden
    rather than face the disturbing truth.
Teach me to admit my faults,
    and so to receive mercy.

Occasionally I may glimpse my darker side,
    but I push it away,
    attempting to deny its existence even to myself,

yet the knowledge of my weakness is always there,
    lurking in the shadows.
Teach me to admit my faults,
    and so to receive mercy.

Help me to open my heart to you,
    in the knowledge that you gave your Son
    to make me whole.
Cleanse, redeem, renew, restore,
    and, by your grace,
    help me to come to terms with the person I am,
    so that, one day, I might become
    the person you would have me be.
Teach me to admit my faults,
    and so to receive mercy.
Amen.

Music   Just as I am from *Our Favourite Hymns 2*

5
Superficial discipleship

Music   Have mercy on us, Lord from *In God Alone*
               (Andrew Moore)

Scripture   You shall love the Lord your God with all your
               heart, soul and mind. This is the first and greatest
               commandment.
                                                Matthew 22:37, 38

               Fashion a new and unblemished heart within me, O
               God; imbue me with a true and faithful spirit.
                                                    Psalm 51:10

Prayer   I've failed to love you, Father, as much as you love me,
               content to offer, rather, a feeble travesty,
               a going through the motions, a playing of the part;
               too often my devotions not springing from the heart.
               I offer songs of worship, kneel down to you in prayer,
               appeal for help and guidance, and read your word
                   with care.
               I go to church each Sunday resolved to walk your way,
               to love and serve you better, to follow and obey.
               To everyone around me my life must look the part –
               yet one thing, Lord, is lacking: true worship
                   from the heart.
               Accept my supplications, have mercy and forgive;
               see past the limitations that scar the love I give.
               Remould, renew, remake me, that I might learn
                   your way,
               responding with the passion you show to me each day.

               Silence

Faith can too easily look the part but be only skin-deep, a bit like carefully applied make-up, as explored in the following prayer:

It was remarkable:
    a touch of lipstick,
    dab of eye-shadow,
    new outfit,
    change of hairstyle,
    and she looked a new person,
    unrecognisable from the woman she'd been before.

Lord, it's different, I know,
    but I too am good at putting on appearances,
    looking the part,
    the face I show to the world
    so often concealing the reality beneath.
Help me to change not so much the outside
    but deep within –
    to become the person you would have me be.
Amen.

Silence

Final prayer Lord Jesus Christ,
    I talk about belonging to you,
    and offering you my service,
    but so often the reality falls short of the ideal.
For the shallowness of my faith,
    forgive me.

Instead of making you an integral part of my life
    I treat you as an optional extra,
    there to turn to as and when it suits me.
Instead of working for your kingdom
    I strive chiefly to serve my own interests.

My deeds deny my words;
    my life betrays the weakness of my commitment.
For the shallowness of my faith,
    forgive me.

When discipleship involves sacrifice,
    putting demands upon me
    or calling for a change in lifestyle,
    I'm found wanting,
    preferring instead the way of least resistance
    and smallest cost.
For the shallowness of my faith,
    forgive me.

Draw me closer to you,
    and fill me with your love,
    so that instead of being skin-deep
    my faith may be real,
    shaping every aspect of who I am.
In your name I ask it.
Amen.

Music   Have mercy on us, Lord from *In God Alone*
(Andrew Moore)

6

Our abuse of creation

Music   What a wonderful world from *Favourite Memories*

Scripture   The heavens proclaim the glory of God: the universe
testifies to his handiwork. Each day witnesses eloquently and each night communicates knowledge,
without need of speech, language or any other voice.
Psalm 19:1-3a

The earth dries up and withers; the world languishes
and shrivels up and the heavens suffer with it. The
earth's own inhabitants despoil it, for they have flouted
God's law, violated his statutes and desecrated the
eternal covenant.   *Isaiah 24:4, 5*

Prayer   You've given a world, Lord, of untold delight,
that moves me to worship and praise;
that speaks of your glory by day and by night –
so much there to thrill and amaze.
The peak of a mountain, the shade of a tree,
the colour and scent of a flower,
the peace of a river or wrath of the sea –
each gives me a glimpse of your power.
The laughter of children, the crunching of leaves,
or delicate song of a bird,
the hum of a city, the whispering breeze –
in so much your voice can be heard.
Forgive me, I pray, the indictment I share
for failing to steward this Earth,
neglecting to give it due honour or care,
and losing a sense of its worth.
I squander resources, betraying your trust,

yet somehow I don't seem to learn.
Lord, help me to treasure this world as I must –
that others might share it in turn.

Silence

Too easily we live today with no thought of tomorrow, but that is to abdicate our responsibility to our
children and our children's children – to forget, in
other words, those who will inherit this world after
us. We do not own this planet but simply hold it in trust
for a moment, and alongside privilege that brings an
awesome responsibility. I explore that in this next
prayer, inspired by my sister's time as trustee of a
major pension fund:

It was an honour,
　　but an onerous one,
　　the future of thousands
　　dependent on her stewardship,
　　for the resources she administered were held on trust,
　　representing not just assets but people –
　　their savings and investments,
　　lives and livelihoods.

You've honoured *us*, Lord,
　　each and every one,
　　placing in our care not just land or money
　　but the world itself,
　　an asset beyond price.
Forgive my share in squandering its resources,
　　living today with no thought of tomorrow.
Forgive my betrayal of your trust,
　　living with little thought
　　for present and future generations.
Teach me to live wisely,
　　mindful of all your creation,
　　and grant that others may do the same.
Amen.

Silence

O merciful Creator,
    thy hand is open wide
    to satisfy the needs of every living creature:
    make us, we beseech thee,
    ever thankful for thy loving providence;
    and grant that we,
    remembering the account that we must one day give,
    may be faithful stewards of thy good gifts;
    through Jesus Christ our Lord,
    who with thee and the Holy Spirit lives and reigns,
    one God, for ever and ever.
Amen.   *Book of Common Prayer* (1979)

Silence

Final prayer   Creator God,
    I forget sometimes
    that I have a duty not just to you
    but to the whole of creation,
    to nurture and protect rather than exploit it,
    to faithfully steward what you have given.
For my part in abusing creation,
    forgive me.

I share in a society that has too often lived for today
    with no thought of tomorrow;
    that unquestioningly accepts economic structures
    that plunder this world's resources
    with little regard for the consequences.
For my part in abusing creation,
    forgive me.

I have lived wastefully,
    giving scant thought
    to those who will come after me.

Concerned chiefly with myself,
   I have squandered natural resources,
   consuming more than I need.
For my part in abusing creation,
   forgive me.

Help me more fully to understand
   the wonder yet fragility of this planet you've given,
   and to do what I can to honour it,
   seeing it not as a possession to treat as I wish
   but as a priceless gift held on trust.
For my part in abusing creation,
   forgive me.
Amen.

Music   What a wonderful world (from *Favourite Memories*)

7
One-sided faith

Music
Life of Christ, renew me from *River of Peace*
(Margaret Rizza)

Scripture
God proved his love for us by sending Christ to die
for us who were yet sinners.   *Romans 5:8*

Do not hold back your mercy from me, Lord, but
keep me safe through your constant and unfailing
love. For innumerable evils have besieged me; my
iniquities have engulfed me such that I can see nothing
else; my heart fails me for they outnumber the very
hairs of my head.   *Psalm 40:11, 12*

Prayer
My sinnes are like the haires upon my head,
And raise their Audit to as high a score:
In this they differ: these doe dayly shed;
But ah! my sinnes grow dayly more and more.
    If by my haires thou number out my sinnes;
    Heaven make me bald before the day begins.

My sinnes are like the sands upon the shore;
Which every ebbe layes open to the eye:
In this they differ: These are cover'd o'er
With every tide, My sinnes still open lye.
    If thou wilt make my head a sea of teares,
    O they will hide the sinnes of all my yeares.

My sinnes are like the Starres within the skies,
In view, in number, even as bright as great:

In this they differ: these doe set and rise;
But ah! my sinnes doe rise, but never set.
    Shine Son of glory, and my sinnes are gone
    Like twinkling Starres before the rising Sunne.

Francis Quarles (1592–1644)

Silence

These words of the Elizabethan Poet Francis Quarles
beautifully capture the contrast between the faithfulness of God and the faithlessness of our response. We
will go on confessing that to our dying day, but we
need to do so remembering that God's love will not
fail. The sight of a wedding ring reminded me of that
wonderful truth and inspired the following prayer:

It was nothing fancy,
    just an ordinary ring,
    worth little in monetary terms,
    but in terms of the reality it represented, priceless,
    speaking of a love that had stood the test of time –
    of an ongoing relationship,
    enduring commitment
    and bond that would not be broken.

Thank you, Lord, for the relationship I enjoy with you –
    your faithfulness across the years,
    your enduring love,
    your companionship through the journey of life –
    and forgive me that all too often
    it has been one-sided,
    you having to do all the running.
Renew my commitment and deepen my devotion,
    so that I may respond in kind,
    offering something back to you
    who has given so much for me.
Amen.

Silence

Lord God,
    sovereign Father,
    creator of all,
    giving me body and soul
    and creating me in your image
    before time even began,
    I confess my faults to you,
    for I have sinned before you and heaven,
    my sins being as numerous
    as the sand on the seashore.
In your love, O God,
    do not turn your face from me and let me perish,
    but have mercy.
I dare to ask it not because I deserve forgiveness
    but because of your grace.
Look down on me, Lord, from your heavenly throne,
    and lighten the shadows of my heart
    with the radiance of your splendour.
Protect me, Lord, with the shield of truth and faith,
    so that the fiery darts of the evil one
    may not pierce me.
Saviour of the world, who lives and reigns for ever,
    have mercy upon me.
Amen.   *Latin prayer (Tenth century)*

Silence

Final prayer   For the one-sidedness of our relationship,
      the way I leave it to you to do all the work
      and make all the running,
      Lord Jesus Christ,
      forgive me.

For expecting you to be there for *me*
    though I am all too rarely there for *you*,
    Lord Jesus Christ,
    forgive me.

For so often going astray,
    clinging to what ultimately can never satisfy,
    Lord Jesus Christ,
    forgive me.

For doubting you when times are hard,
    questioning your ability to lead me safely through,
    Lord Jesus Christ,
    forgive me.

For reaching out only when I have need of you,
    failing to live each day in simple trust,
    quiet confidence and eager expectation,
    Lord Jesus Christ,
    forgive me.

For forgetting that though I let go of *you*,
    you will never let go of *me*,
    Lord Jesus Christ,
    forgive me.
Amen.

Music   Life of Christ, renew me from *River of Peace*
               (Margaret Rizza)

8
Betraying our calling

Music   Miserere nobis, Domine from *Awakening in Love* (Margaret Rizza)

Scripture   Lord God, great and awesome, faithful in your covenant and constant in love towards those who love you and honour your commandments, we have sinned and done wrong, wicked and rebellious in our actions, turning our backs on your commandments and instructions. We plead for mercy not because we have any merit, but recognising your great mercy. Hear, O Lord, and forgive. Listen and act.

Daniel 9:4, 5, 18b, 19a

From your dwelling place in heaven, listen to us, and when you hear, forgive. Hear us in heaven and forgive the people of Israel, your servants, their sins, teaching them instead the true way they should walk. Forgive, act and deal with all appropriately, for you alone know what goes on in human hearts.

1 Kings 8:30b, 36a, 39

Prayer   Lord of my life, have mercy I pray,
I've failed you again, abandoned your way.
My vows I've betrayed, commitment denied,
Intending to serve, I've strayed from your side.
Deal kindly I ask, redeem and renew,
See not what I've done, but all I *would* do.

Silence

Ultimately we will always be dependent on God's grace, his willingness to show mercy however little we deserve it, but that doesn't mean we can simply sit back and leave it all to him. We need to purge our lives, so far as we are able, of whatever gets in the way of faithful discipleship. The following prayer, inspired by the sight of wheelie bins lined up for collection, asks for God's help in doing just that:

They lined the streets,
    regiments of wheelie bins on their weekly parade,
    waiting to be relieved of their load
    and returned to duty.
Another day's work completed,
    another week's rubbish consigned to the tip.
An unglamorous business, perhaps,
    but as I watched the refuse lorry trundle on its way
    I asked myself where we'd be without it,
    what dirt, disease, stench and squalor
    would take hold
    had we no such simple service.

Lord, there's all kinds of rubbish in my life, too,
    emotional baggage and mental clutter
    that I should have discarded long ago
    but that I've allowed to build up inside,
    suffocating,
    scarring,
    polluting,
    poisoning.
Help me to recognise the litter in my life,
    the dross that disfigures and despoils,
    and teach me to dispose of it,
    before it disposes of me.
Amen.

Silence

Words next of St Francis of Assisi (1182–1226), moving
from acknowledgement of sin to a plea for renewal:

Almighty, eternal, just and merciful God,
> give us miserable ones the grace to do for you alone
> what we know you want us to do,
> and always to desire what pleases you.
Inwardly cleansed,
> interiorly enlightened and inflamed
> by the fire of the Holy Spirit,
> may we be able to follow
> in the footprints of your beloved Son,
> our Lord Jesus Christ,
> and, by your grace alone,
> may we make our way to you,
> Most High,
> who live and rule in perfect Trinity and simple Unity
> and are glorified,
> God almighty,
> for ever and ever.
Amen.

Silence

Final prayer Merciful God,
> I have done what I shouldn't have done,
> thought what I shouldn't have thought
> and said what I shouldn't have said.
In so much I have betrayed my calling.
Forgive me.

I have sinned against you and others,
> in thought, and word, and deed.
Greed, selfishness, pride and envy,
> together with carelessness in discipleship
> and shallowness of faith,
> leading me repeatedly to fail you.

In so much I have betrayed my calling.
Forgive me.

I long to serve you better,
    to live as a follower of Christ,
    but though my heart says one thing
    my body says another,
    the spirit willing but the flesh weak.
In so much I have betrayed my calling.
Forgive me.

Deal kindly with me through your grace
    and put a clean heart and right spirit within me.
Assure me of your forgiveness,
    renew me through your love,
    and help me to walk more faithfully
    in the days ahead,
    through Jesus Christ our Lord.
Amen.

Music   Miserere nobis, Domine from *Awakening in Love*
(Margaret Rizza)

9
Finding forgiveness

Music

O Lord, listen to my prayer from *Light in Our Darkness* (Margaret Rizza)

Scripture

While I remained silent, my body grew weary with my constant groaning, for day and night your hand weighed heavily upon me; my strength dried up like sap in the heat of summer. Then I acknowledged my sin and did not conceal my guilt from you; I said, 'I will confess my disobedience to the Lord,' and you absolved me from my guilt and sin. *Psalm 32:3-5*

If we claim that we do not sin, we are deceiving ourselves, and do not have the truth within us. If we confess our sins, God is faithful and just, and will not only forgive our sins but also cleanse us from all unworthiness. *1 John 1:8, 9*

Prayer

Lord, I come to worship, not because I should,
not to claim I'm worthy, virtuous or good,
not because I'm special, different from the crowd,
having any merit, reason to be proud –
Rather, I come humbly, conscious of my need,
knowing I've been faithless, false in word and deed.
Day by day I stumble, miss the goals I seek;
though I mean to serve you, inwardly I'm weak.
Lord, I can't deceive you, hide what's deep inside,
yet you bid me welcome, arms extended wide.
Gratefully I worship, coming not in fear,
but responding gladly, thankful to be here.
I will *try* to follow, walk the Christian way,
not because I have to, but because I may.

Silence

Undeserved mercy – if one thing sums up the Christian message, it is surely this. However much we fail him, God is ready to show forgiveness, not because we deserve it but because his nature is constantly to show love. That wonderful truth is taken up in the well-loved words of the hymn-writer Frederick C. Maker (1844–1927):

Beneath the cross of Jesus
I fain would take my stand,
the shadow of a mighty rock
within a weary land;
a home within a wilderness,
a rest upon the way,
from the burning heat at noontide
and the burden of the day.

Upon that cross of Jesus
mine eyes at times can see
the very dying form of One
who suffered there for me;
and from my stricken heart, with tears,
two wonders I confess –
the wonders of redeeming love,
and my unworthiness.

Silence

A prayer attributed to St Basil the Great (329–79) celebrates God's mercy and asks for help in responding to it:

O God and Lord of the Powers,
    and Maker of all creation,
    who, because of thy clemency
    and incomparable mercy,
    didst send your only-begotten Son
    and our Lord Jesus Christ

for the salvation of mankind,
and with his venerable cross
didst tear asunder the record of our sins,
and thereby didst conquer
the rulers and powers of darkness;
receive from us sinful people, O merciful Master,
these prayers of gratitude and supplication,
and deliver us
from every destructive and gloomy transgression,
and from all visible and invisible enemies
who seek to injure us.
Nail down our flesh with fear of you
and let not our hearts be inclined
to words or thoughts of evil,
but pierce our souls with thy love,
that ever contemplating you,
being enlightened by you
and discerning you,
the unapproachable and everlasting Light,
we may unceasingly render confession
and gratitude to you:
the eternal Father,
with your only-begotten Son,
and with your all-holy, gracious, and life-giving Spirit,
now and ever, and unto ages of ages.
Amen.

Silence

Final prayer   Can you forgive me, Lord?
I say you can,
   but in my heart I'm not sure,
   for I've failed you so often
   that I feel I must exhaust your patience,
   putting myself beyond your love.
Forgive me,
   and open my heart to your grace.

I acclaim you as a God of love,
   yet tend to see you instead
   as stern, angry, judgemental,
   reaching out to discipline and punish.
Forgive me,
   and open my heart to your grace.

Instead of celebrating the freedom you offer in Christ,
   I struggle instead with a burden of guilt,
   oppressed by the weight of past mistakes
   and present weakness.
Forgive me,
   and open my heart to your grace.

Lord, I want to honour you,
   and I will strive each day to love and serve you better,
   but remind me that you love me
   not for what I might become,
   but as I am.
Forgive me,
   and open my heart to your grace.
Amen.

Music   O Lord, listen to my prayer from *Light in Our Darkness* (Margaret Rizza)

10
Failure to live life to the full

Music   Kyrie, eleison (Mass of the Angels) from *Sublime Gregorian Chants*

Scripture   I have come that you might have life, and have it abundantly.   *John 10:10*

You prepare a table before me in the presence of my foes; you anoint my head with oil; my cup brims over.   *Psalm 23:5*

Prayer   Have I failed to live as I ought to,
to serve you as I should?
Have I flouted your will and denied you,
and turned my back on good?
Am I thoughtless, selfish and greedy,
concerned with self alone,
expecting the hungry and needy
to get by on their own?
The answer, Lord, hardly needs saying –
it all is true and more:
my life far too often displaying
mistakes I've made before.
But though such betrayals may grieve you,
they cause you hurt far less
than how often I undervalue
the ways you long to bless.
You offer me life overflowing,
more blessed than words can say.
Lord, help me to thank you by showing
how much it means, each day.

Silence

We talk often as Christians, don't we, of abundant, overflowing life, but what does it actually mean and do we even begin to live it? That's the theme of the following prayer:

It sounds so wonderful, Lord,
    so rich and replete with promise:
    life in all its fullness –
    abundant,
    overflowing.
But do I live in such a way as to show that,
    in a way that makes people sit up and take notice,
    desiring such life for themselves?
Is each day a celebration of your goodness,
    each moment a joyful response
    to the blessings you so freely bestow?
Or do people see in me instead a denial of life,
    a taking refuge in creed and doctrine,
    religion and ritual,
    retreating into the safe environment
    of church and fellowship
    rather than embracing all that is good in your world,
    the inestimable treasures it has to offer?
Forgive me, Lord,
    for I all too easily dwell on the pain, sorrow
    and evil of this world,
    forgetting that life is still your gift,
    fashioned by your hand and bearing your stamp;
    a bequest to be savoured, sanctified and celebrated.
Teach me to live in the world
    yet not be conformed to it,
    to affirm the best and challenge the worst,
    living each day,
    each moment,
    in joyful thanksgiving.
Teach me to anticipate your promise of life to come
    by consecrating life *now*
    and living it to your praise and glory.
In Christ's name I pray.
Amen.

Silence

Final prayer Does your life speak, above all, of celebration at everything God has given? Mine doesn't, or at least not as often as it should do. Finally, then, a prayer acknowledging our failure to appreciate what God has given and seeking his help for the future:

I've failed to appreciate the wonder of life, Lord,
  the beauty, variety and fascination
of this world you've made,
  offering so much to live for, enjoy and celebrate.
You have blessed me so richly;
  forgive me that I fail to respond as I should.

I've failed to appreciate the message of the gospel,
  the good news of your unfailing love,
  unchanging purpose and unending mercy.
You have blessed me so richly;
  forgive me that I fail to respond as I should.

I've failed to appreciate everything you've given,
  growing over-familiar and unmoved by it all,
  more concerned with what I don't have
  than what I do.
You have blessed me so richly,
  forgive me that I fail to respond as I should.

I've failed to appreciate the wonder of your love
  or the fullness of the life you promise –
  a gift not just for now but always,
  poured out, spilling over, abundant beyond words.
You have blessed me so richly;
  forgive me that I fail to respond as I should.

Teach me to celebrate each day,
  to rejoice in each moment,
  receiving and living life to the full,
  through Jesus Christ my Lord.
Amen.

Music   Kyrie, eleison (Mass of the Angels) from *Sublime Gregorian Chants*

11
Renewed, restored, forgiven

Music   Forgiveness from *Music for Quiet Prayer*

Scripture   Happy is the one whose mistakes are forgiven, whose faults are buried, and against whom the Lord imputes no sin.   *Psalm 32:1, 2a*

The Lord is merciful and gracious, abounding in steadfast love and not easily riled. He does not keep on accusing us or for ever nurse his anger, nor does he deal with us according to our sins or repay us for our mistakes. His unswerving love towards those that revere him is as great as the heavens are high above the earth; he banishes our faults from us as far as the east is from the west.   *Psalm 103:8-12*

Prayer   Praise, my soul, the King of heaven!
To his feet thy tribute bring;
ransomed, healed, restored, forgiven,
who like me his praise should sing?
Praise him! Praise him!
Praise him! Praise him!
Praise the everlasting King!

Praise him for his grace and favour
to our fathers in distress;
praise him, still the same for ever,
slow to chide and swift to bless.
Praise him! Praise him!
Praise him! Praise him!
Glorious in his faithfulness!

Father-like he tends and spares us;
well our feeble frame he knows;
in his hands he gently leads us,
rescues us from all our foes.
Praise him! Praise him!
Praise him! Praise him!
Widely as his mercy flows.

Silence

These words of praise from Henry Francis Lyte celebrate God's forgiveness, his willingness to restore and
forgive and so to wash us clean. It is precisely this
idea that lies behind the following reflective prayer.

I tried everything –
    rinsing, rubbing, soaking, scrubbing –
    but to no avail.
It was still there,
    an ugly stain,
    impossible to miss, hard to ignore.

The blots in my life, Lord, are equally unsightly,
    too many to number,
    too many to hide.
I strive in vain to remove them,
    to conquer their hold or conceal their presence,
    but try as I might they still show through,
    impossible to hide.
Take what I am, Lord –
    with all the dirt that sticks so closely,
    the ingrained grime that stains my soul –
    and by your grace, wash me
    and make me clean.
Amen.

Silence

An ancient prayer, written by St Gregory of Nyssa (died c. 385), celebrates that same renewing love:

Lord, from you flows true and continual kindness.
You had cast us off and justly so,
    but in your mercy you forgave us.
You were at odds with us,
    and you reconciled us.
You had set a curse on us,
    and you blessed us.
You had banished us from the garden,
    and you called us back again.
You took away the fig leaves
    that had been an unsuitable garment,
    and you clothed us in a cloak of great value.
You flung wide the prison gates,
    and you gave the condemned a pardon.
You sprinkled clean water on us,
    and you washed away the dirt.
Amen.

Silence

Final prayer Though we have no claim on your love,
        no right to expect mercy,
        you reach out to us in love,
        eager to forgive and forget.
Gracious God,
    renew us now.

Though we repeatedly fail you,
        selfishly and stubbornly resisting your will,
        you go on wiping the slate clean,
        offering us new beginnings,
        a fresh start.
Gracious God,
    renew us now.

Though we have been narrow in our horizons,
    weak in our commitment,
    careless in our worship
    and half-hearted in our service,
    still you are glad to call us your children.
Gracious God,
    renew us now.

Though we have been swift to complain
    and slow to thank you,
    taking your gifts for granted,
    taking *you* for granted,
    you continue to bless us,
    showering our lives with good things.
Gracious God,
    renew us now.
We ask it by the grace of Christ.
Amen.

Music   Forgiveness from *Music for Quiet Prayer*

12
A closed mind

Music   Confiteor from *Sublime Gregorian Chants*

Scripture   Oh how deep are the riches, wisdom and understanding of God – how far beyond us are his judgements and unfathomable his ways! 'Who has figured out the Lord's mind, or been his adviser?' 'Who has offered him gift deserving repayment?'

Romans 11:33-35

I pray for this . . . that Christ may so dwell in your hearts through faith that you will be able to grasp with all the saints the breadth, length, height and depth of the love of Christ; and that you may know this all-surpassing love in such a way that you will be filled with the very fullness of God!

Ephesians 3:14a, 17-19

Prayer   We limit not the truth of God
to our poor reach of mind,
by notions of our day and sect,
crude, partial and confined.
No, let a new and better hope
within our hearts be stirred:
the Lord has yet more light and truth
to break forth from his word.

Who dares to bind to his dull sense
the oracles of heaven,
for all the nations, tongues, and climes,
and all the ages given?

That universe, how much unknown!
That ocean unexplored!
The Lord has yet more light and truth
to break forth from his word.

Silence

Those words of the hymn-writer George Rawson (1807–89) remind us of the danger of closing our minds to what we'd rather not hear, imagining we know all there is to know. As I stood outside a locked door the other day, I was reminded of how often and easily we do that:

It wasn't just closed,
    it was locked and bolted,
    an impenetrable barrier denying access,
    ensuring intruders were kept at bay.

I like to think, Lord, that I'm different,
    friendly, receptive and welcoming,
    even to outsiders . . .
    but I'm not.
All too often the shutters go up
    when my view of the world is questioned,
    my mind closed to customs and convictions
    that threaten my own.
Forgive me,
    and instead of automatically locking the door,
    teach me to open it to others,
    recognising that you may speak through their words,
    teach through their insights
    and meet me through their presence.
Amen.

Silence

Lord, I know that I have failed you,
too familiar with your word –
even though you've spoken clearly
all too often I've not heard.
Closed to truths which stretch horizons
or which go against the grain –
help me, Lord, to stop and listen,
give me grace to start again.

Silence

The following prayer, its source unknown, reminds us of just some of the ways we close our minds against God and those around us.

Our insensitivity to the needs of others,
O Lord, forgive.

Our prejudice and fear that prevent us from loving,
O Lord, forgive.

The narrowness of our vision and our shrinking from your demands,
O Lord, forgive.

Our resentment against those who have hurt us,
O Lord, forgive.

Our desire to do your work in our way,
O Lord, forgive.

Our impatience with those who are different from us,
O Lord, forgive.

Our failure to listen properly to other points of view,
O Lord, forgive.

Our fear of coming out of the fortress
of our own souls into fuller life and deeper love,
O Lord, forgive.
Amen.

Silence

Final prayer   Gracious God,
you speak in all kinds of ways,
through all kinds of people,
but I am sometimes closed to what you have to say,
avoiding that which challenges
my comfortable complacency.
Forgive me for shutting my ears
to what I don't agree with,
for being so sure of what is right
and so set in my ways
that I resent anything unfamiliar
that questions or disturbs the status quo.
Open my mind to your presence,
your word, your truth,
through Jesus Christ my Lord.
Amen.

Music   Confiteor from *Sublime Gregorian Chants*

13
Inward-looking faith

Music   Change my heart, O God from *Music for Quiet Prayer*

Scripture   It is more blessed to give than to receive.

Acts 20:35

I tell you the truth, whenever you offered service to
the least of individuals you offered it also to me.

Matthew 25:40

Silence

Prayer   I'm not an angel, nowhere near,
I often go astray,
but though my faults are all too clear
I *try*, Lord, to obey.
Avoid what's evil, strive for good,
that's been my daily aim –
to live the sort of life I should
in keeping with your name.
But now I see that this alone
can never fully do;
instead, it's how much love I've shown
that matters most to you:
If, when I saw a friend in need,
a person in despair,
I paid their plight sufficient heed,
enough to show I care.
My times of worship, hymns and prayers,
each have their part to play,
but only if my life declares
the truth of what I say;

if what I am and what I do
stays faithful to your call,
in showing love not just to *you*
but equally to all.

Silence

Who is your faith all about – you or others? A signifi-
cant strand of biblical teaching, emphasised by Jesus
himself, suggests that true love of God shows itself in
love of others, and that a commitment turned in on
itself is in danger of being no commitment at all. The
following prayer acknowledges how hard we find it to
deny ourselves and think rather of others:

I'm good at giving, Lord . . . in theory.
I thought, only the other day,
    how wonderful it would be to make a difference:
    to bring hope to the poor,
    food to the hungry,
    medicine to the sick
    and shelter to the homeless; and I resolved,
    as soon as the bank balance could stand it,
    to do something to make it happen –
    to give, and give generously.
I thought of other things besides money –
    of giving my time to write to someone,
    ring them, visit;
    my skills to help others, serve the Church,
    contribute towards the community;
    my energy to share someone's load,
    support a cause,
    advance the growth of your kingdom –
    only each remained just a thought,
    a good intention,
    time somehow always too short,
    skills already called on,
    energies turned inwards rather than outwards.

Forgive me, Lord,
   for I've deprived not just others but myself too,
   each one of us the loser.
I intended much, but achieved little,
   saw the need but failed to respond,
   so wrapped up in self
   that what I thought I possessed
   now in fact possesses me.
Teach me to recognise the joy of giving,
   the privilege of sharing,
   the fulfilment that comes through letting go,
   and so help me, in my own small way,
   to offer something to others
   in grateful response to you
   who offered so much for me.
Amen.

Silence

Words now of William Walsham Howe (1823–97),
acknowledging a failure to look outwards and asking
God to help him change:

Most merciful Father,
   I confess that I have done little
   to promote your kingdom
   and advance your glory.
Pardon my shortcomings
   and give me greater enthusiasm in serving you.
Make me more ready and conscientious by my prayers,
   my giving and my example,
   to spread the knowledge of your truth
   and extend your kingdom;
   and may I do everything to your glory.
Amen.

Silence

Final prayer
For speaking of serving you and others,
    but ultimately serving only myself,
    Loving God,
    forgive me.

For being more concerned
    with what I can get out of my faith
    than what I put into it,
    more concerned with what you can do for *me*
    than with what *I* can do for *you*,
    Loving God,
    forgive me.

For being so concerned with my own affairs,
    welfare and pleasure
    that I've ignored the needs of those around me,
    Loving God,
    forgive me.

For the love I've failed to show,
    care failed to express,
    support failed to give
    and pardon failed to offer,
    Loving God,
    forgive me.

Teach me to look outwards rather than inwards,
    seeking the good of others before my own
    and your glory above all.
Teach me to let go of self,
    that I may find true fulfilment in Christ.
Amen.

Music
Change my heart, O God from *Music for Quiet Prayer*

14
Failure to love

Music   It is a thing most wonderful – *Our Favourite Hymns 1*

Scripture   You shall love the Lord your God with your entire heart, soul, mind and strength . . . and love your neighbour as yourself.   *Mark 12:30, 31*

If I speak in the tongues of ordinary people or of angels, but do not have love, I am nothing more than a blaring trumpet or a clashing cymbal.

1 Corinthians 13:1

Prayer   I try so hard to love, Lord,
to reach out in your name;
to know the worst in people
but cherish them the same.
I strive to show compassion,
to show I really care –
yet measured by your goodness
such love cannot compare.
For what I give is partial,
a prize that must be earned;
its constancy dependent
on whether it's returned.
The love you give, in contrast,
is free and unreserved;
poured out with no restrictions,
although it's undeserved.
Lord, come and work within me,
transform my heart of stone,
until the love I offer
grows closer to your own.

Silence

Discipleship without love is like a meal without seasoning; an idea developed in the following reflective prayer:

They ate dutifully enough,
   smiling politely
   and making the odd appreciative noise,
   but I knew they were enjoying it no more than I was.
The meal was bland,
   all but tasteless,
   and with good reason,
   for I'd forgotten to add seasoning –
   so small an ingredient,
   so large an effect.

Forgive me, Lord, for the insipid fare I offer you,
   looking the part,
   and with so many of the components right,
   yet lacking the one thing needful:
   the savour of love.
Teach me that the poorest of dishes
   with that one vital ingredient
   is worth far more than the finest of feasts without it.
Amen.

Silence

Next a prayer of St Augustine of Hippo (354–430) in which he brings to God the weakness of his love and asks him to deepen it:

Give me yourself, O my God,
   give yourself to me.
Behold I love you,
   and if my love is too weak a thing,
   grant me to love you more strongly.

I cannot measure my love
    to know how much it falls short of being sufficient,
    but let my soul hasten to your embrace
    and never be turned away until it is hidden
    in the secret shelter of your presence.
This only do I know,
    that it is not good for me when you are not with me,
    when you are only outside me.
I want you in my very self.
All the plenty in the world which is not my God
    is utter want.
Amen.

Silence

Final prayer
For speaking so easily of love,
    yet so rarely actually loving,
    Lord,
    have mercy.

For everything in my life that denies your love –
    angry words and unkind comments,
    thoughtless words and careless deeds –
    Lord,
    have mercy.

For reserving my love for the exclusive few –
    family and friends –
    Lord,
    have mercy.

For loving myself beyond all others,
    putting me first and you second,
    Lord,
    have mercy.

Take the little love I have,
 and nurture, deepen and expand it,
 until I have learned what love really means,
 until your love flows through my heart,
 until your love is all in all.
Lord,
 have mercy.
Amen.

Music   It is a thing most wonderful from *Our Favourite Hymns 1*

15
Temptation

Music   All we, like sheep from *Messiah* (Handel)

Scripture   Search me, O God, and know my heart. Test me and know my thoughts. Look to see if there is any wickedness within me, and lead me in your everlasting way.
Psalm 139:23, 24

You know my folly, O God; there can be no hiding my wrongs from you. I have wandered astray like a lost sheep. *Psalm 69:5; 119:176a*

Prayer   Going astray like sheep – it's an image picked up in a prayer by St Jerome (331–420):

O Lord, show your mercy to me
   and gladden my heart.
I am like the man on the way to Jericho
   who was overtaken by robbers,
   wounded and left for dead.
O Good Samaritan,
   come to my aid.
I am like the sheep that went astray.
O Good Shepherd,
   seek me out and bring me home
   in accord with your will.
Let me dwell in your house
   all the days of my life
   and praise you for ever and ever
   with those who are there.
Amen.

Silence

Can God forgive us as we repeatedly give in to temptation? That's the question posed in a poem by the Elizabethan writer John Donne (1573–1631):

Wilt thou forgive that sin where I begun,
Which was my sin, though it were done before?
Wilt thou forgive that sin through which I run,
And do run still, though still I do deplore?
When thou hast done, thou hast not done;
    For I have more.

Wilt thou forgive that sin which I have won
Others to sin, and made my sins their door?
Wilt thou forgive that sin which I did shun
A year or two, but wallow'd in a score?
When thou hast done, thou hast not done;
    For I have more.

I have a sin of fear, that when I've spun
My last thread, I shall perish on the shore;
But swear by thyself that at my death thy Son
Shall shine as he shines now and heretofore:
And having done that, Thou hast done;
    I fear no more.

Silence

Temptation's a strange thing, isn't it? We resolve to resist it, and occasionally succeed, yet time and again, as the following reflective prayer highlights, we're drawn to it like a moth to a candle:

It fluttered around the flame,
    inexorably drawn –
    surely sensing the danger,
    yet unable to resist –
    and it was only a matter of time
    before its wings were scorched,
    and the hapless creature fell.

Like the moth, Lord,
    I too am attracted by what destroys,
    promising life yet delivering death.
I try to fight it,
    aware of the danger,
    but the lure is too strong,
    all sense forgotten when temptation strikes.
Draw me close to you,
    the true light,
    and shine in my darkness,
    bringing life indeed.
Amen.

Silence

Finally, then, a prayer asking for help from the one who understands our temptations, offers forgiveness, and helps us to begin again:

Lord Jesus Christ,
    forgive me
    that I find it so much harder than you did
    to resist temptation,
    the spirit willing but the flesh weak.
Have mercy,
    and help me to walk your way.

Forgive me that all my resolve
    can be undermined in just a few seconds,
    temptation time and again catching me unawares,
    so that I go astray again,
    indulging my desires,
    ignoring your will,
    excusing what I know to be inexcusable.
Have mercy,
    and help me to walk your way.

Renew and refashion me in your image,
    so that when temptation strikes
    I will have sufficient strength to say no.
Touch my heart and put a right spirit within me,
    that I may stay true to you, as you stay true to me.
Have mercy,
    and help me to walk your way.
Amen.

Music   All we, like sheep from *Messiah* (Handel)

16
Undeserved mercy

Music Amazing grace from *Our Favourite Hymns 1*

Scripture If you, Lord, were to keep an account of our sins, which of us could lift up our head before you? In you, though, is forgiveness, and consequently you are worshipped. *Psalm 130:3, 4*

God demonstrated his love for us like this: through Christ offering his life for us even though our lives were steeped in wrongdoing. *Romans 5:8*

Prayer I have no claim on your love at all,
no grounds to seek clemency;
I mean to serve, but repeatedly fall,
my faithlessness plain to see.
The vows I've made, the faith I've professed
all seem to have been in vain,
as faults and flaws so often confessed
return to haunt me again.
You see the worst, all my ugliness,
all that poisons deep inside,
but still you love, always eager to bless,
refusing to be denied.
No words, O Lord, can begin to say
how much I will always owe;
no sacrifice even start to repay
the mercy and grace you show.
I give you thanks, bring my all to you,
amazed that such love can be –
so rich and full, so constant and true,
so priceless and yet so free.

Silence

If we have eyes to see, the ordinary things of life can point to Christ. Take, for example, a credit card statement:

It was there in black and white,
    chilling,
    inescapable.
He'd spent more than he realised,
    more than he could afford,
    and was left now with a debt round his neck,
    an amount owing that would take months,
    even years, to repay.

Lord, I can never earn your love,
    still less repay your goodness towards me,
    but you do not ask me to.
You have cancelled the debt,
    writing it off as though it had never been.
Though I owe so much,
    you ask me simply to receive.
Though I deserve so little,
    you offer new life in Christ,
    free and overflowing.
For the awesome generosity of your gift,
    Lord, I thank you.
Amen.

Silence

To who or what can we compare the merciful love of Christ? St Anselm (1033–1109) found the answer in a mother's love for her children:

Jesus, as a mother you gather your people to you:
    you are gentle with us as a mother with her children;
    often you weep over our sins and our pride:
    tenderly you draw us from hatred and judgement.

You comfort us in sorrow and bind up our wounds:
   in sickness you nurse us,
    and with pure milk you feed us.
Jesus, by your dying we are born to new life:
   by your anguish and labour we come forth in joy.
Despair turns to hope through your sweet goodness:
   through your gentleness we find comfort in fear.
Your warmth gives life to the dead:
   your touch makes sinners righteous.
Lord Jesus, in your mercy heal us:
   in your love and tenderness remake us.
In your compassion bring grace and forgiveness:
   for the beauty of heaven may your love prepare us.
Amen.

Silence

Final prayer   Almighty God,
   I have no claim on your goodness,
   no reason to expect your mercy
   for I repeatedly fail you,
   preferring my way to yours.
I depend on your grace –
   forgive me, I pray.

I say one thing, yet do another.
   declare allegiance, yet openly flout your will.
Try as I might I cannot help myself.
I depend on your grace –
   forgive me, I pray.

Time and again I throw love back in your face,
   taking your goodness for granted,
   ignoring your guidance.
I depend on your grace –
   forgive me, I pray.

Restore me through your Spirit,
  redeem me in Christ,
  remake me through your great love,
  so that I may live and work for you,
  to the glory of your name.
I depend on your grace –
  forgive me, I pray.
Amen.

Music   Amazing grace from *Our Favourite Hymns 1*

17
Hollow discipleship

Music   Kyries from *Sacred Weave* (Keith Duke)

Scripture   Do not recollect my former mistakes and wrongdoings,
Lord, but, in your unfailing love and great goodness,
remember *me* instead.   *Psalm 25:7*

These people honour me with their words, but are
estranged from me in their hearts.   *Matthew 15:8*

Prayer   For turning faith to outer show,
to what I say and do,
my focus more on what I know
than truly knowing *you*;
for all the ways my faith is flawed
and understanding skewed,
I ask your pardon, gracious Lord,
and beg to be renewed.

Silence

New life, new beginnings, new meaning, new hope –
we make great claims about life in Christ, don't we – but
do our lives testify to the truth of them? I found myself
asking that one day as I watched advertisements on
television, and the following reflective prayer was the
result:

It was laughable,
    the claims more exaggerated by the day:
    new,
    enhanced,

improved;
the most advanced formula ever,
the finest and fastest of its kind;
great value,
great quality,
great everything –
quite simply, the best that money can buy.

Lord, I too make extravagant claims –
about the way you've changed my life,
the person you've helped me become,
and the life you've called me to lead.
Forgive me when the walk denies the talk,
what people see in me
leading them to dismiss the faith I profess
as empty hype,
more spin than substance.
Work within me,
so that who I am
may more closely resemble who you want me to be.
Amen.

Silence

Of all the prayers written on the theme of penitence,
few can have been used more often than the following,
taken from the *Book of Common Prayer*. It expresses
beautifully the gulf between what we long to be and
what we are:

Almighty and most merciful Father;
we have erred, and strayed from thy ways
like lost sheep.
We have followed too much
the devices and desires of our own hearts.
We have offended against thy holy laws.

We have left undone
   those things which we ought to have done;
   and we have done those things
   which we ought not to have done;
   and there is no health in us.
But thou, O Lord,
   have mercy upon us, miserable offenders.
Spare thou them, O God, which confess their faults.
Restore thou them that are penitent;
   according to thy promises
   declared unto mankind in Christ Jesu our Lord.
And grant, O most merciful Father, for his sake;
   that we may hereafter
   live a godly, righteous, and sober life,
   to the glory of thy holy Name.
Amen.

Silence

Final prayer   For concerning myself with outer appearance
   rather than inner reality,
   fooling myself that all is well
   when in my heart I know much is wrong,
   have mercy, Lord,
   and deepen my faith.

For turning discipleship into something I do
   rather than something I am,
   a theory to learn
   rather than way of life to put into practice,
   have mercy, Lord,
   and deepen my faith.

For being conscious of my faults,
   aware of my weaknesses,
   yet running from the truth, afraid to face the facts,

have mercy, Lord,
and deepen my faith.

For settling for superficial discipleship,
    what I know to be a veneer,
    affecting part of my life
    but leaving most of it untouched,
    have mercy, Lord,
and deepen my faith.

Help me truly to love and know you,
    so that my commitment may not simply be skin deep,
    but offered with body, mind and soul,
    to the glory of your name.
Amen.

Music   Kyries from *Sacred Weave* (Keith Duke)

18
A plea for forgiveness

Music   Dear Lord and Father of mankind from *Our Favourite Hymns 1*

Scripture   I lift up my voice to the Lord; crying out to him for mercy. Listen to my pleas for mercy, Lord, and in your faithfulness and righteousness, respond to my appeal.
Psalm 142:1; 143:1

From the depths of despair I call out to you, Lord! Hear my voice, I beg you, and listen to my cry as I plead for mercy! *Psalm 130:1, 2*

Prayer   Dear Lord and Father of mankind,
forgive our foolish ways!
Reclothe us in our rightful mind,
in purer lives thy service find,
in deeper reverence praise,
in deeper reverence praise.

Drop thy still dews of quietness,
till all our strivings cease;
take from our souls the strain and stress,
and let our ordered lives confess
the beauty of thy peace,
the beauty of thy peace.

Breathe through the heats of our desire
thy coolness and thy balm;
let sense be dumb, let flesh retire,
speak through the earthquake, wind and fire,
O still small voice of calm!
O still small voice of calm!

Silence

Next, part of a prayer by the theologian Karl Rahner (1904–84), which, as well as acknowledging faults, declares faith and hope in God's assurance of mercy:

I know that there is only one thing that I can say to you:
   have mercy on me.
I need your mercy, because I am a sinner.
I am unworthy of your mercy, because I am a sinner.
But I humbly desire your unfailing mercy,
   for I am a being of this world, not yet lost;
     one who still longs for the heavens of your goodness,
   who willingly and with tears of joy
     receives the inexhaustible gift of your mercy.
Amen.

Silence

Next, a prayer by the celebrated English writer John Donne (1573–1631), asking for God's discipline as a means towards changing his life for the better:

O think me worth thine anger, punish me,
burn off my rusts and my deformity,
restore thine image so much, by thy grace,
that thou mayest know me, and I'll turn my face.

Silence

Final prayer   For failing you time and again,
     Lord,
       forgive me.

For failing to change,
 making the same old mistakes
 despite my resolve to do otherwise,
 Lord,
 forgive me.

For failing to grow in faith,
 being casual or complacent,
 Lord,
 forgive me.

For failing to love you or others,
 too often having time only for myself,
 Lord,
 forgive me.

For failing to appreciate your goodness,
 the wonder of all you have done,
 Lord,
 forgive me.

For failing to respond to your call,
 to faith, to life, to service,
 Lord,
 forgive me.

For failing to trust in your grace,
 doubting your willingness always to show mercy,
 Lord,
 forgive me.

For all the ways I fail you,
 despite your constancy to me,
 Lord,
 forgive me.
Amen.

Music   Dear Lord and Father of mankind from *Our Favourite Hymns 1*

19
Starting again

Music   And he shall purify from *Messiah* (Handel)

Scripture   Create in me a clean heart, O God, and renew a right spirit within me. Cast me not away from your presence, and take not your Holy Spirit from me. Restore to me the joy of your salvation, and uphold me with a willing spirit.   *Psalm 51:10-12*

Sprinkle me with hyssop, and I will be clean; wash me, and I will become whiter than snow. Hide your face from my wrongdoings, and expunge from the record all my faults.   *Psalm 51:7, 9*

Prayer   Lord forgive me, I am weak,
seldom do the things I seek,
rarely serve you as I should –
wrong prevails instead of good.
By your grace come make me whole –
mind and body, heart and soul.
where I'm false help me be true,
wash me clean and make me new.

Silence

What's done cannot be undone, we sometimes say, and sadly that's often true. Mistakes leave a legacy of hurt, guilt and disappointment, which can be hard, if not impossible, to overcome. The message of the gospel, however, is that God does not hold our mistakes against us, but puts them behind us as though they never were. The following reflective prayer, inspired by a game of chess, brings home the contrast:

I spotted the mistake almost immediately,
    but it was too late to do anything about it,
    for the move was made
    and the damage done.
There could be no turning the clock back
    and trying again,
    no second chance or court of appeal.
I'd blundered,
    and had to face the consequences,
    salvaging the situation as best I could.

So easily, Lord, I act in haste
    and live to regret it,
    errors of judgement
    having repercussions I never considered,
    affecting not just me but others too.
And, much though I wish it were otherwise,
    I too can't put the clock back,
    undoing what's once been done.
Yet *you*, Lord, *do* give a second chance,
    ready to put my mistakes behind me,
    as though they have never been.
Teach me, in all I do, to think first,
    considering where it might lead;
    and, when I get things wrong
    as I so often do,
    forgive me,
    and help me to start again.
Amen.

Silence

Next a prayer by the nineteenth-century scholar and clergyman Charles Vaughan; words that remind us God is ready to forgive and forget so long as we are prepared honestly and openly to admit our need of him:

O Lord God, our Father most loving,
  we would not, even if we could,
  conceal anything from you
  but rejoice rather that you know us as we are
  and see every desire and every motive of our hearts.
Help us, Lord, to strip off every mask and veil
  when we come into your presence,
  and to spread before you every thought
  and every secret of our being,
  that they may be forgiven, purified, amended,
  and blessed by you,
  through Jesus Christ our Lord.
Amen.

Silence

Final prayer   Merciful God,
  I thank you that, unlike me,
  you don't dwell on past failures,
  but are always ready to offer a fresh start.
Forgive what I am,
  and direct what I shall be.

I thank you I can acknowledge my mistakes
  openly before you,
  receive your pardon
  and then move on.
Forgive what I am,
  and direct what I shall be.

Teach me to accept your offer for what it is,
  and to rejoice in your mercy
  rather than wallow in guilt.

Forgive what I am,
   and direct what I shall be.

Help me not simply to *talk* about new life
   but to live it joyfully,
   receiving each moment as your gracious gift,
   and celebrating your cleansing, redeeming love.
Forgive what I am,
   and direct what I shall be.
In Christ's name I pray.
Amen.

Music   And he shall purify from *Messiah* (Handel)

20
True repentance

Music O bone Jesu (Marc Antonio Ingegneri) from *Latin Choral Classics*

Scripture Be merciful to me, O God. Through your constant love and overflowing mercy, obliterate my transgressions. Wash away my faults and purify me from my sins, for I am all too aware of my mistakes and my weakness daily stares me in the face.   *Psalm 51:1-3*

I admit my faults and am truly sorry for my sin.
                                                   Psalm 38:18

Prayer It's one thing to acknowledge our mistakes and ask for forgiveness, another to really mean it. How real is the confession we make to God? The following prayer was inspired by an apology:

She didn't find it easy, I could see that,
  words not just hard to find
  but harder still to say.
Yet she'd done wrong
  and was truly sorry,
  had made a mistake
  and wanted to make amends;
  the apology, if not the most gracious,
  nonetheless sincere,
  straight from the heart.

I've no problem saying sorry to *you*, Lord –
  I do it all the time –
  but unless my apologies are real,
  backed up by genuine remorse
  and a true desire to change,

they mean nothing –
all just empty words.
Teach me not just to *say* sorry,
   but to mean it.
Amen.

Silence

Not just to *say* sorry but to mean it – what does that actually involve? Above all, it requires a genuine desire to change, to make amends by avoiding the same mistake in the future. If you're like me though, you confess something one moment only to find yourself doing it again the next. The following prayer asks for help in being *truly* sorry:

I still haven't learned, Lord, have I?
I've made progress –
   a little anyway –
   recognising and confessing my faults,
   but that's about as far as it goes.
Though I've *said* sorry,
   I've not actually *shown* it –
   neither to you nor to others –
   and, to my shame, I've scarcely even tried.
I thought words were all it took,
   one simple expression of regret
   sufficient to put things right,
   but I realise now
   that pious sentiments are not enough,
   exposed as hollow,
   empty,
   meaningless,
   unless there's something more solid
   to back them up,
   some attempt to mend my ways,
   live differently,

correct what I know to be wrong.
I may not succeed in that –
    not even get anywhere close –
    but unless I at least attempt to change
    I can say sorry as often as I like
    and few will take notice,
    for though my lips will say one thing,
    my life will profess another.
Teach me, then, not just to confess my faults
    but also to strive, as far as it lies within me,
    to overcome them;
    to express remorse not just in words but in deeds.
Teach me to *be* sorry,
    in the name of Christ.
Amen.

Silence

A narrowness of vision can ultimately shut out not
just others but God as well, as recognised by St
Augustine of Hippo:

O God, the Light of the heart that sees you,
    the Life of the soul that loves you,
    the Strength of the mind that seeks you:
    may I ever continue to be steadfast in your love.
Be the joy of my heart;
    take all of me to yourself, and abide therein.
The house of my soul is, I confess,
    too narrow for you.
Enlarge it that you may enter.
It is ruinous, but do repair it.
It has within it what must offend your eyes;
    I confess and know it,
    but whose help shall I seek in cleansing it
    but yours alone?
To you, O God, I cry urgently.

Cleanse me from secret faults.
Keep me from false pride and sensuality
   that they do not get dominion over me.
Amen.

Silence

Final prayer   Time after time, Lord, I acknowledge my sins,
       only to make the same mistakes,
       display the same weaknesses,
       all over again.
Help me not just to *say* sorry,
  but to mean it.

I tell you I'm sorry,
    but my actions belie my words,
    for when temptation next strikes I swiftly yield,
    making little if any attempt to stand firm.
Help me not just to *say* sorry,
  but to mean it.

I talk of remorse and penitence,
    but am blasé about my faults,
    telling myself that whatever I do wrong
    you're bound to forgive it.
Help me not just to *say* sorry,
  but to mean it.

I bring you my confession, Lord,
    flawed though it may be,
    for I would truly know, love and serve you better.
Help me not just to *say* sorry,
but to mean it.
Amen.

Music   O bone Jesu (Marc Antonio Ingegneri) from *Latin Choral Classics*

EXPRESSING OUR THANKS

1
For God's strength and help

Music   In God alone my soul is at rest from *Light in Our Darkness* (Margaret Rizza)

Scripture   The Lord is my strength and shield; I trust in him with all my heart and so am sustained. My heart sings for joy within me as I give thanks to him.
Psalm 28:7

Come what may, we can confidently say, 'The Lord is my helper, I will not be afraid. What can anyone do to me?'
Hebrews 13:6

Prayer   Lord, you don't promise us comfort and wealth,
freedom from sickness, immaculate health;
faith brings no pledge of exemption from pain,
troubles oppress us again and again.
Tragedies cause us to grieve and despair,
sometimes their burden too painful to bear.
Visions are shattered and hopes turned to dust,
prayer seems in vain, though we try still to trust.
Yet, though such trials turn out to be true,
still I believe you will help me get through –
there by my side when I can't carry on,
offering strength when all other has gone.
Even in sorrow you somehow bring joy,
peace that no trials can ever destroy.
Light in the darkness continues to shine,
turning the water of life into wine.

Silence

In the storms of life, God is there to defend us, in
much the same way, as the following prayer explores,
that a sea wall holds back the wind and waves:

It had taking a pounding,
    day after day,
    year after year,
    the mighty sea relentlessly renewing its attack
    as wave after wave hurled itself against the wall
    and exploded in a cloud of spray.
Yet still it stood,
    solid and defiant,
    a massive bulwark guarding the town beyond.

Thank you, Lord, for guarding me,
    faithfully providing shelter and protection
    when storms brew
    and waves threaten to sweep me away.
Thank you for the strength of your love
    and certainty of your promise,
    the knowledge that though all else may pass away
    your goodness will continue,
    solid and secure in an ever-changing universe.
Whatever I face, I will not fear,
    for you are with me,
    the same yesterday, today and for ever.
Amen.

Silence

This prayer of St Augustine of Hippo (354–430)
wonderfully expresses faith in God's constancy; a faith
we in turn can share:

O God, who so cares for every one of us
    as if you cared for each one alone;
    and so for all, as if all were but as one,

you are the Life of our lives,
  you are constant through all change.
Blessed are all who love you.
Amen.

Silence

Final prayer For the many ways you've been with me
    across the years,
    equipping,
    enabling,
    supporting,
    sustaining –
    living Lord,
    receive my thanks.

For the knowledge that you're with me now,
    ready to strengthen in times of crisis,
    guide in times of uncertainty,
    hold in times of sorrow
    and provide in times of challenge –
    living Lord,
    receive my thanks.

For the assurance that you'll never let me go –
    that whatever the future may hold
    you will be there to meet my needs,
    renewing,
    redeeming,
    restoring –
    living Lord,
    receive my thanks.
Amen.

Music In God alone my soul is at rest from *Light in Our Darkness* (Margaret Rizza)

2
For God's eternal purpose

Music   Jesus, you are the way from *Fountain of Life*
              (Margaret Rizza)

Scripture   I will offer you thanks, Lord, with all my heart; I will
                  tell everyone of your mighty acts; I will exult and be
                  glad in you.   *Psalm 9:1, 2a*

                  I will give you thanks always, because of the things
                  you have done. In the presence of your people I will
                  honour your name, for it is good.   *Psalm 52:9*

Prayer   God is working his purpose out
                   as year succeeds to year.
               God is working his purpose out,
                   and the time is drawing near;
               nearer and nearer draws the time,
                   the time that shall surely be,
               when the earth shall be filled with the glory of God
                   as the waters cover the sea.

               Silence

               That faith in God's purpose expressed by the Anglican
               vicar and hymn-writer Arthur Campbell Ainger
               (1841–1919) must have taken a bit of a battering in the
               last years of his life which were to see unfolding the
               horrors of the First World War. For us too it can be
               hard to keep believing, yet at the heart of our faith is
               the conviction that God's purpose will finally triumph,
               despite all that conspires against it. We are part not

just of the here and now but of God's eternity, as
explored in the following reflective prayer, called simply
'The dinosaur bones':

They were ancient,
    a reminder of life forms that walked the earth
    not just centuries
    but aeons ago –
    masters for millions of years of all they surveyed –
    the whole of human history, by comparison,
    just a tiny speck,
    a mere drop in the ocean.
Yet now they are gone,
    the only clue to their existence a few fossil remains,
    silent witness to a bygone age.

You alone, Lord, are eternal,
    the same yesterday, today and tomorrow.
You alone are before and beyond all,
    the beginning and end of everything that is,
    has been
    and shall be.
Yet you invite us,
    seemingly here today and gone tomorrow –
    like flowers fleetingly in bloom –
    to share in eternity,
    one with you for evermore.
For the breadth of your purpose
    and wonder of your grace,
    Lord, thank you.
Amen.

Silence

Next, a prayer of Augustine of Hippo (354–430),
reminding us that the same God who brought the

universe into being is concerned with each and every
individual:

Thanks be to you,
    O Creator and governor of the universe,
    for my well-being through the years
      since I arrived at birth.
Thanks be to you, my joy, my confidence, my God,
    for the gifts by which you have preserved me
    and enabled me to grow.
Amen.

Silence

Final prayer   For being a God I can depend on,
    always faithful,
    always true,
    always loving,
    always merciful,
    Lord of all,
    I thank you.

For the way you are constantly at work in my life,
    day after day,
    week after week,
    and year after year leading me
    into new experiences of your love,
    Lord of all,
    I thank you.

For your work across history,
    calling, prompting,
    teaching, leading,
    redeeming and renewing,
    Lord of all,
    I thank you.

For the purpose I'm privileged to be a part of,
    proclaimed by prophets,
    fulfilled in Christ,
    celebrated by countless generations,
    Lord of all,
    I thank you.

For the sense of purpose
    you've brought to me personally,
    the way your love, joy, peace, strength and hope
    have brought shape, meaning and direction
    to my life,
    Lord of all,
    I thank you.

For the knowledge that nothing finally
    can deny your purpose –
    that though my plans come to nothing,
    and heaven and earth pass away,
    your kingdom endures for ever –
    Lord of all,
    I thank you.
Amen.

Music   Jesus, you are the way from *Fountain of Life*
(Margaret Rizza)

3
For the joy of life

Music
Jesu, joy of man's desiring (J. S. Bach) from *Wings of a Dove*, sung by Hannah Mayhew

Scripture
You have turned my tears into dancing; you have removed sackcloth from me and clothed me instead with joy, such that I sing your praises and cannot be silent. Lord God, I will always thank you!
Psalm 30:11, 12

I am contented deep within, like someone who has enjoyed a sumptuous meal. When I lie awake at night, reflecting during the hours of darkness over all you have done, my mouth worships you, songs of joy on my lips, for you have helped me, encircling me in the shadow of your wings. *Psalm 63:5-7*

Prayer
Lord, we thank thee for the pleasure
that our happy lifetime gives,
for the boundless worth and treasure
of a soul that ever lives;
mind that looks before and after,
lifting eyes to things above;
human tears, and human laughter,
and the depths of human love.

For the thrill, the leap, the gladness
of our pulses flowing free;
e'en for every touch of sadness
that may bring us nearer thee;
but, above all other kindness,
thine unutterable love,
which, to heal our sin and blindness,
sent thy dear Son from above.

Teach us so our days to number
that we may be early wise;
dreamy mist, or cloud, or slumber,
never dull our heavenward eyes.
Hearty be our work and willing,
as to thee, and not to men:
for we know our soul's fulfilling
is in heaven, and not till then.

Silence

Those words of the hymn-writer T. W. Jex-Blake
(1832–1915), together with those of the Psalms before,
remind us of the joy at the heart of our faith; a joy
rooted in both life now and life to come. It is a theme
picked up in the following simple prayer of the
Carmelite Monastery, Quidenham:

O God, I know you love me!
My heart is all joy
    because of what you have done for me.
How good you have been to me, O God most high;
    in my joy I shall sing and delight.
I shall sing in your honour.
Amen.

Silence

Final prayer   You have brought me happiness, Lord,
    more than I could ever ask or imagine,
    brimming up within me and running over.
For joy now and yet to come,
    receive my thanks.

You fill each day with blessings too many to number,
    life bringing so much to delight and enthral –
    beauty to captivate,
    love to share,
    horizons to explore,
    pleasures to savour.
For joy now and yet to come,
    receive my thanks.

You give me joy deep within,
    based not simply on present experience
    but on future hope –
    the knowledge that nothing in life or death
    can ever separate me from your love –
    and so, though like anyone else
    I may face tears and sorrow,
    I know that laughter will again fill my soul.
For joy now and yet to come,
    receive my thanks.
Amen.

Music   Jesu, joy of man's desiring (J. S. Bach) from *Wings of a Dove*, sung by Hannah Mayhew

4

For the peace that passes understanding

Music   You, Lord, are in this place from *Sacred Weave*
              (Keith Duke)

Scripture The Lord's my shepherd, I want for nothing. He
               makes me lie down in fertile pastures, he leads be
               beside tranquil waters, he restores my soul. He leads
               me in right paths for his name's sake. Even though I
               walk through the darkest of valleys, I fear no evil, for
               you are with me, your rod and staff a constant source
               of comfort.   *Psalm 23:1-4*

               I leave to you my peace; that's what I give you: a
               peace unlike anything this world can give. So then, do
               not let your heart be anxious or frightened.
                                                    John 14:27

Prayer   In heavenly love abiding,
               no change my heart shall fear;
               and safe is such confiding,
               for nothing changes here.
               The storm may roar without me,
               my heart may low be laid,
               but God is round about me,
               and can I be dismayed?

               Silence

               Those lovely words of Anna Laetitia Waring (1820–
               1910) sum up the inner peace and tranquillity that

God offers us in Christ, and it's that likewise which the
following short and celebrated prayer of St Augustine
of Hippo (354–430) so beautifully celebrates:

Everlasting God,
in whom we live and move and have our being:
you have made us for yourself,
and our hearts are restless
until they rest in you.
Amen.

Silence

Final prayer   For the peace you offer,
founded on the knowledge you are always with me,
ready to support, strengthen, equip and enable,
come what may –
for peace beyond anything this world can give,
Lord, I thank you.

For the freedom you bring from fear and anxiety,
from worries that would otherwise weigh me down
and hold me back,
destroying hope for the future
and happiness in the present –
for your peace beyond anything this world can give,
Lord, I thank you.

For the assurance I have that whatever life may bring,
you will be with me in it,
there to help me through,
however demanding things may prove –
for your peace beyond anything this world can give,
Lord, I thank you.

For the inner contentment you have brought,
a tranquillity of spirit rooted
not just in the here and now

but in your eternal love
from which nothing can ever separate me –
for your peace beyond anything this world can give,
Lord, I thank you.
Amen.

Music   You, Lord, are in this place from *Sacred Weave*
(Keith Duke)

5
Grateful response

Music   Take, Lord from *Awakening in Love* (Margaret Rizza)

Scripture   I will offer the Lord the gratitude that his goodness deserves; I will sing praise to the name of the most high God. Lord, I will bring to you the sacrifice of gratitude and call on your name.   *Psalm 7:17; 116:17*

I will open my mouth and pour out heartfelt thanks to the Lord. I will honour him in the presence of all people. I give thanks to the Lord with all my heart. I offer thanks in your name for your unfailing love and constancy; your name and your love are exalted above everything.   *Psalm 109:30; 138:1a, 2b*

Prayer   Like a bird soaring into flight,
like the moon glowing in the night,
like a flame, radiant with light,
so, O Lord, is your love in my sight.

Like a gift worthy of a king,
like a bud shooting in the spring,
like a bond signalled by a ring,
so each day is the love that you bring.

Like the dawn, fresh with morning dew,
like the sea, old but ever new,
like a dream, somehow coming true,
is the love that I find, Lord, in you.

Like a sign, pointing out the way,
like a field, sweet with summer hay,
like a stream flowing come what may,
so, O Lord, is your love every day.

Silence

Do we appreciate everything that God has given? Sometimes, perhaps, but too often we're so busy coveting what we haven't got that we lose sight of what we have. The following reflective prayer was inspired by the sight of someone collecting their weekly wage packet:

It spoke, Lord, that wage packet:
   of work done and leisure made possible,
   of food on the table and clothes for the kids,
   of presents, treats, holidays and outings,
   of the mortgage and new car,
   of taxes paid and pension contributions –
   of all this and so much more –
   and it spoke too of those with no wage:
   the unemployed,
   asylum seekers,
   refugees,
   millions the world over condemned to poverty
   and a life of need.

I don't earn much, Lord –
   a mere pittance compared to some,
   but it's a king's ransom to others,
   riches beyond their wildest dreams.
However much, then, I may strive for more,
   teach me first to appreciate what I have,
   and gratefully to respond to those with so much less.
Amen.

Silence

A prayer now of Philaret (1782–1867), one-time Metropolitan of Moscow, which exudes grateful and reverent response to all God's goodness:

My Lord, I know not what I ought to ask of you.
You and you alone know my needs.

You love me more than I am able to love you.
O Father, grant unto me, thy servant,
   all which I cannot ask.
For a cross I dare not ask, nor for consolation;
   I dare only to stand in thy presence.
My heart is open to you.
You see my needs of which I myself am unaware.
Behold and lift me up!
In your presence I stand,
   awed and silenced by your will and your judgements
   into which my mind cannot penetrate.
To you I offer myself as a sacrifice.
No other desire is mine but to fulfil your will.
Teach me how to pray.
Do yourself pray within me.
Amen.

Silence

Final prayer   Gracious God,
   no words are enough to thank you
   for your goodness,
   and no deeds can ever express my gratitude
   for your love,
   but I want to respond,
   not because I must but because I *may*.
You have blessed me beyond my deserving.
Gratefully I worship you.

You have poured out your love upon me,
   not only meeting my needs
   but doing far more besides,
   filling my life with good things
   until it overflows with plenty.
You have blessed me beyond my deserving.
Gratefully I worship you.

Though I give so little back to you in return,
    carefully and even grudgingly
    measuring out my response,
    still you care for me,
    your love refusing to be denied.
You have blessed me beyond my deserving.
Gratefully I worship you.

So, then, I bring you my prayer, my life,
    my faith and my worship,
    flawed and feeble though they may be,
    offering them to you as a small but simple way
    of saying thank you
    for all you have done in Christ.
You have blessed me beyond my deserving.
Gratefully I worship you.
Amen.

Music   Take, Lord from *Awakening in Love* (Margaret Rizza)

6
For God's gracious acceptance

Music

O for the wings of a dove (Felix Mendelssohn) from *Wings of a Dove*, sung by Hannah Mayhew

Scripture

I will offer you thanks, Lord, among your people and sing your praises among the nations, for your mercy is greater than the heavens, and your faithfulness reaches up to the very clouds.   *Psalm 108:3, 4*

Give thanks to the Lord, for he is good; his generous love continues for ever.   *Psalm 118:1*

Prayer

And can it be that I should gain
an interest in the Saviour's blood?
Died he for me, who caused his pain?
For me, who him to death pursued?
Amazing love! How can it be
that thou, my God, should die for me?

He left his Father's throne above –
so free, so infinite his grace –
emptied himself of all but love,
and bled for Adam's helpless race.
'Tis mercy all, immense and free;
for, O my God, it found out me!

Silence

Those well-loved words of Charles Wesley (1707–88) find an echo in countless hymns across the years, expressing a sense of wonder, almost disbelief, that God can have time for people like us. Yet, despite all our unworthiness, all our faults, he values us for what we are, as the following prayer, inspired by the sight of people queuing at a department store to return faulty goods, makes clear:

There was a counter set aside,
    dealing solely with faulty items,
    and a crowd stood there,
    queuing to return their goods
    and claim a refund.
They had no need to argue,
    for it was taken as read:
    the product was substandard,
    unacceptable to all.

You could reject *me* just as easily, Lord,
    replace me for another model with equal grounds,
    for I fall short in so many ways
    of the person I ought to be.
Yet, for all my faults, you refuse to let me go,
    counting me instead of inestimable value,
    and working tirelessly to make me new.
For that patient and faithful love,
    thank you.
Amen.

Silence

A prayer now attributed by some to Abu Bakr (c. 573–634), companion and later father-in-law of the prophet Muhammad, one of the first converts to Islam, and also the first of the Muslim caliphs:

I thank you, Lord, for knowing me
    better than I know myself,
    and for letting me know myself
    better than others know me.

Make me, I pray, better than they suppose,
  and forgive me for what they do not know.
Amen.

Silence

Final prayer Almighty God,
    though I have no claim on your love
    and no right to expect forgiveness,
    each day you reach out afresh in love,
    eager to forgive and forget.
  For that wonderful truth,
    I thank you.

  Though I repeatedly fail you,
    time and again flouting your will
    and disobeying your commands,
    you go on wiping the slate clean,
    offering me new beginnings, a fresh start.
  For that wonderful truth,
    I thank you.

  Though my faith is weak,
    my commitment poor,
    my service feeble
    and my love for you flawed,
    you delight to call me your child
    and continue to shower me with blessings.
  For that wonderful truth,
    I thank you.

  Though so much about me is unlovely,
    undeserving,
    unfaithful,
    uncaring,
    still you value me,
    receiving me just as I am.

For that wonderful truth,
I thank you.

Though you recognise the good and the bad in me,
the strengths and the weaknesses,
the faith and the doubt,
the obedience and the waywardness,
you invite me to find in you full forgiveness
and a life changed for ever.
For that wonderful truth,
I thank you.
Amen.

Music   O for the wings of a dove (Felix Mendelssohn) from
Wings of a Dove, sung by Hannah Mayhew

7
For God's faithfulness

Music   Thou art all things from *Fire of Love* (Margaret Rizza)

Scripture   The Lord be thanked, for he is good; his faithful love is eternal. Offer gratitude to the God of gods; gratefully acknowledge the Lord of lords; for he is good, his faithful love is eternal. He alone performs wonderful deeds; his faithful love is eternal.   *Psalm 136:1-4*

I will sing unceasingly of your unfailing love, O Lord; I will declare your faithfulness to all generations. Your constant love is unchanged from the beginning of time, and your faithfulness is as permanent as the heavens.
Psalm 89:1, 2

Prayer   I've talked of trusting, come what may,
of walking where you lead;
I've pledged to follow day by day,
to serve in word and deed;
I've claimed to love you, heart and soul,
enough to give my all –
yet though such faith has been my goal
repeatedly I fall.

Lord, thankfully the love *you* show
is of a different kind –
a love that will not let me go no matter what you find.
However much I fail to be the person I intend,
in you I find true constancy,
one faithful to the end.

Silence

Though we fail him, God will not fail us – that is the message at the heart of the gospel: our faithlessness constantly contrasted to his faithfulness. It's a theme taken up in the prayer of Notker of St Gall (c. 840–912):

Praise to you, O faithful God!
You never fail those who trust in you,
   but you allow them to share in your glory.
You fight for us
   against everything that could attack
   or do us harm.
You are our shepherd,
   and you free us from the snare.
You protect us who honour you, O God;
   great is the sweetness that you give.
Amen.

Silence

Final prayer

For your wonderful and constant love,
   your inexhaustible care
   and incontrovertible purpose,
   faithful God,
   thank you.

For the fulfilment of your promises
   throughout history,
   your constancy
   experienced generation after generation,
   faithful God,
   thank you.

For meeting rejection with love,
   disobedience with mercy,
   faithful God,
   thank you.

For staying true when I prove false,
    seeking me out though I repeatedly go astray,
    faithful God,
    thank you.

For being there for me though I let go of you,
    being ever the same though I daily prove fickle,
    faithful God,
    thank you.
Amen.

Music   Thou art all things from *Fire of Love* (Margaret Rizza)

8
For all God has yet to teach us

Music　　　　O give thanks to the Lord from *Light in Our Darkness*,
　　　　　　　　(Margaret Rizza)

Scripture　　I've never stopped thanking God for you, remembering
　　　　　　　　you when I pray and asking God – the wonderful
　　　　　　　　Father of our Lord Jesus Christ – to grant you his
　　　　　　　　Spirit, who will bring you wisdom, revealing God to
　　　　　　　　you in such a way that you will know him. My prayer
　　　　　　　　is that your minds may be opened to see his light, in
　　　　　　　　order for you to understand the hope he has called
　　　　　　　　you to – the extraordinary value of the breathtaking
　　　　　　　　blessings he promises his people, and the magnitude
　　　　　　　　of his power working within us who believe.
　　　　　　　　　　　　　　　　　　　　　　Ephesians 1:16-19a

　　　　　　　　I will appeal to the Father, and he will grant you a
　　　　　　　　companion to be with you for ever – the Spirit, who
　　　　　　　　reveals understanding about God. Because it can
　　　　　　　　neither see nor know him, the world is unable to
　　　　　　　　receive him, but you know him, since he remains
　　　　　　　　both with and in you. This helper, the Holy Spirit, sent
　　　　　　　　by the Father in my name, will teach you everything
　　　　　　　　and bring to your minds all that I have taught you.
　　　　　　　　　　　　　　　　　　　　　　John 14:16, 17, 26

Prayer　　　　More about Jesus would I know,
　　　　　　　　more of his grace to others show;
　　　　　　　　more of his saving fullness see,
　　　　　　　　more of his love – who died for me.

　　　　　　　　More about Jesus let me learn,
　　　　　　　　more of his holy will discern;

Spirit of God, my teacher be,
showing the things of Christ to me.

More about Jesus; in his Word
holding communion with my Lord;
hearing his voice in every line,
making each faithful saying mine.

More about Jesus; on his throne,
riches in glory all his own;
more of his kingdom's sure increase;
more of his coming – Prince of Peace.

Silence

Those words of the American hymn-writer Eliza
Hewitt (1851–1920) – a woman who suffered for many
years from a debilitating spinal disease yet continued
to write sacred music throughout her life – remind us
that discipleship is not a destination but a journey in
which we are always travelling forward to new horizons.
We should never imagine we have understood more
than a fraction of God's grace and goodness. The
following prayer, inspired by a visit to a local aquarium,
takes up that theme:

They darted this way and that,
   probing, foraging and exploring,
   the fish secure in their own little world.
Were they aware of me looking in,
   conscious of another plane,
   an altogether different dimension,
   beyond the boundaries that confined them?

There's so much, Lord, that *I* don't see,
   the world of my senses not the whole story
   but just a glimpse of reality,
   one aspect of a greater whole.

Save me from being bound by my limited horizons,
    closing my life to wonders beyond
    and riches yet to be revealed.
Open my heart to your infinite love,
    greater than eye has seen or mind conceived.
Amen.

Silence

Words now of St Anselm (1033–1109), taken from
the Preface of his *Proslogium*, which acknowledge
everything God has done while yet seeking greater
faith and understanding:

I acknowledge, Lord, and I give thanks
    that you have created your image in me,
    so that I may remember you,
    think of you, love you.
But this image is so obliterated
    and worn away by wickedness,
    it is so obscured by the smoke of sins,
    that it cannot do what it was created to do,
    unless you renew and reform it.
I am not attempting, O Lord,
    to penetrate your loftiness,
    for I cannot begin to match my understanding with it,
    but I desire in some measure
    to understand your truth,
    which my heart believes and loves.
For I do not seek to understand
    in order that I may believe,
    but I believe in order to understand.
For this too I believe,
    that 'unless I believe, I shall not understand'.
Amen.

Silence

Final prayer   For all I learn of you through your word,
        through prayer
        and through worship,
        Lord,
        I thank you.

For all I learn of you through the indwelling of Christ,
        the prompting of your Spirit
        or your still small voice within,
        Lord,
        I thank you.

For all I learn of you through others,
        their ideas and insights,
        experiences and example,
        Lord,
        I thank you.

For all I learn of you through the beauty of creation,
        the wonder of the universe,
        the miracle of life,
        Lord,
        I thank you.

For all I have yet to learn of you,
        yet to explore,
        yet to understand,
        Lord,
        I thank you.
Amen.

Music   O give thanks to the Lord from *Light in Our Darkness*
(Margaret Rizza)

9
For God's guidance

Music   The Lord is my light and my salvation from *Light in Our Darkness* (Margaret Rizza)

Scripture   You are my rock and stronghold; for the honour of your name you lead and guide me. Through your advice you direct me, and ultimately you will accept me in glory.   *Psalm 31:3; 73:24*

If I set sail on the wings of the morning and settle at the uttermost limits of the sea, even there your hand will lead me, your right hand holding me firm.
Psalm 139:9, 10

Prayer   I do not know what life may hold,
if good or ill I'll see,
what twists and turns may yet unfold,
what trials yet might be.
I cannot say if light will shine
or darkness fall once more,
what destiny might still be mine,
what future lies in store.
But even if the way is tough
and storms begin to blow,
the gales prove strong, the water rough,
one thing, Lord, still I know:
that you'll be there, supporting me,
a faithful, loving guide –
a constant help who will not fail
to strengthen and provide.
I have no need to ask for more
nor any cause to fear:
whatever life may hold for me
I know that you'll be near.

Silence

We all feel in need of guidance sometimes, whether
it's simply to get our bearings when we're lost or for
more complex decisions affecting the course our life
may take. The following reflective prayer moves from
the first to the second, taking as its inspiration the
guidance offered by a compass:

It didn't tell me exactly where I was,
   or spell out the path to follow,
   but it helped me get my bearings,
   enough to work out the next step,
   the direction I should take.
And though the way wasn't always easy
   or the path always clear,
   it was sufficient for my needs,
   leading me safely to my final destination.

Thank you, Lord, for the guidance you offer each day,
   not setting out detailed instructions
   for every aspect of life,
   still less dictating the course I should take,
   but prompting through your word
   and pointing the way forward.
Teach me to travel in faith until the journey is done,
   your love a light to my path,
   a compass through the changing scenes of life.
Amen.

Silence

Final prayer   For your constant guidance throughout our lives –
   the way you encourage, strengthen,
   challenge and renew,
   daily there to lead us,
   Lord, we gratefully respond.

For speaking through your Word, your Son
and your Church –
offering instruction for daily life
and insight into your sovereign purpose,
daily there to lead us,
Lord, we gratefully respond.

For speaking through creation –
the people we meet, sights we see,
things we hear, do and experience,
daily there to lead us,
Lord, we gratefully respond.

For speaking through the inner presence of your Spirit –
inspiring, instructing, reassuring and equipping,
daily there to lead us,
Lord, we gratefully respond.

For all the ways you give guidance,
a light to our path and lamp for our way,
daily there to lead us,
Lord, we gratefully respond.
Amen.

Music   The Lord is my light and my salvation from *Light in Our Darkness* (Margaret Rizza)

10
For the wonder of creation

Music   Bless the Lord, my soul from *Light in Our Darkness*
(Margaret Rizza)

Scripture   Everything you have made and done will offer you
thanks, Lord, and all your faithful people will bless
you!   *Psalm 145:10*

He it was, in his wisdom, who created the universe;
his faithful love is eternal. He it was who laid out the
land above the ocean, and who fashioned the celestial
lights – the sun to govern the day, and the moon and
stars to reign over the night; his faithful love is eternal.
Psalm 136:5-9

Prayer   For summer and autumn, winter and spring,
the breathtaking beauty these faithfully bring –
lengthening days calling new life to birth,
delicate blooms bursting fresh from the earth;
sunshine and showers, heat mist and haze,
fragrance and colour to thrill and amaze;
ripening fruit, golden sheaves in the field,
harvest thanksgiving at Earth's gracious yield;
holly and ivy, a nip in the air,
frost-covered branches, their glory laid bare –
Lord, for this cycle so special and true,
life always changing yet ever made new,
hear now my worship, and help me, I pray,
gladly to honour creation each day.

Silence

Where better to look for inspiration in celebrating creation than in the natural world itself? As the following prayer explores, so much there is special, even though familiarity may inure us sometimes to its wonder.

I caught the movement as I crouched in the hide –
   a sudden flutter of wings –
   and, grabbing my binoculars, I scanned the trees,
   excited, and expectant,
   straining to catch a sight . . .
   but then . . . disappointment . . . dismay,
   for it was nothing interesting,
   nothing rare . . .
   only a sparrow.

Only a sparrow?
What do I mean, Lord?
It may be plain,
   but, like everything else in the world,
   it's a miracle,
   a wonder,
   special beyond words –
   each bone and feather a work of art,
   fashioned by your hands and speaking of you.
However ordinary it may seem or familiar be,
   teach me never to lose my sense of wonder
   at all you have made.
Amen.

Silence

Next, words of the celebrated German mathematician, astrologer and astronomer, Johann Kepler (1571–1630) – a scientist who glimpsed the hand of God in the order and grandeur of the universe:

O thou who through the light of nature
    hast aroused in us a longing for the light of grace,
    so that we may be raised in the light of thy majesty,
    to thee, I give thanks, Creator and Lord,
    that thou allowest me to rejoice in thy works.
Praise the Lord, ye heavenly harmonies,
    and ye who know the revealed harmonies.
For from him, through him and in him, all is,
    which is perceptible as well as spiritual;
    that which we know
    and that which we do not know,
    for there is still so much to learn.
Amen.

Silence

In similar but more poetic vein is an abridged version of a prayer by Edward King (1829–1910), Bishop of Lincoln from 1885 to 1910:

Thank you, O God,
    for the pleasures you have given me
    through my senses.
Thank you for the glory of thunder,
    the mystery of music, the singing of birds
    and the laughter of children.
Thank you for the delights of colour,
    the awe of sunset, the wild roses in the hedgerows,
    the smile of friendship.
Thank you for the sweetness of flowers
    and the scent of hay.
Truly, O Lord, the earth is full of your riches!
Amen.

Silence

Final prayer   Creator God,
thank you for the world you have given,
so full of beauty,
so touched with wonder.
For all its richness,
thank you.

Thank you for the splendour of the heavens
and beauty of the countryside,
the grandeur of mountains and oceans,
the tranquillity of birds singing
and flowers in bloom –
the sheer wonder of life.
For all its richness,
thank you.

Thank you for everything we can see, hear, feel,
smell and touch,
everything that enthrals our senses,
capturing the imagination and stirring the spirit.
For all its richness,
thank you.

Thank you for so much that is good and lovely,
able to move, astonish, inspire and refresh us,
For all its richness,
thank you.
Amen.

Music   Bless the Lord my soul from *Light in Our Darkness*
(Margaret Rizza)

11
For hope that will not fail us

Music   Thank God there's a heaven from *Gentle as a Lamb*
(Christopher Wright)

Scripture   I brim over with happiness, my words overflow with
joy. Human though I am, I rest assured in hope.
Acts 2:26

The hope God has given does not disappoint us, for
through his Holy Spirit – his gift to us – he has
poured his love liberally into our hearts.
Romans 5:5

Prayer   For all the hope that sheds its glorious ray
along the dark and unknown future way,
and lights the path to God's eternal day,
Hallelujah! Hallelujah!

Silence

Words of the hymn-writer and Baptist minister
Leonard James Egerton Smith (1879–1958), through
which he expresses his faith in God's future; but what
does the future hold for us? When we're young it
seems full of promise, but the older we get, the harder
it can be to look forward with any real sense of expectation. The message of the gospel, though, is that we
should eagerly anticipate all that lies in store, for God
offers us hope that will not disappoint us. The following
reflective prayer, titled simply 'The birthday card',
explores that truth:

It was greeted with excitement,
  hastily torn open in anticipation of a gift inside –
  yet another birthday surprise.

It was greeted with pride,
  for it represented a coming of age,
  a personal milestone,
  the start of a new and exciting chapter.

It was greeted with resignation,
  for it meant another year gone by,
  another year older –
  too much of life gone,
  too little yet to come.

Whatever my stage of life, Lord,
  help me to greet it thankfully,
  knowing that as you have blessed me,
  so you will bless me again,
  each moment given by you,
  and with the best yet to come.
Amen.

Silence

Next, part of an ancient prayer – words from Psalm
42:5, 6a – acknowledging the hope that springs from
knowing God:

Why be disheartened, O my soul?
Why should I be troubled in spirit?
In you, O Lord, I place my hope,
  confident that I will again praise you,
  my help and my God.
Amen.

Silence

Final prayer   Thank you, Lord, for the message of hope
　　　　　　　　　at the heart of the gospel,
　　　　　　　　　the assurance that, whatever may conspire against it,
　　　　　　　　　your love will always emerge victorious.
　　　　　　　For hope that will never disappoint,
　　　　　　　　　thank you.

　　　　　　　Thank you for hopes realised across the years:
　　　　　　　　　of deliverance from Egypt,
　　　　　　　　　of entry into the Promised Land,
　　　　　　　　　of the birth of the Messiah,
　　　　　　　　　of resurrection following his death on a cross,
　　　　　　　　　of new beginnings, new life through his Spirit.
　　　　　　　For hope that will never disappoint,
　　　　　　　　　thank you.

　　　　　　　Thank you for the assurance you've given me,
　　　　　　　　　the knowledge that whatever disappointments
　　　　　　　　　I may experience,
　　　　　　　　　whatever difficulties face,
　　　　　　　　　you are able to make all things new,
　　　　　　　　　bringing joy out of sorrow, light out of darkness
　　　　　　　　　and faith out of doubt.
　　　　　　　For hope that will never disappoint,
　　　　　　　　　thank you.

　　　　　　　Thank you that I can live each moment
　　　　　　　　　with confidence,
　　　　　　　　　and look forward to the future with anticipation,
　　　　　　　　　knowing that true happiness lies not in things seen
　　　　　　　　　but in things promised,
　　　　　　　　　more wonderful than I can yet understand.
　　　　　　　For hope that will never disappoint,
　　　　　　　　　thank you.
　　　　　　　　　Amen.

Music   Thank God there's a heaven from *Gentle as a Lamb*
　　　　　　　(Christopher Wright)

12
The constancy of God's love

Music   Love divine, all loves excelling from *Our Favourite Hymns 3*

Scripture   I thank you, Lord God, with all my heart, and will give glory to your name for ever, for great is the constancy of your love to me.   *Psalm 86:12, 13a*

I am convinced that neither death nor life, nor angels or demons, nor the present or the future, nor any powers, nor indeed height or depth or anything else in all creation, will ever be able to separate us from God's love that is made ours through Jesus Christ our Lord.   *Romans 8:38, 39*

Prayer   I've tasted pain and sadness,
the bitterness of tears,
yet also known such gladness,
such joy across the years;
so much that's brought me pleasure,
more blessed than words can say,
experiences to treasure,
enchantment day by day.
Yes, darker times have faced me,
some difficult to meet,
but always you've embraced me
and set me on my feet.
Lord, whether celebration
will mark the days ahead,
or bitter desolation
will be my lot instead,
of one thing I am certain –

experience tells me so –
your love will never fail me
or ever let me go.

Silence

Prayer can be inspired by the simplest of things; in
the prayer that follows even something as ordinary as
an afternoon snooze:

I tried to stay awake,
    fighting to control the creeping lethargy,
    but it was no good,
    the heavy meal and glass of wine,
    coupled with the summer heat,
    causing my head to nod and eyelids to droop,
    sleep closing in.

You, Lord, never tire nor slumber.
Your love is constant each day,
    your faithfulness ever sure.
Whatever I face,
    you are there watching over me –
    guiding,
    protecting,
    loving,
    forgiving –
    your goodness never exhausted,
    your compassion never failing.
For that assurance, receive my praise.
Amen.

Silence

A prayer next of Richard of Chichester (1197–1253), acknowledging God's love in Christ and seeking to offer love in return:

Thanks be to you, my Lord Jesus Christ,
 for all the benefits you have won for me,
 for all the pains and insults you have borne for me,
 O most merciful redeemer, friend and brother.
May I know you more clearly,
 love you more dearly
 and follow you more nearly,
 day by day.
Amen.

Silence

Final prayer Gracious God,
 for the way you watch over me throughout my life,
 continually there to nurture, cherish,
 protect and bless me –
 for the sheer constancy of your love,
 thank you.

For not abandoning me
 though I wander from your side,
 refusing to forsake me
 though I repeatedly desert you,
 remaining faithful though I betray your trust –
 for the sheer constancy of your love,
 thank you.

For choosing me before I ever chose you,
 accepting me just as I am
 with all my faults and failings,
 and daily making me new –

for the sheer constancy of your love,
thank you.

For your awesome commitment
that refuses to let me go,
and that was willing to sacrifice so much
to make me whole –
for the sheer constancy of your love,
thank you.
Amen.

Music   Love divine, all loves excelling from *Our Favourite Hymns 3*

13
For the things we've forgotten to thank God for

Music
Thank you for your love from *Gentle as a Lamb* (Christopher Wright)

Scripture
Sing psalms, hymns and spiritual songs among yourselves, singing and making music in your hearts to the Lord, and in everything giving thanks to God the Father, in the name of our Lord Jesus Christ.
Ephesians 5:19, 20

I will praise the name of the Lord in song; I will magnify him with thanksgiving. I will offer to the Lord whole-hearted thanksgiving: my mouth will constantly utter his praise.
Psalm 69:30; 34:1

Prayer
Lord, today your voice is calling,
lifting thoughts to things above;
life is wonderful, enthralling,
touched by your unfailing love.
Suddenly I see the beauty
often hidden from my gaze,
so I come not out of duty,
but with glad and grateful praise.

Lord, I sometimes fail to value
all your blessings as I should;
slow to make due time to thank you,
blind to so much that is good.
Days are lived in such a hurry
there's no time to stop and stare;
joy is crushed by weight of worry,
happiness obscured by care.

Lord, today I come rejoicing,
vowed to waste your gifts no more;
bringing praise and gladly voicing
what I should have voiced before.
Pouring out my adulation,
scarcely knowing where to start,
with a song of exultation,
Lord, I thank you from the heart.

Silence

Most of us are good at asking God for things but poor
at thanking him when he gives them – a point explored
in the following reflection:

Lord, I sent a card today.
Nothing out of the ordinary,
    just a simple thank-you note for a special gift.
There was no need to send it,
    for it wasn't expected,
    and I very nearly didn't, time as always being short.
But that present had meant something to me,
    touched my heart,
    and I wanted to show my appreciation,
    to make it plain it wasn't just taken for granted,
    but that I was truly grateful.
Yet it struck me, Lord,
    as I popped that card into the post-box,
    that while I'm good on the whole
    at saying thank you to others,
    I'm pretty hopeless when it comes to you.
I'd never considered it before,
    the thought simply not occurring to me,
    but suddenly I realised my prayers
    are all too often 'please'
    and all too rarely 'thank you'.

It's true, isn't it, Lord?
I'm always after something –
  another problem to solve,
  another request,
  another need,
  another desire,
  and I bring them to you without a second thought,
  almost automatically,
  confident you'll help.
But when the crisis is over,
  your answer given,
  it's all forgotten,
  nothing more said until the next time.
There's no excuse, Lord, I know that –
  so today, quite simply, I want to say thank you,
  thank you, for everything.

Silence

Next, a traditional Scottish prayer:

Lord of all mercy and goodness,
  let me not by any ingratitude or hardness of heart
  forget the wonderful benefits
  that you have bestowed upon me
  this and every day,
  but grant that I may be mindful,
  all the days of my life,
  of the incomparable gifts
  which you always give to me.
Amen.

Silence

And now, a short but simple prayer written by George
Herbert (1593–1633):

You, Lord, have given so much to me;
    give me one thing more,
    a grateful heart.
Amen.

Silence

Final prayer

Too often, Lord, I've earnestly begged you
    for something –
    your help, your peace, your mercy, your guidance –
    only to forget your goodness when you grant it.
Today, then, simply but sincerely,
    I say to you, 'Thank you!'

Too often, Lord, I've taken your blessings for granted,
    celebrating daily pleasures,
    the beauty of your world,
    the sheer joy of life
    with little if any thought of you.
Today, then, simply but sincerely,
    I say to you, 'Thank you!'

Too often, Lord, I've received mercy,
    celebrated new beginnings,
    experienced your transforming power,
    yet failed to appreciate all it cost you.
Today, then, simply but sincerely,
    I say to you, 'Thank you!'

Too often, Lord, I'm swift to ask but slow to respond,
    quick to complain but sluggish to show gratitude,
    eager to receive but reluctant to give,
    my relationship with you painfully one-sided.
Today, then, simply but sincerely,
    I say to you, 'Thank you!'
Amen.

Music   Thank you for your love from *Gentle as a Lamb*
(Christopher Wright)

14
For the knowledge
that God watches over us

Music   Come to me from *Fountain of Life* (Margaret Rizza)

Scripture   Even though I walk through the darkest of valleys, I fear no evil, for you are with me, your rod and staff a constant source of comfort.   *Psalm 23:4*

God is our sanctuary and protection, a constant help in times of peril. So we will fear nothing, even if this world should be turned upside down and the mountains crumble into the depths of the ocean – even if the waters of the sea thunder and churn and the mountains quiver amidst the turmoil.   *Psalm 46:1-3*

Prayer   Every single day,
by your side I'll stay,
trust me, come what may,
I'll be there every step of the way.

When you're feeling low,
tears begin to flow,
I want you to know,
I'll be there every step as you go.

When you're in despair,
spirit crushed by care,
life too hard to bear,
I'll be there – every step, everywhere.

When your dreams have died,
hopes have been denied,

nowhere left to hide,
I'll be there every step by your side.

When you need a friend
aching wounds to tend,
broken heart to mend,
I'll be there every step to the end.

Silence

Big brother is watching you, we're sometimes told,
many being concerned that surveillance cameras monitor
our every move. I don't have too many problems with
that, such cameras giving a sense of security. The following prayer picks up that theme:

It was a strange feeling,
    reassuring yet also eerie,
    for I was being watched,
    my every move surveyed,
    the all-seeing eye of the camera taking everything in
    and storing it all away.

You, Lord, watch over me,
    hour after hour,
    day after day,
    not to keep tabs on what I do,
    but as a loving friend and faithful companion –
    there to help in times of need,
    protect in times of danger,
    and comfort in times of hurt.
Thank you for the knowledge that,
    though *I* lose sight of *you*,
    still *you* look out for *me*.
Amen.

Silence

Words now taken from the so-called Universal Prayer of Pope Clement XI (1649–1721):

Lord, I believe in you: increase my faith.
I trust in you: strengthen my trust.
I love you: let me love you more and more.
I am sorry for my sins: deepen my sorrow.
I worship you as my first beginning.
I long for you as my last end.
I praise you as my constant helper,
    and call on you as my loving protector.
Amen.

Silence

Final prayer

For the knowledge that you are not distant
    from my situation,
    removed from my daily experiences,
    but here by my side,
    present every moment of every day,
    Lord,
    I thank you.

For involving yourself in the stuff of life,
    being concerned about joys and sorrows,
    hopes and fears,
    triumphs and disappointments,
    pleasure and pain,
    Lord,
    I thank you.

For caring about my welfare,
    always looking to support, strengthen,
    comfort and encourage,
    Lord,
    I thank you.

For travelling with me in the journey of life,
  eager to lead me into new experiences of your love
  and a deeper understanding of your purpose,
  Lord,
  I thank you.

For being with me now,
  ready to speak, listen, forgive, renew,
  inspire and enable,
  Lord,
  I thank you.

For being with me always,
  no place outside your love,
  no moment beyond your power to transform,
  Lord,
  I thank you.
Amen.

Music   Come to me from *Fountain of Life* (Margaret Rizza)

15
For new beginnings

Music   Laudamus te (Vivaldi) from *Wings of a Dove*, sung by Hannah Mayhew

Scripture   Whoever is united with Christ is a new person; the old is past, the new has dawned.

2 Corinthians 5:17

You need to be made entirely new in heart and mind, putting on the new self created in the likeness of God, in righteousness, holiness and truth.

Ephesians 4:23, 24

Prayer   'Twas battered and scarred, and the auctioneer
Thought it scarcely worth his while
To waste much time on the old violin,
But he held it up with a smile.
'What am I bidden, good folks?' he cried.
'Who will start bidding for me?'
'A dollar, a dollar' – then, 'Two!' 'Only two?'
'Two dollars, and who'll make it three?
Three dollars once, three dollars, twice;
Going for three' – But no,
From the room, far back, a gray-haired man
Came forward and picked up the bow;
Then wiping the dust from the old violin
And tightening the loosened strings,
He played a melody pure and sweet,
As sweet as a carolling angel sings.

The music ceased and the auctioneer,
With a voice that was quiet and low,
Said, 'What am I bidden for the old violin?'

And he held it up with the bow.
'A thousand dollars, and who'll make it two?
Two thousand! And who'll make it three?
Three thousand, once; three thousand, twice;
And going, and gone!' said he.
The people cheered, but some of them cried,
'We do not quite understand.
What changed its worth?' Swift came the reply;
'The touch of the Master's hand.'

And many a man with life out of tune,
And battered and scarred with sin,
Is auctioned cheap to the thoughtless crowd,
Much like the old violin.
A 'mess of pottage', a glass of wine,
A game – and he travels on.
He's 'going' once, and 'going' twice,
He's 'going' and almost 'gone'.
But the Master comes, and the foolish crowd
Never can quite understand
The worth of a soul, and the change that's wrought
By the touch of the Master's hand.

Silence

Celebrated words from the American writer Myra Brooks Welch that speak of the new beginnings God makes possible, what had seemed ordinary suddenly seeming special. For me, a new ream of paper spoke in similar fashion:

It was a mess,
  the page a mass of corrections,
  not just one or two,
  but hundreds,
  and the result was a shambles.
Yet no matter,
  for I'd a *ream* of paper to work with –

not just one clean sheet,
but another . . .
and another . . .
and another . . .
as many, surely, as I could ever want.

Thank you, Lord, for the clean sheet *you* offer
when I make a mess of life;
your invitation to turn over a new leaf
and start again.
Thank you that your mercy is never exhausted,
your patience never at an end;
that you go on offering new beginnings
for as many times as it takes.
Amen.

Silence

Words now from the first letter of Peter (1:3), expressing gratitude for the fresh start we have received in
Christ:

Let us give thanks
to the God and Father of our Lord Jesus Christ,
who, through his great mercy,
has given us new life
by raising Jesus Christ from the dead,
thus filling us with a vibrant hope.
Amen.

Silence

Final prayer   When life brings apparent endings,
defeats, disappointments and despair,
living Lord,
thank you for bringing new beginnings.

When life brings reminders of my weakness,
    temptation once again leading me astray,
    living Lord,
    thank you for bringing new beginnings.

When life brings sorrow,
    grief sometimes too painful to bear,
    living Lord,
    thank you for bringing new beginnings.

When life brings regrets,
    reminders of opportunities overlooked
    or frittered away,
    living Lord,
    thank you for bringing new beginnings.

When life brings hurt,
    injury in body, mind or spirit,
    living Lord,
    thank you for bringing new beginnings.

When life brings confusion,
    questions to which I can find no answers,
    living Lord,
    thank you for bringing new beginnings.

Whatever life brings,
    though it ultimately be death itself,
    living Lord,
    thank you for bringing new beginnings.
Amen.

Music   Laudamus te (Vivaldi) from *Wings of a Dove*, sung by
Hannah Mayhew

16
For all we have received

Music   Take, Lord from *Awakening in Love* (Margaret Rizza)

Scripture   The lines of my life have fallen in pleasant places; truly I have a stunning heritage. So I am glad at heart, at peace in body, celebrating with my whole being. You, Lord, have shown me the way of life; in your presence is complete joy and from your right hand come eternal pleasures.   *Psalm 16:6, 9, 11*

Do not brood over anything, but thankfully acquaint God with all your needs through your prayers and petitions. Whatever you do, whether in word or deed, do it in the name of the Lord Jesus, offering thanks to God the Father through him.

Philippians 4:6; Colossians 3:17

Prayer   New every morning is the love
our wakening and uprising prove;
through sleep and darkness safely brought,
restored to life and power and thought.

New mercies, each returning day,
hover around us while we pray;
new perils past, new sins forgiven,
new thoughts of God, new hopes of heaven.

If on our daily course our mind
be set to hallow all we find,
new treasures still, of countless price,
God will provide for sacrifice.

Old friends, old scenes, will lovelier be,
as more of heaven in each we see;
some softening gleam of love and prayer
will dawn on every cross and care.

The trivial round, the common task,
will furnish all we ought to ask;
room to deny ourselves; a road
to bring us daily nearer God.

Only, O Lord, in thy dear love
fit us for perfect rest above;
and help us, this and every day,
to live more nearly as we pray.

Silence

The words of that well-loved hymn by John Keble
(1792–1866) find an echo in a poem titled 'Thanksgiving', written by the American poet William Stanley
Braithwaite (1878–1962):

My heart gives thanks for many things;
For strength to labour day by day,
For sleep that comes when darkness wings
With evening up the eastern way.
I give deep thanks that I'm at peace
With kith and kin and neighbours, too –
Dear Lord, for all last year's increase,
That helped me strive and hope and do.

My heart gives thanks for many things;
I know not how to name them all.
My soul is free from frets and stings,
My mind from creed and doctrine's thrall.
For sun and stars, for flowers and streams,
For work and hope and rest and play –

For empty moments given to dreams,
For these my heart gives thanks today.

Silence

So much in everyday life has the power to speak of God,
inspiring prayer and thanksgiving. The following, for
example, was inspired by a pensioner showing me a
photograph album:

It had a melancholy feel,
 the dog-eared pages and faded photographs
 speaking of moments long gone,
 past glories and pleasures, for ever tucked away.
But for the pensioner poring over her album
 it was more than an epitaph to distant memories;
 it was a living testimony to special times shared,
 precious people loved,
 and countless experiences enjoyed.

I too, Lord, carry my memories with me,
 if not on paper then in my heart –
 so much I have done,
 so many I have known,
 innumerable people, places, sights and sounds
 that have enriched and enthralled,
 fashioning the person I am today.
For all I have so richly received,
 Lord, thank you.
Amen.

Silence

A classic prayer, known as the General Thanksgiving,
dates back to Tudor times and reflects the genius of

Thomas Cranmer, to whom, in large part, we owe the *Book of Common Prayer*. Cranmer, in turn, drew on Catholic monastic tradition, this prayer being part of the ancient order of Compline:

Almighty God, Father of all mercies,
   we thine unworthy servants
   do give thee most humble and hearty thanks
   for all thy goodness and loving-kindness to us
   and to all men;
We bless thee for our creation, preservation,
   and all the blessings of this life;
   but above all for thine inestimable love
   in the redemption of the world
   by our Lord Jesus Christ,
   for the means of grace, and for the hope of glory.
And we beseech thee,
   give us that due sense of all thy mercies,
   that our hearts may be unfeignedly thankful,
   and that we shew forth thy praise,
   not only with our lips,
   but in our lives;
   by giving up ourselves to thy service,
   and by walking before thee
   in holiness and righteousness
   all our days;
   through Jesus Christ our Lord,
   to whom, with thee and the Holy Ghost
   be all honour and glory, world without end.
Amen.

Silence

Final prayer   For memories of special occasions,
   memories of special people,
   and memories of special places,

God of past, present and future,
gladly I thank you.

For memories of special achievements,
    memories of special blessing,
    and memories of special guidance,
    God of past, present and future,
    gladly I thank you.

For all the events and experiences
    that have gladdened my life in any way,
    God of past, present and future,
    gladly I thank you.
Amen.

Music   Take, Lord from *Awakening in Love* (Margaret Rizza)

17
For God's countless blessings

Music   Now thank we all our God from *Our Favourite Hymns 1*

Scripture   You are my God, and I thank you for it; you are my God; I will acclaim you.   *Psalm 118:28*

Blessed be the God and Father of our Lord Jesus Christ, who has bestowed on us in Christ every spiritual blessing in the heavenly realms.   *Ephesians 1:3*

Prayer   When I fret about the things life might have brought,
when I fail to count my blessings as I ought,
when I moan about my lot,
pine for what I haven't got,
scarcely give what I've received a second thought,
teach me, Lord, to take a second look, and see
all the special gifts you grant so lavishly –
so much beauty everywhere,
so much speaking of your care,
boundless blessing, priceless treasure, going free.
Help me prove I've understood that truth, I pray,
in a way that words alone just can't convey:
may the happiness you give
show itself in how I live –
in a life that shines with thanks and praise each day.

Silence

What is the secret of offering thanks and praise each day, and not just *offering* those but *meaning* them? The answer is very simple, and is spelt out in the well-loved hymn of Johnson Oatman Jr (1856–1922):

Are you ever burdened with a load of care?
Does the cross seem heavy you are called to bear?
Count your many blessings, every doubt will fly,
And you will keep singing as the days go by.

When you look at others with their lands and gold,
Think that Christ has promised you his wealth untold;
Count your many blessings. Wealth can never buy
Your reward in heaven, nor your home on high.

Count your blessings, name them one by one,
Count your blessings, see what God hath done!
Count your blessings, name them one by one,
And it will surprise you what the Lord hath done.

Silence

Next, words of the Elizabethan and Stuart bishop
and scholar Lancelot Andrewes (1555–1626):

For all these, and also for all other mercies,
    known and unknown,
    open and secret,
    remembered by us or now forgotten,
    kindnesses received by us willingly
    or even against our will,
    we praise you,
    we bless you,
    we thank you,
    and will praise and bless and thank you
    all the days of our life,
        through Jesus Christ our Lord.
Amen.

Silence

Final prayer For the countless blessings I've received,
the innumerable good things
that surround me each day,
loving Lord,
thank you.

For a world of awesome beauty and variety,
able to enrich the body,
captivate the mind,
move the heart and inspire the spirit,
loving Lord,
thank you.

For health and strength,
food and clothing,
family and friends,
work and leisure,
loving Lord,
thank you.

For books and music,
sport and entertainment,
hobbies and interests,
holidays and days out,
loving Lord,
thank you.

For education and healthcare,
law and order,
emergency and public services,
shops and factories,
loving Lord,
thank you.

For fellowship and worship,
hymns and songs,
prayer and Scripture,
pastoral care and spiritual guidance,
loving Lord,
thank you.

For the knowledge of your love,
    the outpouring of your mercy,
    the blessing of your peace,
    and the certainty of your promise,
    loving Lord,
    thank you.
Amen.

Music   Now thank we all our God from *Our Favourite Hymns 1*

18
For the gift of laughter

Music   When Irish eyes are smiling from *Favourite Melodies*

Scripture   A happy heart shows itself in a cheerful expression,
whereas heartfelt sorrow breaks the spirit. Though
the life of the poor is hard, those who are happy at
heart will for ever feast. There is no finer medicine
than a merry heart; a miserable disposition, by contrast,
shrivels the bones.   *Proverbs 15:13, 15; 17:22*

There's a time for tears and a time for laughter; a time
to grieve, and a time to dance. In his own time, God
will put laughter into your mouth and joy upon your
lips.   *Ecclesiastes 3:4; Job 8:21*

Prayer   Think of a world without any laughter,
think of a life without any wit;
think of a day without any humour,
think of a sermon without any quips.
We thank you, Lord, for laughter, wit and humour,
we thank you, Lord, and praise your holy name.

Think of a world without any smiling,
think of a party without any fun;
think of a joke without any punch line,
think of a language without rhyme or pun.
We thank you, Lord, for smiling, fun and punch lines,
we thank you, Lord, and praise your holy name.

Think of a world without any comedy,
think of a circus without any clowns;
think of a court without any jester,

think of a home without merry sounds.
We thank you, Lord, for comics, clowns and jesters,
we thank you, Lord, and praise your holy name.

Think of a world where all must be serious,
think of a church were everyone's grim;
think of a life where laughter is frowned upon,
think of a faith where humour is sin.
We thank you, Lord, for all we have to cheer us,
we thank you, Lord, and praise your holy name.

Silence

Words of mine adapting an original hymn by Doreen
Newport. Sadly, some people see little place for laughter
in prayer and worship. Personally, I disagree, seeing it
as one of the most special of God's gifts, as explored
in the following reflection:

'Don't make me laugh,' he said.
And I knew what he meant,
    for I've said it often enough myself.
But today, Lord, I'm asking the opposite –
    make me laugh, please,
    for of all your gifts
    there is none more precious than laughter.
Not the laughter of mockery, I don't mean that –
    jeering at someone in their misfortune –
    but the ability to laugh *with* the world and *at* myself –
    to greet life with a smile,
    a wry grin,
    seeing the funny side of even the darkest moments;
    serious when I have to be,
    but recognising the foolish, the absurd and comical,
    and sharing the joke with you.
Teach me that, Lord,

give me wisdom, confidence, faith and humility,
to look at the solemnity and the tragedy of life,
and yet see the wonderful humour within.

My child,
    thank you for your prayer,
    for seeing me as I am
    rather than as I'm so often painted.
It gladdens my spirit to hear you,
    for all too many regard me as solemn and sombre,
    a tight-lipped, po-faced God,
    with never a smile or chuckle crossing my lips.
I understand why,
    for I can be stern,
    even forbidding,
    the issues I raise and the challenge I bring
    no laughing matter.
And there are times when what passes as humour
    fills me with sadness –
    the cruel jibe,
    the sick joke,
    the heartless teasing,
    the cutting sarcasm.
But there's another side also,
    a part of me that revels in laughter
    and loves to see a smile on your faces,
    that delights in fun and longs to share it with you –
    for I know that happiness breeds happiness,
    and cheer spreads cheer,
    joy aids healing, and sunshine brings life.
So yes, there's a time to weep, but also to laugh,
    a time to mourn, but also to dance,
    and if you lose that balance,
    it's serious indeed,
    for I fear you've lost sight of me.

Silence

Most of us enjoy a joke, so long as it doesn't poke fun at people unkindly. The following prayer takes as its inspiration a joke book I picked up in a second-hand bookshop:

It wasn't side-splittingly funny,
　　not by a long chalk,
　　but the jokes were enough to raise the spirits –
　　bringing a smile in place of a frown,
　　helping to defuse a tense situation,
　　cementing a budding friendship,
　　offering a welcome reminder
　　of the funny side of life –
　　and in so doing they more than proved their worth.

Though much in life, Lord, is touched by pathos,
　　teach me to keep a sense of humour,
　　able to laugh, even through tears,
　　and smile, even in sorrow.
And though much is serious,
　　demanding a measured response
　　and sober judgement,
　　help me to retain a sense of fun,
　　aware that laughter is your gift,
　　as valuable and special as any.
Amen.

Silence

Give me a sense of humour, Lord,
　　and also things to laugh about.
Give me grace to take a joke against myself
　　and see the funny side of the things I do.
Save me from annoyance,
　　bad temper,
　　resentment against my friends.

Help me to laugh even in the face of trouble.
Fill my mind with the love of Jesus,
    for his name's sake.
Amen. *A. G. Bullivant*

Silence

Final prayer

For the things in life that make me laugh,
    bringing a smile to my face and a twinkle in my eye,
    loving God,
    thank you.

For the way laughter can bring comfort,
    release,
    pleasure,
    and even health,
    loving God,
    thank you.

For laughter's capacity to mend a quarrel,
    defuse tension,
    prick pomposity
    and cement friendships,
    loving God,
    thank you.

For those who make me laugh,
    helping me to see the funny side of life,
    bringing a little light relief
    into the routine business of the day,
    loving God,
    thank you.
Amen.

Music

When Irish eyes are smiling from *Favourite Melodies*

19
For a new day

Music   Oh what a beautiful morning from *Favourite Memories*

Scripture   It's a pleasure, Lord, to express my gratitude to you;
                     to acknowledge you as the Most High through songs
                     of praise; to proclaim each morning the constancy of
                     your love and each night your great faithfulness.
                     Through all you have done, Lord, you have brought
                     me gladness, and I sing for joy as I survey your handi-
                     work.   *Psalm 92:1, 2, 4*

                     The constant love of the Lord never fades nor can his
                     mercies be exhausted; each morning they are made
                     new, such is his great faithfulness. 'The Lord is all I
                     need,' declares my soul, 'and so I will trust in him.'
                                                     Lamentations 3:22-24

Prayer   Lord, I woke up this morning,
                         the sun streaming in at the window,
                         birds singing in the garden,
                         a gentle breeze whispering in the trees –
                     and I wanted to sing for joy,
                         to shout your praise from the rooftops,
                         for suddenly life was wonderful,
                         a taste of Eden.
                     I looked round,
                         at the clouds scudding in the sky,
                         children walking to school,
                         bees buzzing among the flowers
                         and the dew glistening on the grass,
                         and I wondered how I could ever fail to notice these,

how my eyes could be blind
and my soul closed to the loveliness of life.
Yet it happens, Lord, all too often.
I wake up and feel pressure rather than promise,
  a sense of burden rather than blessing.
I get dressed,
  go to work,
  talk to friends,
  walk in the park,
  but though my eyes see all, my soul sees nothing,
  thoughts turned inwards instead of out,
  to my own little world instead of the world beyond.
But this morning was different,
  for you opened my eyes to the miracle of life
  and the beauty within it,
  so I bring you my praise
  and offer this prayer:
  teach me to see, Lord, new every morning.

My child,
  it's good to hear you,
  to witness your joy and glimpse your delight.
And believe me, there's nothing I'd like better
  than to answer your prayer,
  to give you always what you feel this moment.
Yet I can't promise that,
  for I know through experience
  that what you see today you will miss tomorrow,
  and what speaks to you now may seem silent then.
It's not your fault,
  just the way of the world –
  your mind distracted by each day's passing cares.
Though the dawn will break and the sun still shine,
  though the birds will sing and the flowers still bloom,
  you may wake tomorrow and be blind to it all,
  unmoved by life's beauty,
  untouched by my presence.
But whether you see me, or whether you don't,

whether morning brings joy, or fills you with dread,
take heart, for I am with you,
close by your side,
from the dawn of the morning
to the end of the day.

Silence

O Lord, the day is yours, and the night is yours;
    you have prepared the light and the sun;
        they continue this day according to your ordinance,
        for all things serve you.
Blessed are you, O Lord,
    for you turn the shadow of death into morning,
    and renew the face of the earth.
Amen.

Bishop Lancelot Andrewes (1555–1626)

Silence

We give you hearty thanks
    for the rest of the past night
    and for the gift of a new day
        with its opportunities of pleasing you.
Grant that we may so pass its hours
    in the perfect freedom of your service,
        that at eventide we may again give thanks to you,
        through Jesus Christ our Lord.
Amen.

Eastern Church

Silence

Next an anonymous prayer, taken from the Baptist service book *Praise God*:

All through this day, O Lord,
    let me touch the lives of others for good,
    by the power of your quickening Spirit,
    whether through the word I speak,
    the prayer I breathe,
    or the life I live.
In the name of Jesus.
Amen.

Silence

Final prayer

For this new day and the opportunities it brings –
    to work and rest,
    think and learn,
    reflect and worship,
    Lord,
    I thank you.

For the things I'll achieve,
    pleasures I'll enjoy,
    and people I'll meet.
    Lord,
    I thank you.

For the company I'll share,
    the love, laughter and conversations they bring,
    Lord,
    I thank you.

For the blessings you give,
    the guidance, strength, peace and hope
    you unfailingly provide,
    Lord,
    I thank you.

For the mercy you show,
  the patience, understanding and pardon
  you daily offer,
  Lord,
  I thank you.

For your love that shapes this and every day,
  in rain or sunshine,
  joy or sorrow,
  pain or pleasure,
  Lord,
  I thank you.
Amen.

Music   Oh what a beautiful morning from *Favourite Memories*

20
For the close of the day

Music   The Blessing of the Three from *Sacred Weave*
               (Keith Duke)

Scripture Accept my prayer as incense, my uplifted hands as a
               night-time sacrifice.   *Psalm 141:2*

               I lie down and sleep, and the Lord protects me
               throughout the night.   *Psalm 3:5*

Prayer   The day thou gavest, Lord, is ended,
               the darkness falls at thy behest;
               to thee our morning hymns ascended,
               thy praise shall hallow now our rest.

               We thank thee that thy Church unsleeping,
               while earth rolls onward into light,
               through all the world her watch is keeping
               and rests not now by day or night.

               As o'er each continent and island
               the dawn leads on another day,
               the voice of prayer is never silent,
               nor dies the strain of praise away.

               The sun that bids us rest is waking
               our brethren 'neath the western sky.
               And hour by hour fresh lips are making
               thy wondrous doings heard on high.

               So be it, Lord; thy throne shall never,
               like earth's proud empires, pass away;
               but stand, and rule, and grow for ever,
               till all thy creatures own thy sway.

               Silence

Those lovely words of the clergyman and hymn-writer John Ellerton (1826–93) have inspired innumerable generations across the years, affirming faith and trust at the end of the day. Much older, but expressing similar trust, is the following prayer from the sixth-century Gelasian Sacramentary:

I thank you, Lord,
    that you have kept me through this day.
I thank you, Lord,
    that you will keep me through the night.
Bring me, in safety, Lord, to the morning hours,
    that you may receive my praise at all times,
    through Jesus Christ my Lord.
Amen.

Silence

A prayer now from the German theologian and pastor Dietrich Bonhoeffer (1906–45):

O Lord my God,
    thank you for bringing this day to a close.
Thank you for giving me rest in body and in soul.
Your hand has been over me
    and has guarded and preserved me.
Forgive my lack of faith,
    and any wrong that I have done today,
    and help me to forgive all who have wronged me.
Let me sleep in peace under your protection,
    and keep me from all the temptations of darkness.
Into your hands I commend my loved ones;
    I commend to you my body and soul.
O God, may your holy name be praised.
Amen.

Silence

Final prayer   At the close of another day,
　　　　　　　　　remembering all that has been
　　　　　　　　　and awaiting all that is yet to come,
　　　　　　　　　Lord,
　　　　　　　　　I thank you.

For the love that's surrounded me,
　　and, above all, *your* love that's supported me,
　　Lord,
　　I thank you.

For the happiness I've enjoyed,
　　and, above all, the joy *you* have put into my heart,
　　Lord,
　　I thank you.

For the help I've received,
　　and, above all, the help *you* unfailingly provide,
　　Lord,
　　I thank you.

For the peace of this night,
　　and, above all, *your* peace that passes understanding,
　　Lord,
　　I thank you.

For the things I've learned,
　　and, above all, everything I've learned of *you*,
　　Lord,
　　I thank you.

For the goals I've achieved,
　　and, above all, what *you've* achieved in Christ,
　　Lord,
　　I thank you.

For new initiatives I've begun,
　　and, above all, for making *me* new,
　　Lord,
　　I thank you.

For the gift of life that I celebrate each day,
   and, above all, for *your* gift of life eternal.
Lord,
I thank you.
Amen.

Music   The Blessing of the Three from *Sacred Weave*
(Keith Duke)

EXPRESSING OUR NEEDS

1
When we first awake

Music   Morning has broken from *Morning Has Broken* (Rick Wakeman)

Scripture   Satisfy us each morning with your unswerving love, so that we may rejoice and celebrate all our days. I will sing of your power; every morning I will loudly sing of your constant love.   *Psalm 90:14; 59:16a*

The enduring love of the Lord never fades, his mercies can never be exhausted; each morning they are made new, such is his great faithfulness.
Lamentations 3:22, 23

Prayer   Awake my soul, and with the sun
thy daily stage of duty run;
shake off dull sloth, and joyful rise
to pay thy morning sacrifice.

Lord, I my vows to thee renew;
disperse my sins as morning dew;
guard my first springs of thought and will,
and with thyself my spirit fill.

Direct, control, suggest, this day,
all I design or do or say;
that all my powers, with all their might,
in thy sole glory may unite.

Silence

Those verses from a hymn by the bishop, poet and hymn-writer Thomas Ken (1637–1711) beautifully consecrate a new day to God's service. Not, of course, that our first thought each morning is necessarily of God; as the following prayer reminds us, our inclination as the morning alarm jangles in our ear may be to roll over and go back to sleep! Yet each day is God's gift, to be received with thanks and lived for him:

It woke me with a start,
    its shrill and insistent beep
    breaking into my dreams and forcing me to stir.
I'd have preferred to ignore it,
    to turn over and go back to sleep,
    but I'd the kids to get to school,
    a bus to catch,
    work to do,
    so I stumbled out of bed
    in readiness for another day.

Rouse me to your call, Lord –
    your summons to faith, service,
    repentance and commitment,
    however disturbing it may be.
Instead of sleepwalking through life,
    ignoring what I'd rather not hear,
    may I hear your voice and wake up to your challenge,
    ready to live each day for you.
Amen.

Silence

Next, the prayer of St Patrick (390–461), a perfect prayer for the new morning:

As I arise today,
    may the strength of God pilot me,
    the power of God uphold me,
    the wisdom of God guide me.
May the eye of God look before me,

the ear of God hear me,
the Word of God speak for me.
May the hand of God protect me,
the way of God lie before me,
the shield of God defend me,
the host of God save me.
May Christ shield me today:
Christ with me,
Christ before me,
Christ behind me,
Christ in me,
Christ beneath me,
Christ above me,
Christ on my right,
Christ on my left,
Christ when I lie down,
Christ when I sit,
Christ when I stand,
Christ in the heart of everyone who thinks of me,
Christ in the mouth of everyone who speaks of me,
Christ in every eye that sees me,
Christ in every ear that hears me.
Amen.

Silence

Another prayer, not as ancient as St Patrick's but historic nonetheless, is that of Jacob Astley (1579–1652), written in 1642 during the English Civil War, just before the battle of Edgehill:

Lord, help me to realise today
that you will be speaking to me
through the events of the day,
through people,
through things,
and through all creation.

Give me ears, eyes and heart to perceive you,
    however veiled your presence may be.
Give me insight to see through the exterior of things
    to the interior truth.
Give me your Spirit of discernment.
O Lord, you know how busy I must be this day.
If I forget you, do not forget me.
Amen.

Silence

Final prayer   God of new beginnings,
    too often I awake forgetful of your presence,
    and closed to the opportunities a new day brings.
Meet me afresh,
    this and every day.

Open my eyes once more
    to the promise of each new morning,
    to the good things you hold in store,
    the joy, love, beauty and interest each day can hold
    in such abundance.
Meet me afresh,
    this and every day.

Open my eyes to your presence with me,
    guiding my footsteps,
    giving your strength,
    revealing your love,
    granting your mercy.
Meet me afresh,
    this and every day.

Open my eyes to the blessings I have received –
    the countless reasons I have to rejoice,
    give thanks
    and look forward to the future.
Meet me afresh,
    this and every day.

Open my eyes to what I can do for others this day –
    the ways I can offer help,
    increase happiness,
    share burdens.
Meet me afresh,
    this and every day.

Open my eyes to opportunities for drawing closer to
    you –
    to reflect,
    pray,
    study your word
    and offer my worship.
Meet me afresh,
    this and every day.

Open my eyes to the wonder of knowing you,
    so that I may awake this and every day
    with joy in my heart
    and a song on my lips.
Meet me afresh,
    this and every day.
Amen.

Music   Morning has broken from *Morning Has Broken*
(Rick Wakeman)

2

When troubled by thoughts of ill health, old age or death

Music   Out of the depths from *Light Divine* (Val Goldsack)

Scipture   Deal kindly with me, Lord, for my health is failing;
               heal me, Lord, for I'm disturbed in my bones, deeply
               agitated in spirit. How long, Lord, until you help me?
               Turn to me, and save my life, rescue me on account of
               your constant love. I am tired of groaning, Lord. Night
               after night I inundate my sickbed with my tears; I soak
               my divan with weeping.   *Psalm 6:2-4, 6*

               We are not discouraged, for although we seem out-
               wardly debilitated, inwardly we are being renewed
               every day. For the inconsequential affliction we endure
               now is preparing for us an eternal weight of glory
               beyond measure.   *2 Corinthians 4:16, 17*

Prayer   When days are filled with struggle
               and nights are racked by pain,
               when faculties are failing
               and health is on the wane,
               when living seems an effort,
               past vigour long since gone,
               and darkness starts encroaching
               where once the sun had shone,
               Lord, teach me you'll be with me,
               to comfort and console –
               that, though time wastes the body,
               it cannot touch the soul.

When youth seems but a memory
and limbs are stiff and sore,
when daily I'm reminded
of things I'll do no more,
when inwardly I'm willing
but outwardly I'm weak,
and succour proves elusive,
no matter how I seek,
Lord, teach me you'll be with me,
to cherish and to mend –
that though this life is passing,
the grave is not the end.

When treasures start to tarnish,
as all things surely must,
when childhood dreams have faded
and hopes lie in the dust,
when life no longer sparkles
quite as it used to shine
and nothing can recapture
the joys that once were mine,
Lord, teach me, you'll be with me,
to strengthen and sustain –
that, though the night is falling,
your light will shine again.

Silence

Those words speak of the infirmity associated with advancing years, but, of course, illness can strike at any time of life. Our natural impulse then is to pray for healing, and, God willing, that prayer will be answered, but there are times when healing doesn't come and people have to come to terms with a lifetime of chronic disease or the stark reality of some terminal illness. I'm not sure how well I'd cope with such a situation, or indeed with any other serious adversity, but a prayer of Cardinal John Henry Newman (1801–90) suggests a way of consecrating even the most testing of experiences to God:

My God, you have created me
    to do you some definite service.
I have my place in your plan.
I may never know what it is in this life,
    but I will be told it in the next.
So I will trust you in all things.

If I am sick, may my sickness serve you.
If I am worried, may my worry serve you.
If I am in sorrow, may my sorrow serve you.
If I am exhausted, may my exhaustion serve you.
If I am sleepless, may my wakefulness serve you.
Amen.

Silence

Any serious illness reminds us of our mortality, increasingly so as we get older. Instinctively we push such thoughts away, but as the following reflective prayer – inspired while dusting the house – reminds us, our perspective on death as Christians should be shaped by our hope in Christ.

It lay everywhere –
    thick upon each surface,
    each nook and cranny of the house –
    a sombre reminder of the fate we share:
    our striving and dreams,
    our very self,
    destined to turn to dust.

Yet from the dust of the earth, Lord,
    you fashioned our bodies and gave us life.
And though to the ground we return –
    dust to dust,
    ashes to ashes –
    you promise us new beginnings:
    love that will neither fade nor perish,
    a kingdom that never ends.
Speak, then, not of death and decay,
    but of your new creation,
    life for evermore.
Amen.

Another celebrated prayer of Cardinal Newman views death in a correspondingly positive light, contrasting God's eternal peace with the ceaseless striving of this world:

O Lord,
    support me all through the long day of my life,
    until the shadows lengthen
    and the evening comes,
    and the busy world is hushed,
    and the fever of life is over,
    and my work is done.
Then, Lord, in your mercy,
    grant me safe lodging,
    a holy rest,
    and peace at the last.
Amen.

Silence

Final prayer   Of course, none of us welcomes illness, still less pain or death, but they are part of what it means to be human, and faith must strive to make sense of them.

Our closing prayer commits every part of life into God's keeping:

Lord God,
> whatever I may face,
> grant, I pray, the sure knowledge of your presence.

Restore me in life,
> **renew me in death.**

Should illness strike,
> reach out to heal, strengthen and comfort.

Restore me in life,
> **renew me in death.**

Should health fail,
> reach out into my frustration, despair and doubts.

Restore me in life,
> **renew me in death.**

Should I face suffering,
> reach out into my pain, weariness
> and longing for release.

Restore me in life,
> **renew me in death.**

Should life be threatened,
> reach out into my fear, sorrow and anxiety.

Restore me in life,
> **renew me in death.**

Assure me, Lord,
> that nothing will ever separate me from your love,
> now or in all eternity.

Amen.

Music   Out of the depths from *Light Divine* (Val Goldsack)

3
When seeking a deeper knowledge of God

Music   Be thou my vision from *Our Favourite Hymns 2*

Scripture   O God, you are my God, and I seek you, my spirit
                  yearns for you, my body craves for you, as in an arid
                  and exhausted land devoid of water.   *Psalm 63:1*

                  Give me insight into your ways, Lord; instruct me in
                  your paths. Guide and educate me in your truth, for
                  you are my saving God, upon whom I wait each day.
                  Train me to do your will, for you are my God. May
                  your good Spirit direct me on smooth ground.
                                              Psalm 25:4, 5; 143:10

Prayer   Breathe on me, Breath of God,
                  fill me with life anew,
                  that as you love, so I may love,
                  and do what you would do.

                  Breathe on me, Breath of God,
                  until my heart is pure:
                  until my will is one with yours
                  to do and to endure.

                  Breathe on me, Breath of God,
                  fulfil my heart's desire,
                  until this earthly part of me
                  glows with your heavenly fire.

                  Breathe on me, Breath of God,
                  so shall I never die,
                  but live with you the perfect life
                  of your eternity.

                  Silence

Those words of the hymn-writer and theologian Edwin Hatch (1835–89) express a longing that has probably inspired more prayers than any other; namely to know and love God better. Here are just a few. First, the prayer of the medieval saint and cardinal-bishop, Bonaventure (1221–74):

Lord Jesus Christ, pierce my soul with your love,
 so that I may always long for you alone,
 who are the bread of angels
 and the fulfilment of the soul's deepest desires.
May my heart always hunger and feed upon you,
 so that my soul may be filled
 with the sweetness of your presence.
May my soul thirst for you,
 who are the source of life, wisdom, knowledge, light
 and all the riches of God our Father.
May I always seek and find you,
 think upon you,
 speak to you
 and do all things for the honour and glory
 of your holy name.
Be always my only hope,
 my peace, my refuge and my help
 in whom my heart is rooted
 so that I may never be separated from you.
Amen.

Silence

Grant me, O Lord my God,
 a mind to know you,
 a heart to seek you,
 wisdom to find you,
 conduct pleasing to you,

faithful perseverance in waiting for you,
and a hope of finally embracing you.
Amen.   *St Thomas Aquinas (1225–74)*

Silence

A prayer now of Alcuin of York (c. 735–804), the eighth-century scholar and advisor to Charlemagne the Great:

Eternal Light, shine into my heart.
Eternal Goodness, deliver me from evil.
Eternal Power, be my support.
Eternal Wisdom, scatter the darkness of my ignorance.
Eternal Pity, have mercy upon me,
    that with all my heart and mind
    and soul and strength
    I may seek your face
    and be brought by your infinite mercy
    to your holy presence,
    through Jesus Christ my Lord.
Amen.

Silence

St Augustine of Hippo (354–430) wrote numerous memorable prayers during his lifetime, including the following:

Lord, let the flame of your love
    set on fire my whole heart.
May I wholly burn towards you,
    wholly love you, set aflame by you.
Amen.

Silence

Finally, a prayer from the Spanish mystic, St John of the Cross (1542–91):

O living flame of love,
    that wounds my soul so tenderly in its deepest centre;
    since, by your grace, I can endure your touch,
    perfect your work in me according to your will.
Amen.

Silence

Final prayer Mighty God,
    create in me, through your Spirit,
    a passionate desire to know you better,
    a genuine hunger to love and honour you
    as you deserve.
Encircle my life,
    and draw me close.

Give me a fresh sense of who you are,
    greater than my mind can fathom,
    able to accomplish more than I can ever ask
    or expect.
Encircle my life,
    and draw me close.

Teach me to see with your eyes,
    to let my thoughts soar to heaven
    rather than being tied to earth,
    and so to appreciate all you are able to do,
    both in my life and that of the world around me.
Encircle my life,
    and draw me close.

Instil in me deeper faith,
  stronger commitment,
  truer devotion,
  and fuller joy,
  my life resounding to your praise in every part.
Encircle my life,
  and draw me close.

Cleanse me from everything that keeps me from you,
  preventing me from being the person
  you would have me be.
Work your miracle of grace within me,
  so that I may know and love you as you do me.
Encircle my life,
  and draw me close.
  Amen.

Music Be thou my vision from *Our Favourite Hymns 2*

4
When in need of patience

Music Prayer of St Teresa from *Awakening in Love* (Margaret Rizza)

Scripture I waited patiently for the Lord; he bent down to me and listened to my cry. *Psalm 40:1*

Do not overlook this key point, my friends: a single day, with the Lord, is comparable to a thousand years, and a thousand years to one day. The Lord is not sluggish in honouring his promise, in the way some might imagine, but deals patiently with you, wanting all to come to repentance rather than for anyone to perish. *2 Peter 3:8, 9*

Prayer I put my foot down, determined to beat the lights,
    but they changed as I approached,
    forcing me to brake,
    and I seethed in frustration,
    bemoaning my luck.

Why, Lord?
What did I hope to gain?
Why did I sour the day
    in search of a few seconds more?
Grant me the gift of patience
    and the ability to celebrate each moment,
    whatever it might bring.
Teach me to savour the here and now,
    and to let go of what might be or could have been.
Amen.

Silence

Few of us find patience easy. Life is short, so we want things now rather than later, and though we try to curb our impetuosity, time and again we succumb:

Lord, I know it's foolish,
    that impatience gets me nowhere,
    but I just can't help it.
I try telling myself, 'What's the hurry?'
I do my best to slow down,
    to take it easy.
I remind myself of what really matters.
Yet, before I know it,
    I find myself fretting once more
    about a few moments wasted here,
    a little delay there.
Touch me by your grace
    and teach me to receive every moment as your gift,
    living each one for what it is.
Put a new and tranquil spirit within me,
    a quiet mind and patient heart,
    so that I may recognise the more I worry about time,
    the less I will enjoy the time I have.
Amen.

Silence

An inner tranquillity of spirit – that's the key to patience, and that's what St John of the Cross (1542–91) asks for in the following prayer:

O blessed Jesus,
    give me stillness of soul in thee.
Let thy mighty calmness reign in me;
    rule me, O King of gentleness, King of peace.
Give me control, great power of self-control,
    control over my words, thoughts and actions.

From all irritability, want of meekness,
   want of gentleness,
     dear Lord, deliver me.
By thine own deep patience, give me patience.
Make me in this and all things
   more and more like thee.
Amen.

Silence

Final prayer   In our final prayer, we commit to God some of those things that most severely test our patience.

When hopes are frustrated, dreams dashed
   and plans thwarted,
   Lord,
     grant me patience.

When nothing seems to change,
   despite all my efforts,
   Lord,
     grant me patience.

When I fume and fret,
   wanting things to happen faster,
   Lord,
     grant me patience.

When I'm irritated by slowness in others,
   real or imagined,
   Lord,
     grant me patience.

When I'm dismayed by my inability to serve you
   as I wish,
   Lord,
     grant me patience.

When I can't find answers
   to problems large and small,
   Lord,
   grant me patience.

In everything help me to look at life in terms
   not of my brief span
   but of your eternity.
   Lord,
   grant me patience.
Amen.

Music   Prayer of St Teresa from *Awakening in Love*
(Margaret Rizza)

5
When feeling up against it

Music   Come to me from *Gentle as a Lamb*
             (Christopher Wright)

Scripture   Save me, O God, for the waters have come up to my
                 neck. Do not keep you distance, for trouble approaches,
                 and there is no one else to help.   *Psalm 69:1; 22:11*

                 Cast all your worries on to him, for he cares about you.
                                                               1 Peter 5:7

Prayer   When I'm feeling crushed by care,
              heavy burdens hard to bear;
              when my heart, oppressed by grief,
              looks in vain to find relief;
              when I find it hard to trust,
              hopes and dreams reduced to dust;
              teach me, Lord, that you are near,
              never mind how things appear,
              reaching out to see me through,
              ever-faithful, ever-true.
              Be there with me, by my side,
              there to help, support, provide.
              Lead me onwards by your grace,
              till I meet you, face to face.

              Silence

              God has different ways of answering prayer when we
              find ourselves up against it. Sometimes he removes the
              problem, but at other times, as a prayer of the sixteenth-
              century bishop Miles Coverdale indicates, he may
              simply give us the strength we need to face it:

O give us patience and steadfastness in adversity,
strengthen our weakness,
comfort us in trouble and distress,
help us to fight;
grant unto us that in true obedience
and contentment of mind
we may give over our own wills unto thee,
our Father in all things,
according to the example of thy beloved Son;
that in adversity we grudge not,
but offer up ourselves unto thee
without contradiction.
O give us a willing and cheerful mind,
that we may gladly suffer and bear all things
for thy sake.
Amen.

Silence

Another old prayer is that of Bishop Thomas Wilson
(1663–1755):

Grant, O God,
that amidst all the discouragements, difficulties,
dangers, distress and darkness of this mortal life,
I may depend upon your mercy
and on this build my hopes, as on a sure foundation.
Let your infinite mercy in Christ Jesus
deliver me from despair,
both now and at the hour of death.
Amen.

Silence

To what can we compare the strength God is able to offer us in times of trial and turmoil? The sight of a suspension bridge spanning a deep gorge seemed to provide a perfect image:

It was a majestic sight:
    a single graceful arch spanning the ravine,
    simple and elegant,
    yet supporting it were massive chains,
    mighty sinews of steel combining to bear the load.

There are times, Lord, when,
    despite the impression I may give to others,
    I feel weighed down by heavy burdens,
    the pressure building until I feel
    unable to take the strain any longer.
Yet even though *I* can't cope,
    teach me that *you* can,
    your strength sufficient for all my needs.
Help me to entrust myself into your gracious arms,
    knowing you will support me,
    whatever life might bring.
Amen.

Silence

Final prayer   When I look at the difficulties and demands of life,
    and question my ability to get through,
    remind me, Lord, of your sovereign power
    and teach me to trust you always.

When I am plagued by fear,
    weighed down by worry and uncertainty,
    remind me, Lord, of your sovereign power
    and teach me to trust you always.

When I feel weary,
    unable to bounce back
    from setbacks and disappointments,
    remind me, Lord, of your sovereign power
    and teach me to trust you always.

When things go wrong,
    bringing hurt, sorrow or trouble,
    remind me, Lord, of your sovereign power
    and teach me to trust you always.

When problems mount up and I see nowhere to turn,
    no way of getting through them,
    remind me, Lord, of your sovereign power
    and teach me to trust you always.

Whenever I lose sight of your love and greatness,
    forgetting all you are able to do,
    remind me, Lord, of your sovereign power
    and teach me to trust you always.
Amen.

Music   Come to me from *Gentle as a Lamb*
(Christopher Wright)

6
When we lose sight of God's presence

Music   Come, my Lord, my light, my way from *Sacred Weave*
                   (Keith Duke)

Scripture   If I sail on the wings of the morning and settle at the
                   uttermost limits of the sea, even there your hand will
                   lead me, your right hand holding me firm.
                   Psalm 139:9, 10

                   I will always be with you, to the very end of time.
                   Matthew 28:20b

Prayer   In vain, great God, in vain I try
                   To escape thy quick all-searching eye:
                   Thou with one undivided view
                   Dost look the whole creation through.

                   My private walks to thee are known;
                   In solitude I'm not alone:
                   Thou round my bed a guard dost keep;
                   Thine eyes are open while mine sleep.

                   Thou art the light by which I see;
                   Be it my joy to live in thee:
                   Beset me, Lord, behind, before;
                   And draw my heart to love thee more.

                   Silence

                   Sometimes, as those lines from a poem by the country
                   parson, poet and philosopher John Norris (1657–1711)

remind us, we consciously evade God's presence, unwilling to meet his searching challenge. More often, though, as explored in the following reflection, we simply fail to see:

You're here, Lord!
How did I never see it before?
How did I go so long,
   aching, thirsting, searching,
   when all the time you were here,
   standing by my side,
   right before my very eyes?
It's astonishing, yet it's true,
   day after day I've gone through life
   oblivious to your presence.
I've knelt in prayer and begged you to hear me,
   I've shared in worship, hungry to meet you,
   I've studied your word, thirsting for guidance,
   yet when you answered,
   when you touched my soul,
   I never knew it, even when you called my name.
Why Lord?
Wasn't I listening?
Was my mind distracted, my attention elsewhere?
I thought I was ready, tuned in and waiting,
   but I wasn't, for somehow I missed you
   when you were there all along.

My child,
   there's no mystery, strange though it all seems to you.
You *were* listening,
   as eagerly and intently as I could have wished for,
   except for one thing –
   it was for *your* answer,
   in *your* time,
   on *your* terms!
That's what muddled you.

When I told you to wait, you wanted to hurry;
    when I answered no, you shouted yes;
    when I asked for patience,
    you chafed with frustration;
    when I urged you forward, you wandered back.
It wasn't me you were looking for,
    much though you thought it,
    but yourself –
    me made in your image
    rather than you made in mine,
    and that's why you never heard.
But I was there for all that,
    just as I always am,
    just as I'll always be,
    speaking my word,
    leading you by the hand,
    offering you my guidance
    and waiting till you respond.
So next time you do not see me,
    when you call my name and I do not seem to answer,
    look within and ask yourself,
    are you really listening,
    and do you want to hear?

Silence

O supreme and inaccessible Light,
    O complete and blessed Truth,
    how far you are from me,
    even though I am so near to you!
How remote you are from my sight,
    even though I am present to yours!
You are everywhere in your entirety,
    and yet I do not see you;
    in you I move and have my being,
    and yet I cannot approach you.

O God, let me know you
   and love you so that I may find my joy in you;
   and if I cannot do so fully in this life,
   let me at least make some progress every day,
   until at last that knowledge, love, and joy
   come to me in all their plenitude.
Amen.

St Anselm (1033–1109)

Silence

Final prayer   Living God,
   as I worship you,
   give me a greater sense of your presence,
   a recognition that you are here by my side,
   aware of my thoughts,
   responding to my prayer,
   watching over my life.
Help me to find you, Lord,
   not just here but everywhere.

Through times such as this, set aside for you,
   help me to realise that you are always present,
   involved in both my life and the life of others,
   daily at work in the world.
Help me to find you, Lord,
   not just here but everywhere.

Save me, then, from losing sight of you,
   either through wilful rejection, forgetfulness
   or misplaced preconceptions,
   but instead may I glimpse your presence
   in the daily round of life,
   discerning your love and purpose through it all.
Help me to find you, Lord,
   not just here but everywhere.

So may I consecrate every minute of every day to you,
    seeking your will, guidance, grace and glory
    in all things.
Help me to find you, Lord,
    not just here but everywhere.
Amen.

Music   Come, my Lord, my light, my way from *Sacred Weave*
(Keith Duke)

7
When feeling dissatisfied with our lot

Music   When I survey the wondrous cross from *Festival of Anthems*

Scripture   Do not amass earthly treasures for yourselves . . . Focus instead on treasures in heaven, vulnerable neither to moth, rust nor larceny. For you can be sure of this; wherever your treasure is to be found, your heart will be found too.   *Matthew 6:19a, 20*

Seek first the kingdom and righteousness of God and you will be given everything else you need in addition.   *Matthew 6:33*

Prayer   In a world awash with greed,
occupied with serving self,
where the overriding creed
honours gain and worships wealth;
where we rarely seem content,
always seeking one thing more,
so much time and effort spent
adding to our worldly store,
gracious Lord, help me to see
where true riches really lie:
teach me that your love is free,
something money cannot buy.
Teach me, then, each day to toil
not for treasures of this earth,
but for that which will not spoil:
gifts of everlasting worth.

Silence

How far do we seek lasting treasures rather than what
this world has to offer? Shopping in a busy supermarket
set me thinking:

Food, drink, clothes, books;
    houseware, electrical goods, even insurance –
    all there under one roof at bargain prices,
    everything we need,
    all we could ask for.
And crowds flocked accordingly
    to this consumer paradise,
    a cathedral of delights.

I'm not knocking it, Lord,
    for the bargains are welcome,
    the range excellent,
    and the convenience a bonus,
    but I can stack my trolley full,
    yet still leave empty,
    if I imagine what I buy can meet my needs.
It may feed the body
    but not the soul,
    delight the senses
    but not the spirit –
    contentment being a gift rather than product,
    a treasure to be received
    rather than a commodity plucked from a shelf.
Teach me where true fulfilment lies,
    and to seek it before all else.
Amen.

Silence

Next, a prayer of St Ignatius Loyola (1491–1556),
words that speak of letting go that we may truly receive:

Take, O Lord, and receive my entire liberty,
   my memory,
   my understanding
   and my whole will.
All that I am and all that I possess you have given me:
   I surrender it all to you to be disposed of
   according to your will.
Give me only your love and your grace;
   with these I will be rich enough,
   and will desire nothing more.
Amen.

Silence

Final prayer   Too often, Lord, I forget how fortunate I am.
I see what others earn or own,
   and I'm jealous,
   asking why *I* shouldn't have the same.
Teach me to seek your kingdom and righteousness,
   treasure in heaven rather than riches on earth.

Instead of appreciating what I have,
   I end up dwelling on the things I don't have,
   wanting more of this,
   more of that,
   more of everything.
Teach me to seek your kingdom and righteousness,
   treasure in heaven rather than riches on earth.

Whatever I acquire, I covet something extra,
   possessions failing to satisfy as I expect,
   pleasing enough for a moment
   but their shine soon fading.
Teach me to seek your kingdom and righteousness,
   treasure in heaven rather than riches on earth.

Time and again, Lord,
    I lose sight of what's truly of value:
    joy, peace, hope and love;
    the knowledge that I'm valued by you,
    accepted for what I am;
    the assurance of your forgiveness;
    the daily experience of your presence
    by my side and deep within.
Teach me to seek your kingdom and righteousness,
    treasure in heaven rather than riches on earth.

Remind me that such blessings are beyond price,
    too wonderful for words
    yet offered by you freely,
    not just now but for all eternity.
Teach me to seek your kingdom and righteousness,
    treasure in heaven rather than riches on earth.

Save me, then, from chasing after illusory happiness,
    from attempting to fill my life
    with what can never truly fulfil.
Teach me simply to look to you
    and to open my heart to your grace,
    recognising that through your many blessings
    I am rich indeed.
Teach me to seek your kingdom and righteousness,
    treasure in heaven rather than riches on earth.
Amen.

Music   When I survey the wondrous cross from *Festival of Anthems*

8
When wrestling with temptation

Music   Circle me, Lord from *Sacred Weave* (Keith Duke)

Scripture   Do not lead us into temptation, but rescue us from evil.
                                            Matthew 6:13

Ours is not a high priest incapable of empathising with our failings; rather, he was tempted in every way just as we are. Because he personally experienced the anguish associated with temptation, he is able to help those being tempted in turn.   *Hebrews 4:15; 2:18*

Prayer   Be thou my guardian and my guide,
            and hear me when I call;
            let not my slippery footsteps slide,
            and hold me lest I fall.

            And if I tempted am to sin,
            and outward things are strong,
            do thou, O Lord, keep watch within,
            and save my soul from wrong.

            Silence

            Those words of the Anglican author, poet, theologian and clergyman Isaac Williams (1802–65) speak of how easily we can slip up as we attempt to walk the way of Christ. An icy path after a recent snowfall graphically brought home that truth to me:

I tried to keep my feet,
  but it was hopeless,
  the ground too slippery to gain a hold.
For each step forward I slid back another,
  my legs giving way beneath me,
  skidding now this way,
  now that,
  any progress all but impossible.

Lord, I try to walk the way of Christ,
  but I repeatedly slip up,
  temptation and weakness causing me to founder,
  and before I know it
  I find myself back where I started,
  the journey of discipleship more demanding
  than I ever imagined.
Guide my footsteps,
  that I may tread the path of faith more surely.
And should I slide backwards,
  take me by the hand,
  lift me up,
  and lead me forward again.
Amen.

Silence

We continue with two memorable prayers. First, a prayer of the thirteenth-century theologian St Thomas Aquinas (1225–74):

Most loving God,
  give me a steadfast heart,
  which no unworthy thought can drag downwards;
  an unconquered heart,
  which no hardship can wear out;
  an upright heart,
  which no worthless purpose can ensnare.

Give me also, O Lord my God,
  understanding to know you,
  diligence to seek you,
  and a faithfulness that will finally embrace you;
  through Jesus Christ my Lord.
Amen.

Silence

And next, a prayer by John Donne (1573-1631):

Eternal and most glorious God,
  suffer me not so to undervalue myself
  . as to give away my soul,
  thy soul,
  thy dear and precious soul,
  for nothing;
  and all the world is nothing, if the soul be given for it.
Preserve therefore my soul, O Lord,
  because it belongs to thee,
  and preserve my body
  because it belongs to my soul.
Amen.

Silence

Final prayer   Lord Jesus Christ,
  you taught your followers to pray,
  'Do not lead us into temptation',
  yet too often I succumb when temptation strikes.
Help me, I pray.

When I'm tempted to go astray –
to indulge my desires,
  ignore your will,
  excuse what I know is inexcusable,

gracious Lord,
help me to stay true.

When I'm tempted to follow the crowd –
to shirk difficult decisions,
water down my principles,
pander to popular opinion,
gracious Lord,
help me to stay true.

When I'm tempted to put myself first –
to seek my own ends,
follow my own inclinations,
live without reference to you,
gracious Lord,
help me to stay true.

When I'm tempted to forget others –
to overlook their needs,
dismiss their opinions,
ignore their rights,
gracious Lord,
help me to stay true.

Lord Jesus Christ,
tempted just as I am, yet standing firm
even to death on a cross,
touch my life,
and grant me strength and courage to stay faithful
to your way;
gracious Lord,
help me to stay true.
Amen.

Music   Circle me, Lord from *Sacred Weave* (Keith Duke)

9

When craving peace

Music   Be still, for the presence of the Lord from *Our Favourite Hymns 2*

Scripture   Be still, and know that I am God.

Psalm 46:10a

My legacy to you is peace – that's what I leave to you, my very own peace, unlike anything the world can offer. So, then, don't let anything disturb or distress you. Put your heart at rest and fear nothing.   *John 14:27*

Prayer   Like a dove come to me, fill me with peace;
Lord, I leave all in your care.
Time now for worry and striving to cease;
always, my God, you are there.
When strength is fading, you heal and renew,
where all seems hopeless, your hand sees me through;
though all else may fail me, your love will stay true:
always, my God, you are there.

Bind up my wounds and in love make me whole;
Lord, I leave all in your care.
Quieten my heart and bring rest to my soul;
always, my God, you are there.
When I am broken you help me rebuild,
with you beside me the turmoil is stilled,
the darkest of moments with light will be filled:
always, my God, you are there.

Silence

A universal human longing is for peace of mind, a peace that endures despite everything life may throw at us. The sight of a city park in the middle of London summed up for me what that peace is all about:

It was such a surprise:
　　there, so close to the roar of traffic
　　and milling crowds,
　　the jostling skyscrapers and throb of city life,
　　a little park,
　　an oasis of tranquillity,
　　a quiet retreat from the hectic world beyond.
Flowers bloomed,
　　trees blossomed,
　　birds sang,
　　squirrels played,
　　oblivious to the incongruity of it all.

The peace you promise, Lord, is equally unlikely,
　　yet just as real,
　　not removed from this world,
　　but found equally amid the hurly-burly of life,
　　the stresses and strains of the daily routine.
Open my heart, Lord,
　　to that special peace beyond understanding;
　　may it touch each moment of every day.
Amen.

Silence

As Christians, then, we believe true peace is found in Christ, but, as the following memorable words of St Augustine of Hippo (354–430) remind us, the tranquillity of which he speaks sometimes eludes us:

Late have I loved you,
　　O Beauty so ancient and so new.
You called, and broke through my defences,

and now I long for you.
You breathed your fragrance on me,
   and I drew in my breath
   and now I pant for you.
I tasted you,
   and now I hunger and thirst for you.
You touched me,
   and I burn for your peace.
Amen.

Silence

Similar thoughts are expressed by the Danish theologian
and philosopher Søren Kierkegaard (1813–55):

O Lord,
   calm the waves of this heart;
   calm its tempests.
Calm thyself, O my soul,
   so that God is able to repose in thee,
   so that his peace may cover thee.
Yes, Father in heaven,
   often have we found that the world
   cannot give us peace.
O but make us feel that thou art able to give peace;
   let us know the truth of thy promises:
   that the whole world
   may not be able to take away thy peace.
Amen.

Silence

If we fail to make God's peace fully our own, we
know the fault lies with us rather than him, and so we
seek it all the more, not through our own efforts but
through his grace. A prayer from the Syrian liturgy of

St Clement of Alexandria (c. 150–215) articulates that
yearning:

O God, you are the unsearchable abyss of peace,
    the ineffable sea of love,
    and the fountain of blessings.
Water us with plenteous streams
    from the riches of your grace;
    and from the most sweet springs of your kindness
    make us children of quietness and heirs of peace.
Amen.

Silence

Final prayer God of peace,
    teach me each day to make time for you –
    time to pause and ponder,
    to take stock of my life, reflect on your goodness
    and hear your word.
Through your still small voice,
    grant me a quiet mind and tranquil spirit.

Silence

Teach me that your peace is truly different
    from anything this world can give,
    rooted not in transitory pleasure
    or short-term satisfaction,
    but in your undying love,
    the knowledge that, come what may,
    you will be with me,
    and that your purpose will finally prevail.
Through your still small voice,
    grant me a quiet mind and tranquil spirit.

Silence

Come, then, and breathe your peace within me,
    calming fears,
    easing frustration,
    healing wounds,
    soothing sorrows.
Through your still small voice,
    grant me a quiet mind and tranquil spirit.

Silence

Lord, I have made time for you in the quietness.
Go with me now as I return to the bustle of life
    with all its trouble, confusion, demands
    and responsibilities;
    and may your peace rest with me there,
    this day and always.
Through your still small voice,
    grant me a quiet mind and tranquil spirit,
    through Jesus Christ my Lord.
Amen.

Music   Be still, for the presence of the Lord from *Our Favourite Hymns 2*

10
When struggling to practise
what we preach

Music   Let your beauty from *Awakening in Love*
(Margaret Rizza)

Scripture   Faith alone, without works, is dead.   *James 2:17*

Be doers of the word, and not those who hear it and
deceive themselves.   *James 1:22*

Prayer   O thou who camest from above
the fire celestial to impart,
kindle a flame of sacred love
on the mean altar of my heart.

There let it for thy glory burn
with inextinguishable blaze,
and trembling to its source return
in humble prayer and fervent praise.

Jesus, confirm my heart's desire
to work and speak and think for thee;
still let me guard the holy fire
and still stir up the gift in me.

Ready for all thy perfect will,
my acts of faith and love repeat,
till death thy endless mercies seal,
and make the sacrifice complete.

Silence

Words of Charles Wesley (1707–88) that sum up the sort of life we yearn to lead. But, as another less well-known hymn reminds us, the reality is often very different:

Dear Master, in whose life I see
all that I long, but fail to be,
let thy clear light for ever shine,
to shame and guide this life of mine.

Though what I dream and what I do
in my poor days are always two,
help me, oppressed by things undone,
O thou, whose deeds and dreams were one.

Silence

Those lovely words of the hymn-writer John Hunter (1848–1917) simply but eloquently sum up the frustration we can feel at failing to live up to our faith. Obedience in discipleship doesn't come easily. As with learning anything, we have to work at it if we are to achieve our goal. Practice, as they say, makes perfect, as I was reminded watching a televised game of snooker:

He made it look so easy,
   rattling in one ball after another,
    and each time the next shot was lined up perfectly,
   the break accumulated
   with quiet but assured precision.
Only, of course, it *wasn't* easy;
   it was the result of years of discipline,
   countless days practising at the table,
   executing those seemingly effortless pots
   time after time,
   until a truly breathtaking skill
   became almost as natural as breathing.

Lord, give me similar commitment in following you,
similar resolve to honour your will,
similar dedication in discipleship.
Teach me truly to practise what I preach,
in the sense of working at it each day,
until walking the way of Christ
becomes second nature,
not the exception but the norm.
Amen.

Silence

Many classic prayers ask for God's help in living more faithfully, among them the following from St Ignatius Loyola (1491–1556):

Teach me, good Lord,
to serve you as you deserve:
to give, and not to count the cost;
to fight, and not to heed the wounds;
to toil, and not to seek for rest;
to labour, and to ask for no reward,
except that of knowing that I do your will;
through Jesus Christ my Lord.
Amen.

Silence

Final prayer   Let us seek God's help, then, in prayer to live up to the faith we proclaim.

Lord Jesus Christ,
I want to follow you,
but I so rarely practise what I preach,
failing to show in my life
the faith I profess with my lips.

Take what I am
and make me what I long to be.

I talk of forgiving others, yet nurse grievances,
 of being content, yet am full of envy,
 of ministering to others, yet serve self,
 of loving truth, yet deal falsely.
Take what I am
and make me what I long to be.

I speak of commitment, but am careless in discipleship,
 of faith, but am full of doubt,
 of vision, but am narrow in outlook,
 of being a new creation,
 but am the same as I've always been.
Take what I am
and make me what I long to be.

Help me not simply to talk about faith
 or speak of love,
 but to demonstrate both
 through the person I am and the life I live.
Grant that my words and deeds may be one,
 a living witness to your renewing, redeeming power.
Take what I am
and make me what I long to be.
Amen.

Music   Let your beauty from *Awakening in Love*
(Margaret Rizza)

11
When seeking guidance

Music   Lead, kindly light from *Light Divine* (Val Goldsack)

Scripture   Pour out your light and truth and let them guide me;
                 let them lead me to your holy hill and your dwelling
                 place.   *Psalm 43:3*

                 Reveal your ways to me, Lord, instruct me in your paths.
                 Guide and teach me in your truth, for you are the God
                 who saves me; I wait for you all day long.   *Psalm 25:4*

Prayer   Lead us, heavenly Father, lead us
                 o'er the world's tempestuous sea;
                 guard us, guide us, keep us, feed us,
                 for we have no help but thee;
                 yet possessing every blessing
                 if our God our Father be.

                 Silence

                 These words of the hymn-writer James Edmeston
                 (1791–1867) find an echo in another celebrated hymn
                 – that of James William Elliott (1833–1915):

                 O Jesus, I have promised,
                 to serve thee to the end;
                 be thou for ever near me,
                 my Master and my friend:
                 I shall not fear the battle
                 if thou art by my side,
                 nor wander from the pathway
                 if thou wilt be my guide.

                 Silence

Two historic prayers now. First, one by the Roman statesman, writer and philosopher Boethius (c. 480–524):

Father,
  help us to climb in spirit
  to the fountain of all light,
  and be purified.
Shine forth in splendour,
  you who are calm weather,
  a place of quietness and serenity
  for all who faithfully make you their goal,
  and break through those earthly things
  that obscure your glory.
You are the end and the beginning –
  our guide and vehicle along the way,
  the journey, and the journey's end.
Amen.

Silence

And next, a prayer of St Teresa of Avila (1515–82):

Lord, grant that I may always allow myself
  to be guided by you,
  always follow your plans,
  and perfectly accomplish your Holy Will.
Grant that in all things,
  great and small,
  today and all the days of my life,
  I may do whatever you require of me.
Help me respond
  to the slightest prompting of your grace,
so that I may be your trustworthy instrument
  for your honour.

May your will be done in time and in eternity
  by me,
  in me,
  and through me.
Amen.

Silence

Final prayer   Loving God
  you have shown me, in Christ, the way to life,
  the path of faithful service and fulfilment.
You promise to lead me
  into new experiences of your love
  and a deeper understanding of your purpose.
Help me to see more clearly,
  and to walk in faith.

Save me from going astray,
  following my own inclinations
  and ignoring your will.
Save me from trusting you when all goes well,
  but questioning the moment life fails to conform
  to my expectations.
Help me to see more clearly,
  and to walk in faith.

Save me from preferring an easy life
  to the way of faith,
  from following the path of this world
  instead of that which leads to life.
Save me from putting myself before you and others,
  from selfishly turning inwards
  rather than reaching out in love.
Help me to see more clearly,
  and to walk in faith.

Show me the way you would have me tread,
    and give me faith to follow,
    looking always to Jesus,
    the pioneer and perfecter of my faith.
Amen.

Music   Lead, kindly light from *Light Divine* (Val Goldsack)

12
When prayers seem unanswered

Music   Desert waters from *Sacred Pathway* (Keith Duke)

Scripture   How much longer, Lord? Are you going to hide yourself away for ever? O God, do not remain silent; please
don't keep quiet or do nothing. Listen and answer me,
Lord, for I'm desperately in need. Let my prayer reach
you; hear my cry, I beg you. Listen to my prayer, Lord,
and answer me when I call.
Psalm 89:46a, 83:1; 86:1; 88:2; 102:1a

My God, my God, why have you forsaken me? Why
are you so far from saving me, so far from the words
of my groaning? O my God, I cry out day and night,
my voice never silent, yet you do not answer.
Psalm 22:1, 2

Prayer   I prayed, Lord.
I watched and I waited,
    trusting,
    expecting,
    hoping . . .
    but nothing happened.
I prayed again,
    crying out for help,
    pleading for guidance,
    and this time I was not only sure you'd answer
    but also confident of what the answer would be.
Only it wasn't what I expected,
    life taking an unforeseen twist,
    shattering my illusions,
    crushing my hopes,

and leaving faith teetering,
balanced over a precipice.
I called again,
begging you this time,
promising you undying loyalty,
total commitment,
if you would just respond to my plea . . .
but yet again the answer was wanting,
and I felt lost,
confused,
frightened;
everything that had seemed so certain
suddenly so insecure.
But then you spoke –
through the counsel of a friend,
the testimony of Scripture,
the prompting of your Spirit,
the circumstances of life –
and I realised you'd been speaking all along,
giving your reply,
except the answer was different
from the one I'd looked for,
your purpose breaking out
of the fetters I'd placed upon it,
refusing to be confined.
I'd prayed,
I'd trusted,
but I'd anticipated the wrong thing,
expecting you to act as I wanted
instead of giving myself to your will.
Forgive me, Lord,
and teach me to open my eyes to the unexpected,
to the constant surprise of your love.
Amen.

Silence

It would be simplistic to suggest that all unanswered prayer is down to a single reason, but, as that prayer suggests, our expectations may prevent us from hearing what God is saying more often than we might imagine. God's answer may be very different from the one we want to hear, as the following anonymous reflection makes clear:

I asked God for strength that I might achieve;
I was made weak that I might learn humbly to obey.
I asked for health that I might do greater things;
I was given infirmity that I might do better things.
I asked for riches that I might be happy;
I was given poverty that I might be wise.
I asked for power that I might have people's praise;
I was given weakness that I might feel my need of God.
I asked for all things that I might enjoy life;
I was given life that I might enjoy all things.
I was given nothing that I asked for;
but everything that I had hoped for.
Despite myself, my prayers were answered;
I am among all people most richly blessed.

Silence

It may be that God doesn't answer us immediately for a reason, or even that he's speaking to us through silence – an idea explored in a prayer by the Danish philosopher and theologian Søren Kierkegaard (1813–55):

Father in heaven,
    you speak to us in many ways.
Even when you are silent, you still speak to us,
    in order to examine us,
        to try us,

and so that the hour of understanding
may be more profound.
Oh, in the time of silence,
when I remain alone and abandoned
because I do not hear your voice,
it seems as if the separation must last for ever,
but, Father, it is only a moment of silence
in the intimacy of a conversation.
Bless, then, this silence,
and let me not forget that you are silent through love,
and that you speak through love,
so that in your silence and in your word
you are still the same Father,
and that you guide and instruct even by your silence.
Amen.

Silence

Final prayer   Loving God,
it's hard to keep praying when you seem silent,
to keep trusting
when my pleas seem to fall on deaf ears.
Help me to believe at such times that you have heard
and that, in your own time and way,
you will respond.
Whatever your answer,
help me to listen and accept.

Help me to be open to *your* answer,
however much it may differ
from what I want you to say.
Help me to be open to your call to wait patiently,
to recognise that your answer may be
'yes, but not yet'.
Whatever your answer,
help me to listen and accept.

Help me to be open to your saying no,
    to recognise that what I ask for
    is not what you desire or is best for me.
Help me to be open to your saying maybe,
    the answer to my prayer
    dependent on the seriousness of my request
    and depth of my commitment.
Whatever your answer,
    help me to listen and accept.

Help me to be open to the possibility
    I'm not truly listening,
    my relationship with you nothing like it should be.
Help me to be open to the fact that in this life
    some prayers can't be answered,
    your hands tied by the rules you have set in place
    until the dawn of your eternity.
Whatever your answer,
    help me to listen and accept.

Loving God,
    however much it may seem you fail to hear us,
    teach me that you both hear *and* respond,
    and may that knowledge sustain me
    this and every day.
Amen.

Music   Desert waters from *Sacred Pathway* (Keith Duke)

13
When finding it hard to trust

Music
Like the deer that yearns from *In God Alone*
(Andrew Moore)

Scripture
I trust in you, Lord. I say, 'You are my God; my times
are in your hand.'   *Psalm 31:14, 15a*

Whenever I feel afraid, I put my trust in you. In God,
whose word I honour, in God who I trust; I will not
fear, for what can flesh do to me? The Lord is a bastion
for the oppressed, a source of strength in times of
trouble. All who revere your name, Lord, place their
trust in you, for you have never abandoned those who
seek you.   *Psalm 56:3, 4; 9:9, 10*

Prayer
I am trusting thee, Lord Jesus,
trusting only thee,
trusting thee for full salvation,
great and free.

I am trusting thee for pardon:
at thy feet I bow,
for thy grace and tender mercy,
trusting now.

I am trusting thee to guide me;
thou alone shalt lead,
every day and hour supplying
all my need.

I am trusting thee for power:
thine can never fail;
words which thou thyself shalt give me
must prevail.

I am trusting thee, Lord Jesus;
never let me fall:
I am trusting thee for ever,
and for all.

Silence

Those lovely words of Frances Ridley Havergal
(1836–79) sum up what Christian trust is, or at least
should be, all about: putting our trust in God for
everything in the confidence that whatever we are called
to face, he will be with us through it. Such trust is
rooted not in ourselves but solely in him, as the following makes plain:

For the truth that day by day
you are present, come what may;
when we see you, when we don't,
when we trust you, when we won't –
for the peace such love imparts,
Lord, we come with grateful hearts.

Silence

True trust entails committing ourselves entirely into
God's keeping, and few prayers express that better
than that of the nineteenth-century Metropolitan of
Moscow, Philaret (1782-1867), from which come the
following lines:

O Lord, I do not know what to ask of you.
You alone know what are my true needs.
You love me more than I myself know how to love.
Help me to see my real needs,
    which are concealed from me.

I dare not ask for either a cross or a consolation;
I can only wait on you.
My heart is open to you.
Come to me and help me, for your great mercy's sake.
I put all my trust in you.
I have no other desire than to fulfil your will.
Teach me how to pray.
Pray yourself in me.
Amen.

Silence

Words of St Augustine of Hippo (354–430) put
things more simply:

Trust the past to the mercy of God,
    the present to his love,
    the future to his providence.

Silence

Final prayer   Eternal God,
    I have put my faith in you,
    but my trust is fragile,
    all too easily threatened
    by the traumas and trials of daily life.
Though all else may fail,
    teach me that *you* will not.

Remind me that you are greater
    than my mind can fathom,
    sovereign over all,
    mighty beyond words,
    able to accomplish
    more than I can ever ask or imagine.

Though all else may fail,
teach me that *you* will not.

Remind me of all you have done across the years,
   renewing and redeeming,
     bringing hope out of despair, joy out of sorrow
   and life out of death.
Though all else may fail,
teach me that *you* will not.

Remind me that, however fierce the storm,
   you promise to see me through it,
   your love unchanging,
   your purpose continuing through life and death.
Though all else may fail,
   teach me that *you* will not.

Remind me of the ways I personally have found
   that to be true,
   the countless experiences I have had of your love,
   goodness, help and strength.
Though all else may fail,
   teach me that *you* will not.

Teach me, then, to put my hand in yours,
   assured that your word is true,
   your grace constant
   and your promises sure.
Though all else may fail,
   teach me that *you* will not.
Amen.

Music   Like the deer that yearns from *In God Alone*
(Andrew Moore)

14
When uncertain how to pray

Music   What a friend we have in Jesus from *Our Favourite Hymns 1*

Scripture   One of his disciples said to him, 'Lord, teach us how to pray.'   *Luke 11:1b*

We do not know how to pray, or what to pray for, but the Spirit pleads on our behalf with entreaties that are beyond words, and the one who searches our hearts knows the Spirit's mind, because he intercedes constantly on behalf of the saints seeking the fulfilment of God's purpose.   *Romans 8:26, 27*

Prayer   Father, teach me how to pray,
for I don't know what to say,
sometimes so unsure I barely say a word.
Grant me strength to persevere,
keeping faith that you are near
even though it often seems you haven't heard.
Help me share what's deep inside,
doubts and fears I try to hide,
faults and weaknesses I hesitate to name.
Give me faith to bare my soul,
trusting you can make me whole,
set me free from any sense of guilt and shame.
Help me share my hopes and fears,
joy and laughter, pain and tears,
knowing every part of life is your concern.
And, if I would know your will,
teach me also to be still,
so that through your Spirit's prompting I might learn.
Bid me come because I *may*,
not because I'm *told* to pray,

but responding to the welcome you extend –
neither nervous nor in dread
but approaching you instead
as a faithful Father, living, loving friend.

Silence

Does prayer need special words? Is there a right way
to pray and a wrong way? I don't think so. As I
understand it, prayer is simply being ourselves before
God, or, as St Teresa of Avila put it, 'nothing more
than a friendly conversation with One whom we
know loves us'. I've attempted to capture that idea in
the following reflection:

It's me, O Lord,
    not the person I pretend to be,
    nor who I want to be,
    but me, as I am –
    with all my strengths, all my weaknesses,
    all my faith, all my doubt –
    me, as I've rarely dared come before,
    reaching out to you in prayer.
I've no right to be here, I know that,
    for I'm nothing special,
    nothing to write home about,
    and I've little idea what I'm going to say,
    still less how to say it.
But you tell us if we truly seek, we shall find,
    if we're really sorry, you'll forgive,
    if we keep on asking, you will answer.
So I'm here, Lord,
    in all my ugliness and sin –
    weak, selfish, greedy, thoughtless –
    but I'm here,
    and I'm asking you, despite it all,
    hear my prayer.

My child,
  don't stop,
  keep talking,
  for I'm here too,
  delighted to listen,
  drinking in your every word.
It's a joy to hear you, believe me,
  music to my ears –
  no need to apologise or excuse yourself.
I've looked forward to this moment for so long,
  your coming openly and honestly to meet me.
For it's *you* I want to talk to,
  not the mask you wear for the world –
  you as you really are –
  the face you show, the face you hide,
  the person you love, the person you hate.
They're both you,
  two halves of the same whole,
  inseparable as light and dark, substance and shadow,
  and unless you bring all,
  openly and honestly before me,
  you bring nothing.
You're not perfect, I know that,
  but I don't ask you to be –
  it's not me who twists the knife, only you.
I love you as you are,
  with all your faults and fragile faith,
  and I'll go on loving you day after day,
  drawing you closer to me not as a condition
  but an expression of that love.
So come now, gladly and confidently,
  bring yourself with head bent low
  but soul held high,
  and find in me your kindest critic
  and truest friend.

Silence

One answer to the question how should we pray was provided by Jesus himself, in the Lord's Prayer. However much words may fail us, we always have these words to turn to.

Our Father, who art in heaven,
   hallowed be thy name.
Thy kingdom come,
   thy will be done,
   on earth, as it is in heaven.
Give us this day our daily bread,
   and forgive us our trespasses
   as we forgive those who trespass against us,
   and lead us not into temptation,
   but deliver us from evil.
For thine is the kingdom, the power and the glory,
   now and for evermore.
Amen.

Silence

Final prayer Loving God,
   when I try to pray but the words won't come,
   or when I'm simply not sure what to pray for,
   open your heart to me,
   and mine to you.

Though my prayers are offered as an afterthought,
   squeezed in at the start or end of a busy day,
   though I'm tempted to talk *at* rather than *with* you,
   my prayers more concerned with *my* will than yours,
   though my mind wanders in prayer,
   my thoughts straying to other more trivial concerns,
   though I don't pray as often as I should do,
   sometimes leaving it for days, even weeks,
   open your heart to me,
   and mine to you.

Loving God,
    though I'm slow to learn,
    teach me to pray,
    to enjoy simply being in your presence.
Open your heart to me,
    and mine to you.
Amen.

Music   What a friend we have in Jesus from *Our Favourite Hymns 1*

15
When feeling anxious

Music   Calm me, Lord from *Fire of Love* (Margaret Rizza)

Scripture   Do not be anxious about anything, but thankfully acquaint God with all your needs through your prayers and petitions. The Lord will protect you from all evil; he will watch over you, body and soul. The Lord will guard your going out and your coming in, now and always.   *Philippians 4:6; Psalm 121:7, 8*

I tell you this: do not vex yourself about life, what you will eat or drink, and do not worry about what you might clothe yourselves with. Is not life more than food and the body more than clothing? Do not brood about tomorrow; you can be sure it will bring its sufficient share of difficulties. Take one day at a time, for each has quite enough problems of its own.   *Matthew 6:25, 34*

Prayer   When days are touched with sadness
and nights are filled with pain;
when every waking moment
your faith is under strain;
when burdens weigh upon you
that seem too hard to bear;
remember then the promise
of Jesus, 'I'll be there.'

When all around forsake you
and you feel left alone;
when those you thought most loyal
have taken wings and flown;

when dreams lie bruised and broken
and no one sheds a tear;
remember then the promise
of Jesus, 'I am here.'

When life is dark with shadows,
its lustre long since gone;
when winter's chill encroaches
where summer sun once shone;
when days that seemed to sparkle
are tarnished now with care;
remember then the promise
of Jesus, 'I'll be there.'

When everything you hoped for
lies trampled in the dust;
when there seems nothing solid
in which to put your trust;
when worry holds you captive –
a slave to every fear;
remember then the promise
of Jesus, 'I am here.'

Silence

The knowledge that God is with us in Christ has
inspired many a poet and hymn-writer, among them
the celebrated John Newton (1725–1807), who as
well as writing many classics produced the following
simple verse:

As a little child relies
On a care beyond his own;
Knows he's neither strong nor wise;
Fears to stir a step alone;
Let me thus with Thee abide,
As my Father, Guard, and Guide.

Silence

Most of us worry at some time or other; it's almost impossible not to. If and when you do, whatever else, don't feel guilty about it. As the following reflection makes clear, God understands:

I'm worried, Lord,
    more than I've ever been in my life.
I know I shouldn't be –
    there are enough people telling me that –
    but I just can't help it,
    the more I struggle to stay calm,
    the more worried I become.
It just adds another anxiety to all the rest,
    and there's enough of those already, aren't there? –
    health,
    money,
    work,
    family –
    never allowing a moment's peace.
Time and again, despite my efforts,
    I catch myself brooding,
    haunted by a multitude of questions
    about the future –
    and all the time the spectre grows
    of life spinning crazily out of control,
    taking all I value with it.
It's easy to say, 'Don't worry',
    that everything will be all right,
    but what if it isn't,
    what if my fears come true?
What then, Lord?

My child,
    you know what I'm going to say, don't you?
That's right – don't worry!
But before you jump down my throat,
    stop and hear me out.

I'm not pretending everything will come good,
    for I know it doesn't sometimes –
    all too rarely for my liking.
And I'm not saying your fears are unfounded,
    for sadly some of them probably aren't.
But what I am telling you is this:
    that the only thing worry will change is *you* –
    for the worse.
It won't make you feel any better,
    that somehow you have everything sorted.
It won't stop your fears coming true,
    still less help you face them if they do.
On the contrary, it will suck you dry,
    sap you of energy,
    rob you of the very strength you will need
    should crisis come.
That's one reason I tell you not to worry –
    because I see what it does to you
    and know it achieves nothing.
But there's another reason, more important still,
    for the main thing is I love you,
    and understand your needs,
    and care about your welfare
    more than you would ever imagine.
No, I can't promise you a bed of roses –
    that's not the way I work –
    but I do guarantee this:
    whatever you face,
    however many nightmares come true,
    I'll be there with you always,
    come what may,
    to see you through.

Silence

Next, words of the American nun St Frances Xavier
Cabrini (1850–1917):

Fortify me with the grace of your Holy Spirit
   and give your peace to my soul
   that I may be free from all needless anxiety,
   solicitude and worry.
Help me to desire always that which is pleasing and
   acceptable to you
   so that your will may be my will.
Amen.

Silence

Final prayer   Teach me, Lord,
   that, in the changes and chances of this life,
   with all the uncertainties it brings,
   one thing is certain:
   you will be with me still.
Whatever the future may hold,
   I will not fear.

Teach me that whatever I may be confronted with,
   your love will continue to reach out –
   your hand still support me –
   and your purpose finally be fulfilled.
Whatever the future may hold,
   I will not fear.

Help me, then,
   to let go of the anxieties that weigh me down,
   destroying confidence,
   undermining happiness,
   and preventing me from living life
   as fully as I should.
Whatever the future may hold,
   I will not fear.

Help me to receive the freedom you offer,
   the freedom that comes

from knowing you hold all things in your hands
and that nothing can finally separate me
from your love.
Whatever the future may hold,
   I will not fear.
Amen.

Music   Calm me, Lord from *Fire of Love* (Margaret Rizza)

16
When wrestling with doubt

Music   Why do the nations from *Messiah* (Handel)

Scripture   O Lord, how long must I cry to you for help before
you will listen? How long must I cry, 'Violence!'
before you will save? Why do you let me witness wrongdoing and endure trouble? Destruction and aggression
are all around me; conflict and disputes spring up
everywhere. The law is watered down such that justice
has no chance of winning through. I will stand at my
sentry post, and position myself on the battlements. I
will keep watch to see what he will say to me, how he
will answer my grievance.   *Habakkuk 1:2-4a; 2:1*

Lord, I believe, help me in my unbelief.   *Mark 9:24*

Prayer   Lord, there are times when I have to ask, 'Why?' –
times when catastrophe gives faith the lie.
Innocents suffer and evil holds sway,
grant me some answers, Lord, teach me your way.

Lord, there are times when I have to ask, 'Where?' –
times when it seems that you simply don't care.
Though I call out, you seem distant, aloof,
grant me some answers, Lord, show me some proof.

Lord, there are times when I have to ask, 'What?' –
times when your love isn't easy to spot.
What is life's purpose and what of me here?
Grant me some answers, Lord, make your will clear.

Lord, there are times when I have to ask, 'How?' –
times when what's preached doesn't square with life now.

Wrestling with doubt I ask, 'How can this be?'
Grant me some answers, Lord, help me to see.

Lord, there are times when the questions run fast –
times when I fear that my faith may not last.
Help me, support me, Lord, help me get through.
Lead me through darkness till light shines anew.

Silence

Is asking questions of God wrong? I don't think so,
for a moment. True faith is strong enough to admit to
doubt, for there is much in life that it is hard to make
sense of in terms of faith. Sometimes we search for
answers in vain. At others times, experience and
hindsight help us to make sense of what once seemed
incomprehensible, as observed in lines from 'Peace
after a Storm', a poem by poet and hymn-writer
William Cowper (1731–1800):

When darkness long has veil'd my mind,
And smiling day once more appears,
Then, my Redeemer, then I find
The folly of my doubts and fears.

Straight I upbraid my wandering heart,
And blush that I should ever be
Thus prone to act so base a part,
Or harbour one hard thought of Thee!

Oh! let me then at length be taught
What I am still so slow to learn,
That God is love, and changes not,
Nor knows the shadow of a turn.

Silence

The opening lines of the following prayer by St Benedict of Nursia (c. 480–547), the founder of Western monasticism, focus on our ability to make sense of the things of God:

Father, in your goodness
   grant me the intellect to comprehend you,
   the perception to discern you,
   and the reason to appreciate you.
In your kindness
   endow me with the diligence to look for you,
   the wisdom to discover you,
   and the spirit to apprehend you.
In your graciousness
   bestow on me a heart to contemplate you,
   ears to hear you,
   eyes to see you,
   and a tongue to speak of you.
In your mercy
   confer on me a conversation pleasing to you,
   the patience to wait for you,
   and the perseverance to long for you.
Grant me a perfect end,
   your holy presence.
Amen.

Silence

Final prayer

Mighty and mysterious God,
   there are so many things I'm uncertain about,
   so many complex areas of life that leave me confused,
   searching in vain for answers.
Grant me faith to live with questions.
Lord, I believe,
   help me in my unbelief.

I struggle to make sense of the events of this world,
    for its pain, sorrow, hatred and evil
    challenge and even contradict my faith,
    undermining trust and eroding confidence.
Lord, I believe,
    help me in my unbelief.

I struggle to reconcile belief
    with modern-day knowledge,
    much in the findings of science and other research
    seeming to squeeze you out.
Lord, I believe,
    help me in my unbelief.

I struggle to relate commitment to the daily routine,
    so much of life seeming divorced from faith.
Lord, I believe,
    help me in my unbelief.

I struggle to let go of the comfortable and familiar,
    to accept that some of my beliefs
    may need stretching or even be wrong.
Lord, I believe,
    help me in my unbelief.

I struggle to recognise that doubts and questions
    are a part of faith,
    able to lead me to new insights
    and a deeper understanding of your purpose.
Lord, I believe,
    help me in my unbelief.
Amen.

Music   Why do the nations from *Messiah* (Handel)

17
When looking to deepen our commitment

Music
Silent, surrendered from *Fountain of Life*
(Margaret Rizza)

Scripture
What shall I offer to the Lord for all the blessings he's given me? I will raise the cup of deliverance and call on the Lord's name. I will present a grateful sacrifice and call on his name. I will honour my promises to the Lord in the sight of all his people.
Psalm 116:12, 13, 17, 18

I heard the Lord's voice, saying, 'Whom can I send? Who will go for me?' I answered, 'Here I am. Send me!'
Isaiah 6:8

Prayer
Take the life I proffer,
loving God, today;
all the gifts I offer,
all I think and say.
What I am and what I do,
these I give you now.
Lord, I want to serve you –
show me where and how.

Silence

What can we offer God in response to his goodness, asked the Psalm writer? According to the hymn-writer and poet Frances Ridley Havergal (1836–79), in one of her most celebrated hymns, the answer, quite simply, is everything:

Take my life, and let it be
consecrated, Lord, to thee;
take my moments and my days,
let them flow in ceaseless praise.

Take my love, my Lord, I pour
at thy feet its treasure-store;
take myself, and I will be
ever, only, all for thee.

Silence

We find much the same sentiments in a prayer of the
bishop and Doctor of the Church, St Francis de Sales
(1567–1662):

Lord, I am yours,
   and I must belong to no one but you.
My soul is yours,
   and must live only by you.
My will is yours,
   and must love only for you.
I must love you as my first cause,
   since I am from you.
I must love you as my end and rest,
   since I am for you.
I must love you more than my own being,
   since my being subsists by you.
I must love you more than myself,
   since I am all yours and all in you.
Amen.

Silence

Another prayer, this one written by J. H. Jowett (1864–1923), reminds us that commitment involves consecrating the small as well as the large:

My Father in heaven,
 teach me the value of little things.
Show me how to consecrate what seems insignificant,
 and to recognise the light of your presence
 in every moment.
May I glory the day by offering each minute
 to be redeemed by your love.
I offer you all my moments.
Amen.

Silence

A prayer familiar to many will be the following, from St Augustine of Hippo (354–430):

Lord God,
 the light of the minds that know you,
 the life of the souls that love you,
 and the strength of the wills that serve you:
 help me so to know you that I may truly love you,
 and so to love you that I may fully serve you,
 whom to serve is perfect freedom.
Amen.

Silence

Final prayer   Gracious God,
 I want to serve you more faithfully –
 to show, in word and deed,
 my gratitude for all you have done.

Take what I am and what I long to be,
　　and, by your grace,
　　use them as you will.

Take my words and deeds,
　　my thoughts and prayers,
　　my time and talents,
　　my energy and enthusiasm,
　　and, by your grace,
　　use them as you will.

Take my work and leisure,
　　my money and possessions,
　　my hands and feet,
　　my body and soul,
　　and, by your grace,
　　use them as you will.

Take my trust and convictions,
　　my hopes and dreams,
　　my faith and commitment,
　　my love and response,
　　poor though they may be,
　　and, by your grace,
　　use them as you will.
Amen.

Music　　　　Silent, surrendered from *Fountain of Life*
　　　　　　　　(Margaret Rizza)

18
When in need of strength and protection

Music   I lift my eyes from *Light Divine* (Val Goldsack)

Scripture The Lord is my strength and shield; my heart trusts in him and finds help. Though my body and heart may fail, God is my inner strength, my portion for ever.
Psalm 28:7a; 73:26

My soul waits quietly for God; my confidence comes from him. He, and he alone, is my rock, my deliverance and my stronghold; nothing will shake me.
Psalm 62:5, 6

Prayer   Help me, Lord, reach out to save;
hold me tight, or I am lost;
storms are breaking, wave on wave,
into turmoil life is tossed.
Answer someone, hear my call,
for I'm sinking like a stone;
faith is feeble, all too small –
I can't face this on my own.
You may tell me not to fear,
say that I should always hope,
but I cannot see you near –
how then am I meant to cope?
Wait! What's this? The tide is turning.
Once again, Lord, I was wrong.
Bit by bit, I'm slowly learning
when I'm weak, then you are strong!

Silence

God's strength in our weakness – it's a recurring theme in the Bible, and one that has been a source of inspiration for many, including William Cowper (1731–1800) in the following poem:

The billows swell, the winds are high,
Clouds overcast my wintry sky;
Out of the depths to thee I call –
My fears are great, my strength is small.

O Lord, the pilot's part perform,
And guard and guide me through the storm;
Defend me from each threatening ill,
Control the waves – say, 'Peace! be still.'

Amidst the roaring of the sea
My soul still hangs her hope on thee;
Thy constant love, thy faithful care,
Is all that saves me from despair.

Silence

Two prayers now of St Augustine of Hippo (354–430), both acknowledging God's help and strength while turning to him:

O my God,
    light of the blind and strength of the weak;
    yes, also light of those that see
    and strength of the strong:
    we turn and seek you,
    for we know you are here in our hearts
    when we converse with you;
    when we cast ourselves upon you;
    when we weep,
    and you do gently wipe away our tears,
    and also when we weep for joy

because you who made us
does remake and comfort us.
Grant that we may entirely love you,
even unto the end.
Amen.

Silence

O God, the deathless hope of all,
we rejoice that you support us both when little
and even to grey hairs.
When our strength is of you, it is strength indeed;
but when our own only, it is feebleness.
With you are refreshment and true strength.
Amen.

Silence

Next, words of Karl Rahner (1904–84) expressing
faith in the strength God will provide:

Wise, merciful, loving God,
do not cast me from your presence.
Keep me in your service all the days of my life.
Ask of me what you will.
Only grant what you command of me.
Even if I tire in your service,
you in your patience will not tire of me.
You will come to help, you will give me the strength
to make a fresh start again and again;
to hope against hope;
in all my defeats to have faith in victory
and in your triumph within me.
Amen.

Silence

Final prayer   When I feel powerless, Lord,
　　　　　　　incapable of meeting the challenges before me,
　　　　　　　unable to cope with the demands of life,
　　　　　　　teach me that though I am weak,
　　　　　　　you are strong.

　　　　　　　When I'm weak,
　　　　　　　unable to resist temptation,
　　　　　　　to be the person I so much want to be,
　　　　　　　teach me that though I am weak,
　　　　　　　you are strong.

　　　　　　　When I can't see past obstacles,
　　　　　　　missing out in consequence
　　　　　　　on opportunities to serve you,
　　　　　　　teach me that though I am weak,
　　　　　　　you are strong.

　　　　　　　When hope seems futile and despair justified,
　　　　　　　truth and love seemingly overwhelmed
　　　　　　　by falsehood and hatred,
　　　　　　　teach me that though I am weak,
　　　　　　　you are strong.

　　　　　　　When my resources seem small and problems great,
　　　　　　　when I question
　　　　　　　if I can accomplish anything in your service,
　　　　　　　teach me that though I am weak,
　　　　　　　you are strong.
　　　　　　　Amen.

Music   I lift my eyes from *Light Divine* (Val Goldsack)

19
When in need of wisdom and discernment

Music   You are the centre from *Fountain of Life*
             (Margaret Rizza)

Scripture   Teach us to make the most of our days and so to
                 discover the secret of inner wisdom.   *Psalm 90:12*

Oh how deep are the riches, wisdom and understanding
of God – how far beyond us are his judgements and
how unfathomable his ways! 'Who has figured out the
Lord's mind, or been his advisor?' 'Who has offered
him gift deserving repayment?' All things are from him,
through him and to him. Glory be to him for ever.
Amen.   *Romans 11:33-36*

Silence

As the following prayer of St Benedict (c. 480–547)
reminds us, wisdom is a gift of God:

Gracious and holy Father,
   give me wisdom to recognise you,
   intelligence to understand you,
   diligence to seek you,
   patience to wait for you,
   eyes to see you,
   a heart to meditate on you,
   and a life to proclaim you,
   through the power of the Spirit
   of Jesus Christ my Lord.
Amen.

Silence

Next, a prayer of Thomas à Kempis (c. 1380–1471), seeking discernment in terms of the daily judgements we make concerning others:

Grant me, Lord, to know what I ought to know,
    to love what I ought to love,
    to praise what delights you most,
    to value what is precious in your sight,
    and to hate what is offensive to you.
Let me not judge according to superficial appearances,
    nor condemn on the basis of what others say;
    but may I have the discernment
    to understand deeper realities,
    and, above all things, to seek your will.
Amen.

Silence

This short prayer, based on words of Reinhold Niebuhr (1892–1971), positively resonates with wisdom:

God grant me
    the serenity to accept the things I cannot change,
    the courage to change the things I can,
    and the wisdom to know the difference.
Amen.

Silence

Gracious God,
    though I yearn to do what is right,
    time and again I go astray,
    ignoring your will,
    disobeying your commands.
Show me your way,
    and grant me true wisdom.

I resolve to follow you,
   but I am swayed by the opinions of others
   and by the norms of this world,
   allowing my convictions to be compromised
   and undermined.
Show me your way,
   and grant me true wisdom.

I rush into hasty judgements and foolish decisions,
   knee-jerk reactions based on first impressions
   or prior prejudice,
   rather than on a true knowledge of the facts.
Show me your way,
   and grant me true wisdom.

I confuse knowledge with understanding,
   imagining sometimes that I've understood
   all I need to know,
   even when it comes to matters of faith.
Show me your way,
   and grant me true wisdom.

Teach me to make time for you each day,
   to study your word,
   reflect on your goodness
   and hear your voice.
Show me your way,
   and grant me true wisdom.

Draw near to me
   and help me to draw near to you,
   so that you may fill my life in every part,
   body, mind and spirit.
Show me your way,
   and grant me true wisdom.
   Amen.

Silence

Final prayer   Now to the One who,
in line with the gospel I preach
and Lord Jesus Christ I proclaim,
is able to build you up
through the unfolding of the mystery –
obscured for so long, but now,
at God's command
and in order to secure obedient faith,
divulged and made known
through prophetic words to all people –
to that God, the only source of true wisdom,
be glory now and always,
through Jesus Christ!
Amen.   *Romans 16:25-27*

Music   You are the centre from *Fountain of Life*
(Margaret Rizza)

20
When the day draws to a close

Music   The day thou gavest from *Our Favourite Hymns 3*

Scripture   I will lie down and sleep in peace, for you alone, O
Lord, make me lie down in safety.   *Psalm 4:8*

By day the Lord decrees his unfailing love, and by
night I offer him song, a prayer to the Lord of my life.
Psalm 42:8

Prayer   Glory to thee, my God, this night
for all the blessings of the light;
keep me, O keep me, King of kings,
beneath thine own almighty wings.

Forgive me, Lord, for thy dear Son,
the ill that I this day have done,
that with the world, myself, and thee,
I, ere I sleep, at peace may be.

Silence

Words of Thomas Ken (1637–1711) that provide an
ideal way of committing each night into God's keeping.
Another poem, 'A Good Night' by the seventeenth-
century writer Francis Quarles (1592–1644) offers
words of assurance, a touch simplistic perhaps, but a
reminder nonetheless of God's enfolding presence:

Close now thine eyes and rest secure;
Thy soul is safe enough, thy body sure;
He that loves thee, He that keeps

And guards thee, never slumbers, never sleeps.
The smiling conscience in a sleeping breast
Has only peace, has only rest;
The music and the mirth of kings
Are all but very discords, when she sings;
Then close thine eyes and rest secure;
No sleep so sweet as thine, no rest so sure.

Silence

Of course, not every night is marked by tranquil unbroken sleep. Sometimes we can't nod off, try as we might, life seeming strangely bleak and our problems hugely magnified as the long hours of the night tick interminably by. Yet even an experience such as this can inspire prayer:

I'd lain there for hours,
    pummelling my pillow and tossing uncomfortably,
    yet I still couldn't settle,
    a thousand ideas turning over in my mind,
    disturbing my peace
    and denying the sleep I craved.

By day, Lord, as well as by night,
    my spirit is all too often restless,
    unable to find true fulfilment or inner tranquility.
Help me to let go of my fears
    and to place every part of life into your hands,
    so that I may know the rest you promise
    and find true contentment –
    a quietness of body, mind and soul
    that, day or night, cannot be shaken.
Amen.

Silence

Next, four classics, beginning with a couple of well-loved prayers from the Order of Compline:

Be present, O merciful God,
> and protect us through the silent hours of this night,
> so that we who are wearied
> by the changes and chances of this fleeting world,
> may repose upon thy eternal changelessness;
> through Jesus Christ our Lord.
Amen.

Silence

Preserve us, O Lord, while waking,
> and guard us while sleeping,
> that awake we may watch with Christ,
> and asleep we may rest in peace.
Amen.

Silence

Now a prayer of the fourth-century bishop and Doctor of the Church, St Gregory of Nazianzen (c. 330–389)

While I sleep, O Lord,
> let my heart not cease to worship you;
> fill my sleep with your presence,
> while creation itself keeps watch,
> singing psalms with the angels,
> and taking up my soul into its paean of praise.
Amen.

Silence

Last, a prayer from the Tudor *Book of Hours* (1514):

God be in my head, and in my understanding.
God be in my eyes, and in my looking.
God be in mouth, and in my speaking.
God be in my heart, and in my thinking.
God be at my end, and at my departing.

Silence

Final prayer   Eternal God,
as I come to the close of another day,
help me to learn
through everything it has brought me,
whether joy or sorrow, pleasure or pain,
fulfilment or frustration,
so that I may be better able to serve and love you
in whatever the future may hold.
Be with me,
tonight, tomorrow, and always.

Assure me now of your presence,
and watch over me and my loved ones
throughout this night,
grant rest now for mind, body and spirit,
the inner quietness and contentment
that comes only from you.
Be with me,
tonight, tomorrow, and always.

Enfold me in your peace,
and encircle me in your love,
that I may awake restored in strength,
renewed in hope,
rekindled in love
and revitalised in faith,

ready to celebrate your gift of life
and to offer each moment back to you
in grateful service.
Be with me,
 tonight, tomorrow, and always.
Amen.

Music   The day thou gavest from *Our Favourite Hymns 3*

Expressing Our Concern

1
For real and lasting change in our world

Music
Send forth your Spirit from *In God Alone*
(Andrew Moore)

Scripture
The Lord seeks the welfare of all and justice for those
who are exploited. *Psalm 103:6*

Then I saw a new heaven and new earth; for the first
heaven and earth had come to an end, and there was
no more sea. And I heard a loud voice from the
throne declaring, 'See, God's home is among humankind. He will live among them and they will be his
people; God himself will be with them and he will
wipe away the tears from their eyes. There will be no
more death or sorrow, weeping or pain, for former
things have passed away. *Revelation 21:1, 3-4*

Prayer
Almighty Father, who dost give
the gift of life to all who live,
look down on all earth's sin and strife,
and lift us to a nobler life.

Lift up our hearts, O King of kings,
to brighter hopes and kindlier things,
to visions of a larger good,
and holier dreams of brotherhood.

The world is weary of its pain,
of selfish greed and fruitless gain,
of tarnished honour, falsely strong,
and all its ancient deeds of wrong.

Hear thou the prayer thy servants pray,
uprising from all lands today,
and o'er the vanquished powers of sin
O bring thy great salvation in.

Silence

Those words of the hymn-writer J. H. B. Masterman (1867–1933) articulate an important truth: the world *is* weary of its pain. Sadly, dealing with the causes of that pain is no easy matter, the mistakes and weaknesses that bring it about endemic to human nature. Without God's transforming power, we are doomed to a vicious circle of fruitless striving. It needs the touch of his hand for there to be real and lasting change, but as the following prayer reminds us (its author unknown), it needs us to catch a vision of what God can do and play our part in making it happen:

Give me, Lord God,
    a vision of the world as your love would make it;
    a world where the weak are protected
    and none are poor or go hungry;
    a world where the benefits of civilised life
    are shared and everyone can enjoy them;
    a world where different races, nations and cultures
    live in tolerance and mutual respect;
    a world where peace is built with justice
    and justice is guided by love;
    and give me the inspiration and courage
    to share in the task of building it,
    through Jesus Christ my Lord.
Amen.

Silence

That's our vision as Christians, but the world as we know it is sadly different. To me, news of an oil tanker breaking up off the coast seemed to provide an all too graphic analogy of the plight in which we find ourselves:

It wasn't quite the disaster of old,
   for advances had been made,
   technology yielding ways to contain the spill
   and limit the damage,
   but the oil was there nonetheless:
   choking, killing, soiling, polluting,
   leaving a stain on all it touched –
   so swift to form,
   so hard to move.

Our world is stained, Lord,
   engulfed by a black tide of injustice, intolerance,
   fear and hatred
   that desecrates and destroys countless lives,
   and, for all our so-called advances,
   we're no nearer containing it than we've ever been.
Come to our aid,
   and cleanse us of all that denies and divides –
   that precludes joy and crushes hope.
Transform what we can never change ourselves,
   and make all things new.
Amen.

Silence

Final prayer   Loving God,
hear my prayer for the world,
troubled still by so many age-old problems.

To those wrestling with abject poverty,
   denied food, housing, water, education,

healthcare and so much else,
and those in lands scarred by war,
day after day enduring suffering, sorrow
and slaughter,
Lord of all,
grant real and lasting change.

To victims of alcohol and drug abuse,
violence and vandalism,
pornography and paedophilia,
crime and corruption –
Lord of all,
grant real and lasting change.

To those fearful of the future –
the lonely, anxious, sick, despairing,
Lord of all,
grant real and lasting change.

To a world in so much need,
lurching from one crisis to another,
hopes raised only to be dashed again,
Lord of all,
grant real and lasting change.
Amen.

Music   Send forth your Spirit from *In God Alone*
(Andrew Moore)

2
For an end to war and hatred

Music   Peace, perfect peace from *Gloria*

Scripture   He will mediate among the nations, and resolve dis-
                 agreements among countless peoples, so that they will
                 hammer their swords into ploughs, and their spears
                 into pruning hooks. No nation will take up arms against
                 another, nor even train themselves any longer for war.
                 Isaiah 2:4

                 The wolf will live with the lamb, the leopard lie down
                 with the kid and the calf, and the lion and fattened
                 calf will also relax together; led by a little child. Cattle
                 and bears will graze peaceably, their young sleeping
                 alongside each other; and the lion will eat straw like
                 the ox. Babies will play above the nest of the cobra,
                 and infants put their hand into the lair of the adder.
                 Nothing will hurt or destroy anywhere on my holy
                 mountain, for, just as the water fills the sea so will the
                 earth be filled with the knowledge of the Lord.
                 Isaiah 11:6-9

Prayer   Grant, Lord, an end to our sorrow,
                 a halt at last to our pain,
                 the hope of a brighter tomorrow,
                 of sunshine, after the rain.
                 Assure us the day is dawning
                 when darkness will be no more,
                 no suffering, dying or mourning,
                 no violence, hatred or war –
                 a kingdom of joy unbounded,
                 of laughter, blessing and peace,

where evil will be confounded
and all divisions cease;
a time of celebration,
a place of rare delights –
Lord, finish your new creation
and set our world to rights.

Silence

Anyone who needs convincing of the horror and cost
of conflict should pay a visit to the war cemeteries of
Belgium or France. Row upon row of headstones offer
there a stark reminder of the millions who perished in
two world wars, most of them young men who should
have had all of life before them:

It was a peaceful, almost pastoral scene,
　　the gravestones standing neatly to attention,
　　row upon row stretching across
　　the crisply mowed lawns.
But the stillness and order belied the truth,
　　masking the turmoil that had scarred those fields,
　　the slaughter and sacrifice,
　　fear and despair –
　　each name a loved one plucked away,
　　each stone a memorial to broken lives
　　and shattered dreams,
　　stark testimony to the horror yet heroism of war,
　　the price paid,
　　the debt owed.

Teach us, Lord, truly to appreciate
　　the freedom we enjoy
　　and never to forget what it cost so many.
Remind us of the awfulness of conflict
　　that we might strive always for peace.

And awaken hearts everywhere
to their part in a broken world
and their responsibility to work for its healing.
Amen.

Silence

A well-known prayer for peace is that by Francis
Paget (1851–1911), one-time Bishop of Oxford:

Almighty God,
from whom all thoughts of truth and peace proceed:
kindle, we pray you, in the hearts of all people
the true love of peace;
and guide with your pure and peaceable wisdom
those who take counsel for the nations of the earth;
that in tranquillity your kingdom may go forward,
till the earth be filled
with the knowledge of your love,
through Jesus Christ our Lord.
Amen.

Silence

Final prayer   Lord of all,
hear my prayer for the victims of war
and for peace in the world.

I pray for those across the world
who bear the scars of conflict –
the injured, maimed and mentally distressed,
those who, through the horrors of war,
have lost their limbs, their reason or their loved ones.
Lord, in your mercy,
hear me.

I pray for those left homeless or as refugees,
    those who have lost their livelihoods and security,
    and those who still live in daily fear for their lives.
Lord, in your mercy,
    hear me.

I pray for youngsters who have been orphaned,
    parents who mourn their children,
    husbands and wives who have lost their partners –
    countless families for whom life
    will never be the same again.
Lord, in your mercy,
    hear me.

I pray for those in the armed forces,
    charged with keeping the peace
    in countries across the world –
    their work involving months away
    from family and friends
    and often danger to themselves.
Lord, in your mercy,
    hear me.

I pray for world leaders and rulers,
    politicians and diplomats –
    those whose decisions and negotiations
    affect the lives of so many
    and in whose hands peace ultimately lies.
Lord, in your mercy,
    hear me.

Lord of all,
    give wisdom to all who work for peace,
    so that a more secure future may be ensured for all.
Give courage to those who strive for justice,
    so that the causes of conflict may be overcome.
Give strength to those who seek to break down barriers,
    that divisions over race, colour, creed and culture
    may be ended.

Grant that wherever war or the threat of war
   continues to haunt lives, a way of reconciliation
   may be found,
   and harmony established between people and nations.
Lord, in your mercy,
   hear me.
Amen.

Music   Peace, perfect peace from *Gloria*

3
For those scarred by life

Music Prayer of St Teresa from *Awakening in Love*
(Margaret Rizza)

Scripture Celebrate with those who celebrate, grieve with those
who grieve. *Romans 12:15*

The Lord is close to those whose hearts are broken and
rescues those who are crushed in spirit. *Psalm 34:18*

Prayer Hear my prayer for others
in the trials they face –
fellow-sisters, brothers:
grant to all your grace.
Heal the crushed and broken,
body, mind and soul –
let your word be spoken,
touch and make them whole.
Chide the rich and greedy,
strengthen the oppressed,
reach out to the needy,
comfort the distressed.
May the humble flourish,
may the poor be fed.
In your mercy nourish
all who crave for bread.
Bring to every nation
harmony once more;
reconciliation,
peace instead of war.
Hear my intercession,
make my life a prayer,
help me give expression
to your love and care.

Silence

A prayer now written by the Scottish clergyman and writer William Angus Knight (1836–1916):

Almighty and most merciful Father,
    who has taught us not to think only of ourselves
    but also of the needs of others,
    I remember before you
    all who are burdened and oppressed,
    those whose hopes have been crushed
    and whose plans have come to nothing.
I remember also those who are afflicted by poverty,
    or worn down by sickness and disease,
    those who are in darkness or despair,
    or who are suffering for righteousness' sake.
Help them all, O God,
    to rest in you for comfort and strength.
Amen.

Silence

Final prayer   Sovereign God,
    hear my prayer
    for those whose experiences have been painful,
    memories causing grief, revulsion, regret or despair.
Bring healing,
    bring hope.

Hear my prayer for victims of violence, crime,
    abuse and neglect –
    all whose lives are scarred
    by what they've been through.
Bring healing,
    bring hope.

Hear my prayer for the lonely –
    those who ache for a friend or companion
    to brighten their day
    and give meaning to their life.
Bring healing,
    bring hope.

Hear my prayer for the elderly –
    those coming to terms with infirmity
    or declining faculties,
    happy memories tinged with sadness
    for what will never be again.
Bring healing,
    bring hope.

Hear my prayer for those
    whose lives have been shattered by war and conflict –
    those haunted by scenes of hatred and brutality,
    death and destruction.
Bring healing,
    bring hope.

Hear my prayer for the bereaved –
    those who mourn loved ones,
    memories bringing pleasure, yet pain,
    laughter, yet tears.
Bring healing,
    bring hope.

Hear my prayer, Lord,
    for all who long to find renewal and wholeness.
Bring healing,
    bring hope.
Amen.

Music   Prayer of St Teresa from *Awakening in Love*
        (Margaret Rizza)

4
For those seeking peace

Music   Deep peace from *Sacred Pathway* (Keith Duke)

Scripture   May the Lord strengthen his people; may he bless
them with peace.   *Psalm 29:11*

You keep in perfect peace those whose minds are
focused on you, because in you they find their trust.
Isaiah 26:3

Prayer   Listen, stranger, Christ is near,
hear him calling, have no fear.
Bring your troubles, bring your care,
bitter burdens, hard to bear.
He'll give strength to see you through;
from the old he'll bring the new.
Toiling, striving, let them cease,
Come to Jesus, *go* in peace.

Silence

Like light, love, joy and hope, peace is a universal
aspiration. The following, for example, is an Indian
prayer, taken from the Vedas:

May there be peace in the higher regions;
    may there be peace in the firmament;
    may there be peace on earth.
May the waters flow peacefully;
    may the herbs and plants grow peacefully;
    may all the divine powers bring unto us peace.

The supreme Lord is peace.
May we all be in peace, peace, and only peace;
 and may that peace come unto each of us.

Silence

The peace of God,
 which surpasses all understanding,
 guard every heart and mind,
 this day and always,
 through Jesus Christ our Lord.
Amen.   *Philippians 4:7 (adapted)*

Silence

Final prayer Hear my prayer, Lord, for those yearning
 for inner peace yet unable to find it,
 those who long for quietness of mind
 and tranquillity of spirit
 yet whose souls are restless within them.
Grant stillness deep within;
 your peace that passes understanding.

To those troubled by fears, phobias, anxieties
 and uncertainty,
 unable to escape from terrors, real or imagined,
 grant stillness deep within;
 your peace that passes understanding.

To those trapped in the rat race,
 with no time to stop and stare,
 to take stock of what really matters,
 to reflect on who they are and what life is all about,
 grant stillness deep within;
 your peace that passes understanding.

To those tormented by regrets, disappointments,
    hurts and frustration,
    their enjoyment of life undermined by bitterness,
    envy and resentment,
    grant stillness deep within;
    your peace that passes understanding.

To those in lands ravaged by war,
    caught up in a cycle of hatred, suspicion,
    violence and slaughter,
    grant stillness deep within;
    your peace that passes understanding.

To those living in the shadow of death –
    troubled at the prospect of dying,
    mourning loved ones or fearful for their safety,
    grant stillness deep within;
    your peace that passes understanding.

To all those whose minds are in turmoil
    and live in chaos,
    bring your gentle touch,
    an inner calm and tranquillity
    even in the fiercest storm.
Grant stillness deep within;
    your peace that passes understanding.
Amen.

Music   Deep peace from *Sacred Pathway* (Keith Duke)

5
For those seeking help and strength

Music   Exaudi nos, Domine from *Fire of Love* (Margaret Rizza)

Scripture   Happy are those whose help is the God of Jacob, who
                   put their hope in the Lord their God who created the
                   heavens and the earth, the oceans, and everything
                   within them; who keeps faith for ever; who achieves
                   justice for the exploited, and provides food for the
                   starving. The Lord releases the prisoners, gives sight
                   to the blind, and lifts up those who are humbled; he
                   loves the righteous.   *Psalm 146:5-8*

                   Isn't this the fast I want from you: to untie the knots
                   of evil, to undo the straps of the yoke, to allow the
                   exploited freedom, and to break every form of oppres-
                   sion? Isn't it to share your bread with the hungry and
                   offer hospitality to the homeless; to clothe the naked
                   when you see them, and not to turn your back on your
                   own flesh and blood?   *Isaiah 58:6, 7*

Prayer   Where love is met with hatred,
                   and dreams have been snuffed out,
                   where days are full of suffering
                   and faith has turned to doubt,
                   where evil conquers goodness
                   and life is full of care,
                   grant through it all the knowledge
                   that you, O Lord, are there.

                   Where joy has turned to sorrow
                   and hope gives way to fear,
                   where peace is cruelly shattered
                   as sudden storms appear,

where life belies convictions
on which we once relied,
grant through it all the knowledge
you're always by our side.

Where darkness like a shadow
extinguishes the light,
where plans are brought to ruin
and nothing quite goes right,
where health begins to falter
and life begins to fade,
grant through it all the knowledge
we need not be afraid.

To those enduring trouble
with which they cannot cope,
to those for whom disaster
has put an end to hope,
to those who carry burdens
too difficult to bear,
grant through it all the knowledge
that you, O Lord, are there.

Silence

Our next prayer is an ancient one, coming from the
fourth-century Liturgy of St Basil:

Lord,
   the help of the helpless,
   the hope of those past hope,
   the rescuer of the storm-tossed,
   the harbour of the voyagers,
   the healer of the sick:
   I ask you to become all things to all people,
   for you know the needs of each one.

Accept us all into your kingdom,
    making us children of light;
    and give us your peace and love,
    Lord our God.
Amen.

Silence

Final prayer   To those, Lord, who call out to you,
    longing to hear your voice of reassurance,
    inspiration and guidance,
    may your grace bring help,
    your love give hope.

To those who feel lost,
    life seeming devoid of meaning,
    never offering the fulfilment they seek,
    may your grace bring help,
    your love give hope.

To those wrestling with chronic pain,
    debilitating disease or terminal illness,
    crying out for relief,
    yearning for healing,
    may your grace bring help,
    your love give hope.

To those enduring inner turmoil,
    struggling with depression,
    coping with divorce
    or other breakdowns in relationships,
    oppressed by real or imagined fears,
    crushed by bereavement,
    may your grace bring help,
    your love give hope.

To those suffering deprivation –
    the poor, homeless and unemployed;
    all who feel trapped by circumstances,
    denied a stake in society,
    may your grace bring help,
    your love give hope.

To the millions in abject poverty across the world,
    denied the essentials we take for granted,
    deprived of resources to help themselves,
    defeated by market forces beyond their control,
    may your grace bring help,
    your love give hope.

To those in lands broken by war –
    scarred by brutality,
    ravaged by hatred
    and engulfed by fear,
    may your grace bring help,
    your love give hope.

Loving God,
    speak into each and every such situation,
    and, in your mercy,
    may your grace bring help,
    your love give hope.
Amen.

Music   Exaudi nos, Domine from *Fire of Love* (Margaret Rizza)

6
For our broken world

Music   Creator Spirit, come from *Sacred Weave* (Keith Duke)

Scripture   I know that the Lord will uphold the rights of the vulnerable, and secure justice for the needy.
Psalm 140:12

Let justice pour down like waters, and righteousness flow like a never-failing stream.   *Amos 5:24*

Prayer   Lord, to our world in its madness –
broken, bemused and concussed,
crushed by a burden of sadness,
ravaged by fear and mistrust –
grant your renewal and healing,
courage where hope seems in vain,
reach out to all who are reeling,
bring them relief from their pain;
break down the roots of division,
walls that destroy and estrange;
overcome hate and suspicion,
grant us the prospect of change.

Silence

Can our broken world ever be made whole? In an age of indiscriminate terrorist attacks it's hard to believe it, yet faith must somehow hold on, even through these:

It was carnage,
   sickening and horrific,
   like a scene out of hell,

injuries too awful to contemplate,
lives, like the twisted wreckage around them,
shattered beyond repair.
A morning full of promise
   had become the stuff of nightmares,
   yet it was all too real.

Where were you, Lord, when it happened?
What were you thinking of?
How could you let it be?
I look for answers,
   yet search in vain,
   the quest raising more questions than it solves,
   but if one thing is clear, it's that here,
   in this mindless maiming and murder,
   we need you more than ever.
Come to our broken, bleeding world, Lord,
   and bind up its wounds.
Assure us, despite how things seem,
   that hope is mightier than fear,
   right stronger than wrong,
   and love greater than all.
Amen.

Silence

We may think that the ills which beset our world are worse than ever before, but division and conflict are nothing new. The following prayer of St Dionysius dates back, for example, to the sixth century:

O God the Father,
   source of all that is good and true,
   in whom is calmness, peace and harmony,
   heal the dissensions which divide people
   from each other, and bring us back
   to a unity of love

which may bear some likeness to your divine nature.
And as you are above all things,
   make us one by unity of thought,
   that through the bonds of love we may be one,
   both with ourselves and with each other;
   through that peace of yours
   which makes all things peaceful,
   and through the grace, mercy and love of your Son,
   Jesus Christ.
Amen.

Silence

Final prayer Finally, we pray for an end to everything that divides
and fractures our world:

In a world of inequality
   hear my prayer, Lord, for the poor
   denied the essentials of life I take for granted.
Provide the resources they need
   to build a better future,
   and help me to play my part
   in promoting a fairer and more loving world.
Lord of all,
   may your love bring hope, healing and harmony.

In a world of religious tension,
   where faith so often polarises rather than unites,
   inciting hatred, persecution, violence and war,
   hear my prayer, Lord, for dialogue,
   respect and reconciliation –
   a willingness to see beyond differences
   to values and aspirations held in common.
Lord of all,
   may your love bring hope, healing and harmony.

In a world of racial inequality
  in which so many still face discrimination,
  rejection, hostility or abuse,
  hear my prayer, Lord,
  for an end to barriers of bigotry and ignorance,
  so that all may be accorded their true worth.
Lord of all,
  may your love bring hope, healing and harmony.

In a world of political instability,
  troubled by divisions, hatred, suspicion and conflict,
  hear my prayer, Lord, for reconciliation,
  a willingness on the part of all
  to work for justice and peace.
Lord of all,
  may your love bring hope, healing and harmony.

In a battered, bruised and broken world,
  racked by problems to which there sometimes
  seem to be no answers,
  and in which it can be hard to keep on hoping,
  bring new beginnings,
  new life.
Lord of all,
  may your love bring hope, healing and harmony.
Amen.

Music   Creator Spirit, come from *Sacred Weave* (Keith Duke)

7
For the sorrowful and suffering

Music   O Lord, listen to my prayer from *Light in Our Darkness*
               (Margaret Rizza)

Scripture All who sow in tears will harvest with exclamations of
               joy. Those whom the Lord redeems will return to Zion
               singing; eternal ecstasy will rest upon their heads;
               they will receive delight and pleasure, for grief and
               regret will take flight.   *Psalm 126:5; Isaiah 35:10*

               Glory to the God and Father of our Lord Jesus Christ,
               the source of all mercy who comforts us in all our
               suffering, so that we can comfort those experiencing any
               kind of suffering with the comfort God has given us.
                                                  2 Corinthians 1:3, 4

Prayer   An urgent voice is calling, a voice from far away;
               it's crying out for justice, and yearning for that day
               when no one need go hungry, despair will be no more –
               a day at last that heralds a new start for the poor.

               An urgent voice is calling, a voice from somewhere near;
               it's crying out with longing, yet no one seems to hear;
               despite long years of witness, a multitude still search –
               forgive us, Lord, and grant now a new start for the
                    Church.

               An urgent voice is calling, a voice from all around;
               it's crying out in anguish, the grim and tragic sound
               of God's creation groaning, stripped bare, denied her
                    worth –
               Lord, curb our greed, and bring now a new start for the
                    earth.

An urgent voice is calling, a voice from close at hand;
it's crying out in anger, campaigning for a land
where all will be respected, and war will find no place –
a world of peace and friendship, a new start for our race.

An urgent voice is calling, the voice of God above;
it's crying out in sorrow, and urging us to love,
for still a world lies bleeding, the weak go to the wall –
Lord, help us build together a new start for us all.

Silence

Do we think of others as often as we should, making
time, amongst other things, to remember them in
prayer? If you're anything like me, the answer is no.
Most of the time, we're too busy thinking of ourselves,
as acknowledged in the following reflective prayer:

It was nothing major,
    more of a dull ache than a pain,
    but I felt sorry for myself, nonetheless,
    enough to reach for the headache tablets,
    and mope around miserably
    until the last trace had gone.

Forgive me, Lord,
    for I forget those who live in constant pain,
    longing for release
    yet finding no end to their suffering,
    each day blighted by its stranglehold.
Give them strength not just to get through,
    but also to find joy and fulfilment in life,
    and grant the assurance that,
    just as you shared our sufferings in Christ,
    so, through him,
    we will all finally enter a brighter kingdom
    in which pain and sorrow will be at an end.
Amen.

Silence

One of the loveliest prayers for the sick and suffering that I've come across is the following, from St Augustine of Hippo (354–430):

Watch, dear Lord,
 with those who wake, or watch, or weep tonight,
 and give your angels charge over those who sleep.
Tend your sick ones, O Lord Christ,
 rest your weary ones,
 bless your dying ones,
 soothe your suffering ones,
 pity your afflicted ones,
 shield your joyous ones,
 all for your love's sake.
Amen.

Silence

Final prayer Our final prayer commits to God all those wrestling with grief, illness or pain.

Grant your comfort, Lord, to those facing sorrow –
 the heartache of being rejected, deceived or betrayed;
 of watching a loved one suffer;
 or of enduring bereavement.
In your love,
 reach out to help.

Grant strength and support, Lord,
 to those facing suffering –
 the trauma of accident or injury,
 the unrelieved pain of chronic illness,
 the misery of life-threatening disease.
In your love,
 reach out to help.

Grant hope and justice, Lord, to the destitute –
  those not knowing
  where their next meal will come from,
  having nowhere to call their home
  and no way of supporting themselves
  or working for a better future.
In your love,
  reach out to help.

Grant help, Lord, to those whose lives are troubled –
  blighted by the threat of war or violence,
  disturbed by fear and anxiety,
  overwhelmed by loneliness and despair.
In your love,
  reach out to help.
  Amen.

Music   O Lord, listen to my prayer from *Light in Our Darkness*
(Margaret Rizza)

8
For those wrestling with questions

Music Cantique de Jean Racine (Fauré) from *Wings of a Dove*, sung by Hannah Mayhew

Scripture 'I will gain wisdom,' I declared, but it eluded me. Everything that has been is far off, and deep, incredibly profound. Who can hope to discover it?
Ecclesiastes 7:23b, 24

If you cry out for insight, and call for understanding, if you seek for it as for hidden treasures, then you will understand the fear of the Lord and find the knowledge of God. For the Lord brings wisdom; from his mouth come discernment and understanding;
Proverbs 2:3-6

Prayer Where were you, Lord, when the planes struck
and the towers came crashing down?
What did you do to stop it?
Why were you out of town?
Where were you in the Balkans
when the streets ran red with blood?
And how about the shanty town
engulfed by streams of mud?
Why don't you end the famine?
Why don't you stop the war?
How can you let these happen?
What can it all be for?
Lord, is it wrong to ask you,
faithless to speak my mind?
Shouldn't I look for answers?
Don't you say 'seek and find'?
Yes, I know much is beyond me,

truth often hard to discern,
but I'm ready and willing to listen,
eager and hungry to learn.
Don't think I'm daring to judge you,
set myself up in your place –
some things, I know, must stay hidden,
at least till we meet face to face –
yet in a world where so many
feel faith and hope are in vain,
give us some sign, Lord, I beg you
to prove you are here in our pain.

Silence

How can anyone make sense of the tragedies and catastrophes that so many experience? There are no easy answers, yet we need to wrestle with the questions, and to remember those who find them an obstacle to faith. As the sight of surfers riding the waves reminded me, faith must try to make sense of both the beauty and ugliness of this world God has given:

I watched them riding the waves,
   their exhilaration plain as,
   in glorious harmony with the elements,
   they ducked, dived, twisted and turned,
   and I marvelled at the beauty and grandeur
   of creation,
   its power to uplift the body and transport the spirit
   wonderful beyond words.
But I couldn't help recalling *other* waves,
   destructive
   terrifying,
   engulfing homes,
   obliterating communities –
   a merciless torrent overwhelming countless lives –

and I marvelled at the savagery of creation,
its power to *crush* the body and *shatter* the spirit,
dreadful beyond words.

Why, Lord, did you create a world so awesome
yet so awful,
enriched by joy yet cursed by sorrow;
a world in which so much speaks of your care,
but so much else denies it,
giving your love the lie?
Help us to wrestle honestly with the good and bad,
the best and the worst in life,
and somehow to make sense of you in each.
Amen.

Silence

Questions of faith are nothing new. The respected
English scholar and clergyman Charles John Vaughan
(1816–97) acknowledges such in the following prayer,
yet prays for help in keeping faith despite all that seems
to deny it:

Look in mercy, heavenly Father,
on this troubled and divided world.
Though we cannot always trace your footsteps
or understand your working,
give us grace to trust you with an undoubting faith.
And when the time you have set has come, Lord,
show us the new heaven and the new earth,
where righteousness lives
and where the Prince of Peace rules,
your Son, our Saviour Jesus Christ.
Amen.

Silence

Final prayer Let us pray, then, for all who struggle to reconcile their experiences or those of others with faith in a loving God or divine purpose.

Loving God,
   I pray for those who have more questions
   than answers,
   things they cannot make sense of threatening
   to undermine their faith
   or having destroyed it already.
Where life brings puzzles too hard to live with,
   grant answers, O Lord.

I pray for those overcome by tragedy,
   their lives shattered by circumstances
   affecting themselves or their loved ones.
Where life brings puzzles too hard to live with,
   grant answers, O Lord.

I pray for those crushed by need and poverty,
   their lives overwhelmed by famine, warfare,
   terrorism or natural disaster.
Where life brings puzzles too hard to live with,
   grant answers, O Lord.

I pray for those yearning to believe,
   yet unable to resolve the questions they have,
   and equally for those struggling to cling on to faith
   or whose commitment has grown cold.
Where life brings puzzles too hard to live with,
   grant answers, O Lord.
Amen.

Music Cantique de Jean Racine (Fauré) from *Wings of a Dove*, sung by Hannah Mayhew

9
For our loved ones

Music   O God, be gracious from *Awakening in Love*
(Margaret Rizza)

Scripture   Above all, therefore, I would advocate that you offer
requests, intercessions and thanksgiving in your prayers
for everyone.   *1 Timothy 2:1*

Pray for one another.   *James 5:16*

Prayer   It's important in our prayers to remember the needs
of the world, but it's important also to think of those
closer to home, including our nearest and dearest, for
too easily we take them for granted. As the following
prayer, inspired by the sight of a large brick wall,
reminds us, what would life be without them?

It rose before me,
    high and imposing,
    built to withstand the ravages of time,
    that wall's solid bulk somehow reassuring,
    suggestive of security and permanence
    in an ever-shifting world.
Yet what now was one had once been many –
    a heap of bricks, sand and cement,
    each of no consequence until they were assembled,
    the one supporting the other –
    weak alone but strong together.

Teach me, Lord, that I too need others –
    that you created me not to exist in isolation
    but to enjoy company,
    interacting with those around me.

Cement, then, the ties of friendship
   and build up the relationships I share,
     for it is so often through these that you give shape
     and purpose to life.
Amen.

Silence

There are many old prayers committing friends and
loved ones to God. I've chosen three: the first by St
Anselm (1033–1109), the second by the Anglican
Bishop and hymn-writer Jeremy Taylor (1613–67), and
the third that of the medieval saint Edmund of
Abingdon (c. 1175–1240):

O Blessed Lord,
   who commanded us to love one another,
   grant us grace that,
   having received your undeserved bounty,
   we may love everyone *in* you and *for* you.
We implore your clemency for all;
   but especially for the friends
   whom your love has given to us.
Love them, O Fountain of love,
   and make them to love you with all their heart,
   that they may will, and speak,
   and do those things only
   which are pleasing to you.
Amen.

Silence

Be pleased, O Lord, to remember my friends,
   all who have prayed for me,
   and all who have been good to me.
Do good to them,
   and return all their kindness twofold,
   rewarding them with blessings,

sanctifying them with your grace,
and bringing them to glory.
Amen.

Silence

Into your hands, O Father and Lord,
I commend my soul and body,
my parents and home,
my family, friends and neighbours,
all people of faith and love,
and all who stand in special need.
Lighten our lives with your holy grace,
and the knowledge of your constant presence,
O Lord in Trinity, God everlasting.
Amen.

Silence

Final prayer   In our final prayer, commit quietly to God those who
are part of your daily life:

Hear my prayer for those most precious to me, Lord,
those whose presence brings me such love,
laughter and light.

Silence

In your love,
bless and keep them.

Hear my prayer for relations,
those I rarely see but who are part of my story
as I am part of theirs.

Silence

In your love,
   bless and keep them.

Hear my prayer for friends,
   those whose company
   has enriched and illuminated my life in so many ways.

Silence

In your love,
   bless and keep them.

Hear my prayer for colleagues and acquaintances,
   those I meet in the course of my work and leisure,
   with all their joys and sorrows, hopes and fears,
   known and unknown.

Silence

In your love,
   bless and keep them.

Hear my prayer for all whose being there
   in some way shapes my life,
   and in whatever they face
   grant them your strength and support,
   help and guidance,
   health and happiness.

Silence

In your love,
   bless and keep them.
Amen.

Music   O God, be gracious from *Awakening in Love*
(Margaret Rizza)

10
For those in despair

Music   Kum ba yah from *Our Favourite Hymns 3*

Scripture   Happy are those who weep now, for they will laugh.
                                                                Luke 6:21b

                     Sorrow may last for the night, but joy will come with
                     the morning.   *Psalm 30:5b*

Prayer   If we have eyes to see, so much in our world speaks of
                     the needs of others and the sense of hopelessness so
                     many feel. The following prayer, for example, was
                     inspired by the sight of a social security benefit office:

                     The numbers flashed up on the screen,
                         summoning 'clients' to the appropriate booth,
                         and obediently they responded,
                         their forms processed,
                         their claims dealt with.
                     Only they weren't numbers,
                         they were *people*,
                         with joys, sorrows, hopes and fears,
                         just like me.

                     Reach out, Lord, to the people behind the statistics:
                         the mother whose partner has walked out
                         on her and the children,
                         the worker whose factory has closed down,
                         the trader whose business has folded,
                         the victim of the industrial accident,
                         the manager made redundant,
                         the casual labourer whose services
                         are no longer required.

However hopeless they may feel,
> however disheartened, disillusioned or despondent,
> assure them of their worth as individuals,
> and help us as a society to do the same.

Amen.

Silence

The following prayer, based upon words of J. H. Jowett (1864–1923), entrusts all to God's care, but focuses especially on those pushed to the fringes of society:

Father of all,
> hear me when I pray for people
> of every race and nation.

May the light of your love break upon them,
> lightening their burdens and easing their anxieties.

Especially I pray for the marginalised and the neglected.
May my vision, and the vision of others,
> be increased that we become more aware
> of forgotten and unwanted people.

Help us so to order our lives and our societies
> that no one is excluded.

Amen.

Silence

Final prayer   Finally, a prayer for those brought by life to the brink of despair.

Hear my prayer, Lord,
> for those whose hearts are heavy –
> those to whom life brings tears
> rather than laughter.

Touch their lives,
and bring them joy.

Hear my prayer for the disillusioned –
victims of broken relationships or broken dreams.
Touch their lives,
and bring them joy.

Hear my prayer for the troubled in mind –
those in the grip of depression and despair.
Touch their lives,
and bring them joy.

Hear my prayer for the unwell in body –
those facing injury, illness or terminal disease.
Touch their lives,
and bring them joy.

Hear my prayer for those who mourn –
those who have lost parents, children, partners
or other loved ones.
Touch their lives,
and bring them joy.

Hear my prayer, Lord, for all experiencing pain
rather than pleasure,
heartache instead of happiness.
Touch their lives,
and bring them joy.
Amen.

Music   Kum ba yah from *Our Favourite Hymns 3*

11
For the sick and those who care for them

Music   Prayer for peace from *River of Peace* (Margaret Rizza)

Scripture   When they disembarked from the boat, the crowd realised immediately who he was and, racing throughout the district, they started to bring people from their sickbeds to wherever word said he was. Everywhere he went – whether village, city or out in the countryside – they brought those who were unwell and laid them in the marketplaces, begging that these be allowed to touch the hem of his clothes, if nothing more. And those who did so were made well.

Mark 6:54-56

Is anyone unwell among you? Then let them summon the church elders, who should pray over them, anointing them with oil in the Lord's name.

James 5:14

Prayer   Thou to whom the sick and dying
ever came, nor came in vain,
still with healing words replying
to the wearied cry of pain,
hear us, Jesus, as we meet,
suppliants at thy mercy-seat.

Still the weary, sick, and dying
need a brother's, sister's care;
on thy higher help relying
may we now their burden share,
bringing all our offerings meet,
suppliants at thy mercy-seat.

Silence

Words of the hymn-writer Godfrey Thring (1823–1903). Ill health, of course, can strike any of us at any time, in a trice turning our world upside down. I wrote the following prayer after sitting in the crowded waiting room of my local health centre – one of many people waiting there to see the doctor:

Why were they here, Lord?
A bad back, perhaps,
   heavy cold,
   twisted muscle?
A bout of indigestion or hacking cough?
Or perhaps something worse,
   more pressing.
An unexplained lump, discovered that morning,
   sending an icy chill down the spine?
A diagnosis anxiously awaited,
   spelling relief or panic,
   acquittal or sentence?
A failed pregnancy,
   dreams dashed again?
Calm expressions and averted eyes
   belie the maelstrom beneath,
   each story locked away until, one by one,
   our names are called,
   and, like penitents at confession,
   we enter the sanctum and blurt out all,
   craving absolution.

Lord, for those troubled about their health,
   and those with the responsibility of ministering
   to them,
   grant your help, guidance and love.
Amen.

Silence

Next, a Jewish prayer for healing:

Heal us, Lord, and we shall be healed;
   save us, and we shall be saved;
   for it is you we praise.
Send relief and healing for all our diseases,
   our sufferings and our wounds,
   for you are a merciful and faithful healer.
Blessed are you, Lord,
   who heals the sick.
Amen.

Silence

Final prayer

Finally, then a prayer for those who are sick in body, mind or spirit, asking for God's blessing upon them:

Loving God,
   I bring before you the sick and suffering of the world,
   all those wrestling with illness in body, mind or spirit.
In your mercy,
   hear my prayer.

I pray for those afflicted in body –
   enduring physical pain,
   overwhelmed by disabling disease,
   waiting for an operation or further treatment,
   fearful of what the future may hold,
   or living with knowledge of a terminal illness.
In your mercy,
   hear my prayer.

I pray for those disturbed or troubled in mind –
   those whose confidence has broken down,
   those unable to cope with the pressures of daily life,
   those oppressed by false terrors of the imagination,
   those facing the dark despair of clinical depression.
In your mercy,
   hear my prayer.

I pray for those afflicted in spirit –
    those who feel their lives to be empty,
    those whose beliefs are threatened
    or who have lost their faith,
    those who worship gods of their own making
    with no power to satisfy,
    those whose hearts have become bitter and twisted,
    and their minds dark.
In your mercy,
    hear my prayer.

I pray for all who work to bring help, wholeness
    and healing to the sick –
    doctors and nurses, surgeons and medical staff,
    psychiatrists, counsellors, clergy and therapists.
Support and strengthen
    those who share in the work of healing,
    all who strive to bring relief,
    all who minister to others.
Equip them in all they do,
    and bring wholeness through them.
In your mercy,
    hear my prayer.
Amen.

Music   Prayer for peace from *River of Peace* (Margaret Rizza)

12

For the environment
and all responsible for its upkeep

Music

Send forth your Spirit, Lord from *Fountain of Life*
(Margaret Rizza)

Scripture

The earth pines away and shrivels up; the world
languishes and withers. It lies polluted by its inhabitants; for they have disobeyed the laws, violated the
statutes, broken the eternal covenant. The earth in all
its fullness is the Lord's, as are all its inhabitants. The
universe is yours; this world also and everything
within it, for you made it all.

Isaiah 24:4, 5; Psalm 89:11

The earth is hopelessly damaged, torn apart, violently
shaken so that it lurches like a drunken man and totters
like a shack. Its wrongdoing hangs heavily upon it,
and it collapses, and will not rise again.

Isaiah 24:19, 20

Prayer

At long last society has woken up to the importance
of respecting and safeguarding our environment, but
are any of us doing as much as we should? The sight
of a local recycling centre, which just a few years earlier
had simply been a tip, set me pondering that question:

It was a heart-warming sight,
    all kinds of items recycled for further use –
    clothes, plastic, paper, glass
    and so much else that had been thrown away –
    humbling but sobering to see so much saved
    that would otherwise have been lost for ever.

We've made progress, Lord,
   but not enough,
   each of us still being part of a disposable culture,
   a society that consumes resources
   with little thought for tomorrow,
   and still less for others.
Give to all in your world
   a greater sense of responsibility –
   to future generations
   and to you –
   an appreciation of the countless blessings
   we have received
   and the duty we have to use them wisely,
   so that others may enjoy them in turn.
Amen.

Silence

Lord, thank you for creation, the wonder of this earth,
the majesty and beauty your love has brought to birth.
Forgive the way we use it without a second thought,
and teach us to be stewards who tend it as we ought.

Forgive the way we plunder the legacy you give;
the waste, abuse, pollution that marks the way we live.
Instil in every person who lives upon this earth
a proper sense of wonder and due sense of its worth.

Silence

Final prayer Hear my prayer, Lord, for this wonderful planet,
         and for all responsible for maintaining
         its health and balance:
      To conservationists, ecological groups
         and environmentalists,

all who work and campaign to safeguard
sites of special interest and natural beauty
or endangered species and habitats,
grant your guidance,
so that our children and our children's children
may inherit a whole and healthy world.

To international, national and local leaders,
all who must weigh up ecological considerations
against a host of others,
their decisions having long-term implications,
grant your guidance,
so that our children and our children's children
may inherit a whole and healthy world.

To farmers, landowners, planners and developers,
all on whom preservation of the countryside depends,
grant your guidance,
so that our children and our children's children
may inherit a whole and healthy world.

To entrepreneurs and multinational corporations,
economic agencies and business leaders,
all with a stake in harvesting natural resources
but with a responsibility equally
to steward them wisely,
grant your guidance,
so that our children and our children's children
may inherit a whole and healthy world.

To all developing recycling initiatives,
striving to reduce waste, re-use materials,
save energy and cut pollution,
grant your guidance,
so that our children and our children's children
may inherit a whole and healthy world.

To people everywhere, us included,
on whose lifestyles, and willingness to change,

the well-being of this earth finally depends,
grant your guidance,
**so that our children and our children's children
may inherit a whole and healthy world.
Amen.**

Music   Send forth your Spirit, Lord from *Fountain of Life*
(Margaret Rizza)

13
For all who work for a better world

Music　　　　Make me a channel from *Our Favourite Hymns 2*

Scripture　　　Doing right and seeking justice is more pleasing to the Lord than offering a sacrifice.　　*Proverbs 21:3*

'When, Lord, did we see you hungry and give you food, or thirsty and give you a drink? When did we see you a stranger and make you welcome, or naked and clothe you? When was it that we saw you sick or in prison and visited you?' The king will answer, 'I tell you the truth, whenever you did it to the least of your brothers and sisters, you did it also to me.'

Matthew 25:37b-40

Prayer　　　　For those who fight injustice
and make a stand for good,
who strive to give the poor a chance
to live life as they should,
for all who labour, heart and soul,
to make our world more fair,
I ask your courage, succour, strength –
Lord, answer, hear my prayer.

For those who show compassion,
who work to heal and mend,
who nurse the sick, support the weak,
encourage and befriend,
for all who reach out in your name
to offer love and care,
I ask your blessing, power, help –
Lord, answer, hear my prayer.

For those who tackle conflict,
where wounds run red and raw,
who strive to conquer hatred
and put a stop to war,
who work to foster dialogue
despite the scars we bear,
I ask your guidance, vision, faith –
Lord, answer, hear my prayer.

For those who try to witness
to Christ through word and deed,
to show his love embraces
each colour, culture, creed;
who point to light and life and hope
in which we all can share,
I ask your wisdom, grace and truth –
Lord, answer, hear my prayer.

Silence

How far do we practise what we preach? That's a
question which we, as Christians, should always be
asking ourselves if we are not to be guilty of hypocrisy.
It's easy enough to talk of love, much harder to actually
show it. But as the words of Jesus remind us, serving
him very often involves serving others. The following
prayer was inspired by a circular from a national charity,
asking for a special donation:

It was another appeal,
  yet one more begging letter thrust through my door,
  tugging at the heartstrings and seeking my support.
A worthy cause, no doubt,
  as deserving as any other,
  but I'd done my bit, hadn't I? –
  already given more than generously.
What more could people ask?

Is that true, Lord?
Have I done enough?
I've given, certainly,
    but was each donation a meaningful gift
    or a token gesture,
    a response from the heart
    or an attempt to salve my conscience?
I've offered a little, but no more,
    what I spare for others over a lifetime
    being just a fraction of what I spend on myself.
Forgive me,
    and teach me to deal generously,
    as you have dealt generously with me.
Amen.

Silence

Caring enough to show it – that's the theme of the so-called Christopher Prayer:

Father, grant that I may be a bearer
    of Christ Jesus, your Son.
Allow me to warm the often cold, impersonal scene
    of modern life with your burning love.
Strengthen me by your Holy Spirit
    to carry out my mission of changing the world
    or some definite part of it for the better.
Despite my lamentable failures,
    bring home to me that my advantages
    are your blessings to be shared with others.
Make me more energetic in setting right
    what I find wrong with the world
    instead of complaining about it.
Nourish in me a practical desire to build up
    rather than tear down,
    to reconcile instead of polarise,
    to go out on a limb rather than crave security.

Never let me forget
　　that it is far better to light one candle
　　than to curse the darkness,
　　and to join my light, one day, with yours.
Amen.

Silence

Final prayer　Hear my prayer, Lord,
　　for those who work to create a better world,
　　putting others before themselves,
　　offering their time, money, energy and skills
　　to enhance people's lives.
To and *through* them,
　　grant your blessing.

Hear my prayer for all who strive to bring happiness,
　　caring for the sick, lonely and elderly,
　　offering opportunities to the disadvantaged,
　　providing facilities for youngsters,
　　or simply helping to put a smile on people's faces.
To and *through* them,
　　grant your blessing.

Hear my prayer for all who endeavour to build peace,
　　overcoming barriers of prejudice, hatred
　　and suspicion,
　　and working to establish dialogue, understanding
　　and harmony instead.
To and *through* them,
　　grant your blessing.

Hear my prayer for all who seek to bring help –
　　carers, doctors and nurses,
　　aid and charity staff,
　　counsellors, social workers
　　and those in the emergency services.

To and *through* them,
   grant your blessing.

Hear my prayer for all who seek a fairer world –
   working to bring justice, opportunity
   and resources for self-help,
   so that all may have a proper share
   in this earth's resources.
To and *through* them,
   grant your blessing.
Amen.

Music   Make me a channel from *Our Favourite Hymns 2*

14

For those shattered by the demands of life

Music   Hear my prayer (Felix Mendelssohn) from *A Feast of Anthems*

Scripture   The spirit of the Lord God is upon me, for he has anointed me. He has sent me to announce good news to the oppressed; to bind up the broken-hearted, to proclaim freedom to those held captive and release for all who are imprisoned; to proclaim the year of the Lord's favour and the day of our God's retribution. He has sent me to comfort those who grieve, to adorn them with garlands instead of ashes, oil instead of mourners' tears, a garment of praise instead of a heavy heart.   *Isaiah 61:1-3a*

He rescues the needy when they call, the poor and those who have no one else to help them. Do not allow then, Lord, the oppressed to be humiliated, but let the poor and needy praise your name.
                    Psalm 72:12; 74:21

Prayer   In a world of hurt and need,
scarred by selfishness and greed;
touched by sorrow, racked by pain,
such that hope can seem in vain;
in this mix of toil and strife
where so much devalues life;
gracious Lord, I pray be there,
show to all how much you care.

Silence

Most people chug along fairly contentedly most of the time, but it takes less than we might imagine to shatter our contentment and security. The following prayer was inspired by the sight of a broken window:

One throw, that's all it took –
    one stone hurled by a thoughtless child
    and suddenly the window was shattered,
    reduced to jagged shards and splintered glass.

So many, Lord, find their lives shattered –
    broken by the loss of a loved one,
    the onset of disease,
    accident and injury,
    or the breakdown of relationships –
    and though sometimes they can be restored,
    the pieces put back together,
    often they can't,
    in this life, at least, the damage too great to mend.
Reach out into fragmented lives,
    bringing healing and hope,
    until that day when your kingdom comes,
    and all is made whole.
Amen.

Silence

Final prayer   Lord Jesus Christ, broken for all,
    for those broken in body –
    overcome by sickness or disease,
    emaciated through starvation,
    maimed or injured through accident
    or acts of violence –
    I bring you my prayer.
Grant them wholeness and healing.

For those broken in mind –
oppressed by depression and despair,
mentally disturbed or disabled,
or victims of senile dementia –
I bring you my prayer.
Grant them wholeness and healing.

For those broken in spirit –
their confidence crushed by failure and rejection,
their trust in others and the future
broken by betrayal,
their faith in you destroyed by tragedy –
I bring you my prayer.
Grant them wholeness and healing.

For all casualties of life, Lord –
victims of this bruised, battered and broken world –
I bring you my prayer.
Grant them wholeness and healing.
Amen.

Music Hear my prayer (Felix Mendelssohn) from *A Feast of Anthems*

15
For hope, help and healing
in a fractured world

Music   Come, Lord from *Fountain of Life* (Margaret Rizza)

Scripture   Those in need will not be overlooked for ever, nor will the dreams of the poor be allowed to die.

Psalm 9:18

You hear, Lord, the pleas of the lowly, you give ear to them and will strengthen their heart.   *Psalm 10:17*

Prayer   Can I see another's woe,
And not be in sorrow too?
Can I see another's grief,
And not seek for kind relief?

Can I see a falling tear,
And not feel my sorrow's share?
Can a father see his child
Weep, nor be with sorrow filled?

Can a mother sit and hear
An infant groan, an infant fear?
No, no! never can it be!
Never, never can it be!

And can he who smiles on all
Hear the wren with sorrows small,
Hear the small bird's grief and care,
Hear the woes that infants bear –

And not sit beside the next,
Pouring pity in their breast,

And not sit the cradle near,
Weeping tear on infant's tear?

And not sit both night and day,
Wiping all our tears away?
Oh no! never can it be!
Never, never can it be!

He doth give his joy to all:
He becomes an infant small,
He becomes a man of woe,
He doth feel the sorrow too.

Think not thou canst sigh a sigh,
And thy Maker is not by:
Think not thou canst weep a tear,
And thy Maker is not near.

Silence

Words of William Blake (1757–1827) from the poem
'On Another's Sorrow', reminding us that, just as God
shares the pain of others, so we too are called to respond
wherever we are confronted by human need. That
theme is taken up in one of the most celebrated prayers
of all time – that of St Francis of Assisi (1182–1226):

Lord, make me an instrument of your peace:
    where there is hatred, let me sow love,
    where there is injury, pardon,
    where there is doubt, faith,
    where there is darkness, light,
    where there is despair, hope,
    and where there is sadness, joy.

Divine Master,
    grant that I may not so much seek to be consoled
    as to console,

to be understood as to understand,
to be loved as to love.
For it is in giving that we receive,
   it is in pardoning that we are pardoned,
   and in dying that we are born to eternal life.
Amen.

Silence

Whatever we do can never be enough, barely scratching the surface of human sorrow and suffering. Our world lies in constant need of God's healing touch, like an accident victim dependent on expert medical care. The following prayer builds on that analogy:

It was a painstaking business,
   the bones shattered by the impact,
   needing to be pieced together like a jigsaw,
   then carefully supported
   while the breaks began to knit.
Would the injury heal,
   the body mend?
We could only hope and pray.

Lord, our world lies equally broken,
   fractured by prejudice,
   splintered by hate,
   scarred by fear,
   and for all our efforts we cannot make it whole.
Pick up the pieces and bind them together,
   bringing healing where there is hurt
   and unity where there is division.
Hear our prayer and honour our hopes.
Amen.

Silence

Final prayer Hear my prayer, Lord, for those in sorrow or need,
their lives overshadowed by sickness, tragedy,
worry or want –
turn their mourning to dancing,
their dismay to delight.

Reach out to those who are unwell:
worried about unexplained symptoms,
in hospital waiting for surgery,
or living with permanent illness or disability –
turn their mourning to dancing,
their dismay to delight.

Reach out to those who are sad:
those for whom life has brought hurt in relationships,
the loss of loved ones,
the end of dreams –
turn their mourning to dancing,
their dismay to delight.

Reach out to those who are troubled:
worried about family and friends,
fearful of the future,
consumed by all kinds of anxiety and insecurity –
turn their mourning to dancing,
their dismay to delight.

Reach out to those enduring daily hardship:
victims of famine, disaster, oppression or war,
each day a struggle for survival –
turn their mourning to dancing,
their dismay to delight.
Amen.

Music Come, Lord from *Fountain of Life* (Margaret Rizza)

16
For the poor

Music   When I needed a neighbour (Sydney Carter) from
No Organist? No Problem 1

Scripture   Whoever exploit the poor insult their Maker, whereas
those who deal kindly with the needy honour him.
Those who close their ears to the cry of the poor will
not be heard when they themselves call out.

Proverbs 14:31; 21:13

When the poor and those in need look for water but
can't find any, so that their tongues are shrivelled
with thirst, I the Lord God of Israel will answer them;
I will not abandon them.   *Isaiah 41:17*

Silence

Prayer   Recent years have seen a campaign to make poverty
history, but in reality, as the following prayer explores,
it's history in a very different sense:

They were shocking pictures,
   indescribably awful –
scenes of appalling suffering and abject misery
that brought tears to the eyes
and a lump to the throat –
yet I was no longer truly shocked,
for I'd seen them before –
different people,
different emaciated bodies and haunted faces,
yet the same scenes,
history repeating itself time and again.

We *have* made poverty history, Lord,
    but not in the way intended.
We've made it part of our world,
    an accepted norm,
    a fact of life . . . and death . . . for countless millions,
    and though it's not all our doing,
    much of it down to forces beyond our control,
    we're still complicit in the crime,
    none of us able to absolve ourselves fully
    of responsibility.
Forgive the evil of our world,
    and my share within it,
    and give us all a common resolve to tackle poverty
    and *truly* consign it to history.
Amen.

Silence

Listen to words of Mother Teresa (1910–97), that great servant and supporter of the poor:

Lord,
    take away my indifference and insensitivity
    to the plight of the poor.
When I meet you hungry, thirsty or as a stranger,
    show me how I can give you food,
    quench your thirst,
    or receive you in my home –
    and in my heart.
Show me how I can serve you
    in the least of your brothers and sisters.
Amen.

Silence

Final prayer   Loving God,
hear my prayer for the have-nots of this world.
Grant justice,
   grant hope.

I pray for those who have no homes,
living as refugees or sleeping rough on our streets.
Grant justice,
   grant hope.

I pray for those who live in inadequate housing,
the shacks and huts of shanty towns,
or in bed and breakfast accommodation
because there is nowhere else for them to go.
Grant justice,
   grant hope.

I pray for those who have no food,
their crops having failed,
their economies burdened by debt,
or their labours not fairly rewarded.
Grant justice,
   grant hope.

I pray for those who have no fresh water,
daily facing the threat of disease
and the nightmare of drought;
I pray also for those who have scant resources,
condemned to a life of poverty
with no prospect of respite,
no opportunity to help themselves.
Grant justice,
   grant hope.

I pray for those who have no access to education,
a health service or a welfare system;
no one to turn to for help or support.
Grant justice,
   grant hope.

Stir all like me who enjoy plenty
   to respond to the have-nots of this world.
Help us to be ready to say no to ourselves
   so that we may say yes to them,
   to sacrifice a little that they may receive much.
Grant justice,
   grant hope.
Amen.

Music   When I needed a neighbour (Sydney Carter) from
No Organist? No Problem 1

17
For victims of prejudice

Music   A new commandment from *Festival of Anthems*

Scripture   The Lord your God is the God of gods and Lord of lords, awesome, almighty, and wonderful, impartial and takes no bribe. He ensures a fair deal for the orphaned and widowed, and loves strangers, providing them with food and clothing.   *Deuteronomy 10:17, 18*

There can be neither Jew nor Greek, slave nor free, male nor female, for you are all one in Jesus Christ.
Galatians 3:28

Prayer   Lord, for using labels to decide on people's worth:
their age, their sex, their class, their roots,
their faith or place of birth,
their politics or culture, the colour of their skin,
the outward signs that mark them out
instead of what's within;
for summing people up by what nobody can change –
allowing background, creed or race
to poison and estrange –
for all such prejudice, forgive, and from it set me free
to meet the person underneath –
to look and really see.

Silence

We shouldn't label people, but, despite ourselves, we all do, it being almost impossible not to pigeonhole them subconsciously. But, of course, labels can be misleading, just as they can be at our local super-market:

I assumed it would be good,
   the best of its kind,
   for it was a familiar label,
   synonymous, to my mind, with quality.
But I was wrong,
   for the product was poor,
   the workmanship shoddy –
   not a patch on models half the price
   though less well known.

Come to our divided world, Lord,
   and help us to look behind
   the labels we attach to people,
   recognising that the terms so often used –
   East, West,
   black, white,
   Christian, Muslim –
   can only tell part of the story,
   never the whole.
Help us, in all our dealings with others,
   to see the person first,
   and the label second.
Amen.

Silence

Let us ask God's help in overcoming the prejudice that scars our world. First, a prayer from the Liturgy of the Hours:

Almighty God, ever-loving Father,
   your care extends beyond the boundaries
   of race and nation
   to the hearts of all who live.

May the walls, which prejudice raises between us,
   crumble beneath the shadow
   of your outstretched arm.
We ask this through Christ our Lord.
Amen.

Silence

Final prayer   Lord of all,
     I pray today for victims
     of prejudice and discrimination,
     all who are rejected because of their colour, creed,
     convictions or culture,
     subjected to verbal abuse or physical assault,
     social exclusion and deprivation.
Reach out in love
and heal our divisions.

I pray for those who live each day
     with the automatic attaching of labels,
     negative attitudes,
     denial of opportunities
     and offensive remarks.
Reach out in love
and heal our divisions.

Give to all courage to face the prejudice
     that lurks within them –
     the naive assumptions and hidden biases –
     and grant each the ability to appreciate
     the true worth of all.
Reach out in love
and heal our divisions.

Prosper the work of those who work for change –
     campaigning for equality of opportunity,
     striving to break down preconceptions,

building bridges across divided communities.
Encourage them in their efforts
and grant that through bringing people together
prejudices may be overcome.
Reach out in love
and heal our divisions.
Amen.

Music A new commandment from *Festival of Anthems*

18
For the oppressed and disadvantaged

Music   Judge eternal (Malcom Archer) from *Festival of Anthems*

Scripture Grant justice to the weak and orphaned; uphold the
               entitlements of the deprived and destitute. Save the
               vulnerable and disadvantaged; redeem them from the
               clutches of the corrupt.   *Psalm 82:3, 4*

               Learn to do good; look to deal fairly, put right
               exploitation; ensure justice to the orphan, and support
               the cause of the widowed.   *Isaiah 1:17*

Prayer   Where restless crowds are thronging
               along the city ways,
               where pride and greed and turmoil
               consume the fevered days,
               where vain ambitions banish
               all thoughts of praise and prayer,
               the people's spirits waver:
               but thou, O Christ, art there.

               In scenes of want and sorrow
               and haunts of flagrant wrong,
               in homes where kindness falters,
               and strife and fear are strong,
               in busy street of barter,
               in lonely thoroughfare,
               the people's spirits languish:
               but thou, O Christ, art there.

O Christ, behold thy people –
they press on every hand!
Bring light to all the cities
of our beloved land.
May all our bitter striving
give way to visions fair
of righteousness and justice:
for thou, O Christ, art there.

Silence

As those words of the hymn-writer Thomas Curtis
Clark (1877–1953) remind us, nowhere is outside of
Christ's love and purpose, but that doesn't mean we can
leave everything to him. For too many, life is a constant
and demanding struggle, the plight of millions calling
for a response. The sight of lichen growing on a wind-
swept rock brought home to me just how hard life is
for some:

How it grew there was beyond me,
    for it was bare rock –
    rough,
    windswept,
    barren –
    yet the lichen had colonised its surface:
    nothing fancy or luxuriant,
    but, somehow,
    surviving against all odds.

It reminded me, Lord,
    that so many in this world simply *survive*,
        struggling each day to get by as best they can.
Not for them the trappings of life we take for granted,
    the accoutrements we see as ours by right.
They are happy to find even the bare essentials,
    let alone more.

Help me to remember how lucky I am,
> how much I have to celebrate,
> and teach me to respond,
> generously and lovingly,
> so that others may rejoice in turn.
Amen.

Silence

A wonderful prayer for those who are oppressed and disadvantaged is that of St Anselm (1033–1109):
I bring before you, O Lord,
> the troubles and perils of people and nations,
> the pain of prisoners and captives,
> the sorrows of the bereaved,
> the needs of strangers,
> the vulnerability of the weak,
> the downheartedness of the weary,
> the diminishing powers of the aged.
O Lord, draw near to each,
> for the sake of Jesus Christ our Lord.
Amen.

Silence

Final prayer Finally, a prayer for all those who find themselves up against it:

To all facing sorrow,
> their lives marred by tragedy, hurt and bereavement,
> transforming God,
> **bring fresh hope and new beginnings.**

To all facing suffering,
    their lives scarred by injury, disability or disease,
    transforming God,
    bring fresh hope and new beginnings.

To all facing injustice,
    their lives undermined by oppression,
    prejudice or exploitation,
    transforming God,
    bring fresh hope and new beginnings.

To all facing need,
    their lives wrecked by poverty, hunger
    or homelessness,
    transforming God,
    bring fresh hope and new beginnings.

To all facing hatred,
    their lives ruined by violence, terrorism or war,
    transforming God,
    bring fresh hope and new beginnings.

To all facing evil,
    their lives scarred by greed, corruption or crime,
    transforming God,
    bring fresh hope and new beginnings.

To all for whom life brings trouble and distress
    rather than joy and blessing,
    the valley of tears rather than summits of joy,
    transforming God,
    bring fresh hope and new beginnings.
Amen.

Music   Judge eternal (Malcom Archer) from *Festival of Anthems*

19
For those in need of God's touch

Music   When I feel the touch (Keri Jones and David Matthew)
                 from *No Organist? No Problem 1*

Scripture   The Lord is his people's strength; the safe haven of his
                 anointed. Rescue your people and bless your heritage!
                 Be a shepherd to them and bear them always in your
                 arms.   *Psalm 28:8, 9*

                 Jesus came and touched them, saying, 'Get up, you
                 have nothing to fear.'   *Matthew 17:7*

Prayer   To all beset by fears,
                 by sickness, pain or tears,
                 reach out and make them whole,
                 in body and in soul.

                 To all who long for peace,
                 bid inner turmoil cease;
                 reach out and touch their life
                 and put an end to strife.

                 To all oppressed by care,
                 regrets, dismay, despair,
                 reach out and touch their mind;
                 help put the past behind.

                 To all who've gone astray,
                 give light to point the way;
                 reach out and touch their heart,
                 your love and life impart.

                 Silence

Throughout his earthly ministry Jesus showed his love through touch, reaching out to heal and help. He continues to touch lives today, but sometimes, as the following two reflective prayers explore, he needs us to be his hands. The first is called 'The Aids sufferer':

They avoided him,
    shrinking back when he approached,
    well aware the response was foolish,
    but controlled by half-formed fears,
    suspicion and prejudice like a wall between them.
No comment was made – none was needed:
    he walked forlornly away,
    condemned to carry his burden alone.

Some say it's a punishment, Lord, a sign of your anger.
Others pity him.
Most keep their distance; but not you.
As you touched the untouchables
    throughout your ministry,
    so you reach out still,
    seeing not the affliction, but the person underneath.
Forgive, Lord, the feebleness of our love,
    and teach us to do the same.
Amen.

Silence

Secondly, a prayer inspired by the sight of an injured footballer being carried off the pitch on a stretcher:

They eased him on gently,
    mindful of his wounds,
    and as they lifted and carried him
    to the waiting ambulance
    he smiled gratefully through the pain.

Thank you, Lord,
    for the knowledge that you are always there,
    ready to carry me when I cannot continue,
    to tend my wounds when I lie bruised and broken,
    to provide healing and renewal
    in body, mind and spirit.
Teach me to minister to life's casualties in turn,
    reaching out with supportive hands and caring touch,
    in your name.
Amen.

Silence

Final prayer   In our final prayer we commit to God all those needing
the touch of his hand in their lives:

Hear my prayer, Lord, for all in need,
    all who cry to you for help.
I think of the lonely –
    yearning for companionship,
    the reassurance of a friendly face,
    the knowledge that someone cares.
Reach out your hand,
    and touch their lives with your love.

I think of the poor, oppressed and hungry –
    battling for survival,
    desperate for help,
    crying out for justice and compassion.
Reach out your hand,
    and touch their lives with your love.

I think of the sick –
    those suffering in body and mind,
    needing comfort, support, hope and wholeness.
Reach out your hand,
    and touch their lives with your love.

I think of the dying –
    wrestling with fear,
    battling with suffering,
    oppressed by sorrow.
Reach out your hand,
    and touch their lives with your love.

I think of the bereaved –
    consumed by grief,
    numbed by shock,
    struggling with anger,
    crushed by helplessness.
Reach out your hand,
    and touch their lives with your love.

I think finally of those needs I know of personally –
    those among family, friends, neighbours,
    acquaintances or colleagues
    going through hard times,
    grappling with their own problems.
Reach out your hand,
    and touch their lives with your love.
Amen.

Music   When I feel the touch (Keri Jones and David Matthew)
from *No Organist? No Problem 1*

20
For the Church
and its ministry in the world

Music   Father, may they be one from *In God Alone*
              (Andrew Moore)

Scripture My commandment is this: that you love each other as
              I have loved you.   *John 15:12*

              This is how people will know you are my disciples:
              through whether you have love for each other.
                                                          John 13:35

Prayer   You've called us as your Church, Lord,
              your people here on earth,
              a fellowship of equals
              where all are given worth,
              a family together,
              distinguished by our care,
              one faith, one hope, one gospel,
              one vision that we share.
              Yet we have been divided
              by doctrine, dogma, creed,
              estranged from one another –
              your body left to bleed.
              Too full of our convictions,
              believing others wrong,
              we've lost sight of the body
              to which we all belong.
              Our differences deny you,
              betray the faith we claim;
              instead of love uniting,
              we squabble in your name.

Lord, heal the wounds that scar us –
suspicion, fear and pride;
reveal the good in others
that all our labels hide.
May cords of love unite us,
too strong to be undone –
although we may be many,
equip us to be one.

Silence

Of all the prayers for the Church, few are more celebrated than that of Archbishop William Laud (1573–1645):

Gracious Father,
    I pray for your holy Christian Church.
Fill it with all truth, in all truth with all peace.
Where it is corrupt, cleanse it.
Where it is in error, direct it.
Where it is superstitious, rectify it.
Where anything is amiss, reform it.
Where it is right, strengthen and confirm it.
Where it is in want, supply its need.
Where it is divided and torn apart, heal the divisions,
    O Holy One of Israel.
Amen.

Silence

A much more ancient prayer is the following, from the Didache, dating back to the first century and rediscovered in 1883:

Be mindful of your Church, O Lord.
Deliver it from all evil,
    perfect it with your love,
    sanctify it,

and gather it together from throughout the world
into the kingdom which you have prepared for it.
For yours is the power and the glory for ever and ever.
Amen.

Silence

Final prayer   Father God,
I thank you for the family
to which you have called me,
the congregation to which I belong
and the great company of your people,
past, present and future.
For your Church everywhere,
hear my prayer.

I pray for my own fellowship,
those who have moved away,
those confined to their homes
through age and infirmity,
those who are unwell,
those who have become disillusioned
or lost their faith.
For your Church everywhere,
hear my prayer.

I pray for the churches of this town,
striving through word and deed
to make known locally the love of Christ.
Give faith and wisdom to those in positions of oversight,
and give vision to each fellowship,
so that together they may respond gladly
to opportunities for service,
making vision become reality.
For your Church everywhere,
hear my prayer.

I pray for the wider family of the Church,
    remembering especially
    those who are persecuted for their beliefs,
    all for whom commitment to Christ
    is dangerous and costly.
Grant them courage in adversity,
    and help them to stand up for their convictions
    against all the odds.
For your Church everywhere,
    hear my prayer.

I pray for the unity of the Church,
    for the breaking down of barriers
    and a further growing together,
    so that through the life of your people
    your kingdom may be brought closer.
For your Church everywhere,
    hear my prayer.

I pray for those involved in mission,
    either at home or overseas –
    evangelists, preachers, chaplains, missionaries,
    all who seek to proclaim the gospel
    and make known the love of Christ.
For your Church everywhere,
    hear my prayer.

Father God,
    guide, strengthen, equip and inspire
    your people for service,
    so that they may joyfully serve you,
    sensitively proclaim you,
    and faithfully express your love for all.
For your Church everywhere,
    hear my prayer.
    Amen.

Music   Father, may they be one from *In God Alone*
(Andrew Moore)

Scriptural Index

Index of Authors